Doing Good Together

101 Easy, Meaningful Service Projects for Families, Schools, and Communities

Jenny Friedman, Ph.D.
Jolene Roehlkepartain

free spirit
PUBLISHING®

Library of Congress Cataloging-in-Publication Data
Friedman, Jenny Lynn.
  Doing good together : 101 easy, meaningful service projects for families, schools, and communities /
Jenny Friedman and Jolene Roehlkepartain.
    p. cm.
  Includes bibliographical references and index.
  ISBN 978-1-57542-354-8 (alk. paper)
  1. Voluntarism. 2. Child volunteers. 3. Young volunteers in social service. 4. Service learning.
I. Roehlkepartain, Jolene L II. Title.
  HN49.V64F75 2010
  302'.14—dc22

2010020272

Edited by Eric Braun
Cover and interior design by Michelle Lee
Cover photos, top to bottom: Rick Augsburger/Church World Service; liquidlibrary/Jupiterimages; courtesy of Doing Good Together; Tim Pannell/Corbis/Jupiterimages
Interior photos, top to bottom: page ix: © Anpet2000/istockphoto.com; courtesy of Doing Good Together; © Stellajune3700/istockphoto.com; page 3: courtesy of the USO, 2010, www.uso.org; © ImageegamI/istockphoto.com; © JeanellNorvell/istockphoto.com; © RapidEye/istockphoto.com; pages 15, 57, 97, 153, 170: courtesy of Doing Good Together; page 36, © Monkey Business Images/Dreamstime.com; page 68: © Ioannis Syrigos/Dreamstime.com; page 77: © Viorika/istockphoto.com; page 115: © lostinbids/istockphoto.com; © Anke Van Wyk/Dreamstime.com; page 119: © asiseeit/istockphoto.com; page 128: © alexeys/istockphoto.com; page 135: courtesy of the USO, 2010, www.uso.org; page 156: Edith Held/Fancy/Jupiterimages; page 200: liquidlibrary/Jupiterimages; © robcruse/istockphoto.com

10 9 8 7 6 5 4 3 2 1
Printed in the United States of America

Free Spirit Publishing Inc.
217 Fifth Avenue North, Suite 200
Minneapolis, MN 55401-1299
(612) 338-2068
help4kids@freespirit.com
www.freespirit.com

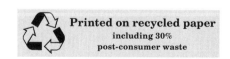
Printed on recycled paper
including 30% post-consumer waste

As a member of the Green Press Initiative, Free Spirit Publishing is committed to the three Rs: Reduce, Reuse, Recycle. Whenever possible, we print our books on recycled paper containing a minimum of 30% post-consumer waste. At Free Spirit it's our goal to nurture not only children, but nature too!

green press INITIATIVE

Dedication

To our families:

Rocky, Jessica, Rachel, and Nick

Gene, Micah, and Eli

for believing in us—and in the power of family service to make our world a better place.

Acknowledgments

We appreciate all the donors, volunteers, board members, and partners of Doing Good Together for all you have done to inspire, encourage, and equip families to volunteer together. This book would not exist if it hadn't been for your ongoing support and unwavering belief that family service is a unique and powerful way to cultivate a new generation of compassionate, generous, engaged citizens.

We'd also like to thank Eric Braun, Michelle Lee, and Margie Lisovskis of Free Spirit Publishing for their thoughtful work on this book.

Contents

Reproducible Pages

Preface
The Benefits of Family Service

In just two hours, families from Cornelia Elementary School in Edina, Minnesota, prepared 300 sandwiches and attached personal notes for a homeless shelter, made 46 blankets for children in need of comfort, created and mailed 50 cards to chronically sick children, packaged reading aid kits for 50 students, organized 32 birthday bags for children living in poverty, and stuffed 100 breakfast bags for families at a Ronald McDonald House.

"This was the best school event ever," commented one mother.

In Ohio, the Rotary Club of Garrettsville-Hiram had seen its membership dwindle to 10 members, with lagging enthusiasm, when the club president decided to take a different approach. "The idea that caught fire with club members was to recognize and celebrate the benefits that strong families offer our community," she says. "The family is universal. Everyone belongs to a family. If we did something for families, we had the potential of reaching every person in the community."

The club created the annual Family Week Celebration that included a family service project. Since its inception in 2002, the club has watched its membership grow as families get together to help others and make a difference in the community. Now a number of people in the organization and community shake their heads and say, "This was such a simple idea. Why didn't we think of this before?"

What's attracting families to get involved—and stay involved—in an organization? Family service. Many families yearn for meaningful ways to spend time together. They want easy, worthwhile projects that help them pass on key values to their children. They're eager to help the places they care about. They like making a difference while doing good together. And more and more organizations have been capitalizing on this growing trend: recruiting families to volunteer together.

The benefits are clear. A successful family service project can change everything. It can boost the number of families getting involved with your school or organization. It can change the way families and staff members feel about making a difference in the world. It can change your organization by giving it a new sense of purpose and direction.

Schools, businesses, and organizations that organize family service projects on a regular basis are discovering that there are many more benefits than helping those in need. They're also seeing positive changes within their organization and within their organization's families. If you are a leader in a youth group, community group, faith community, school, before- and after-school program, workplace, civic group, or any other organization, you can discover these benefits, too.

How Family Service Helps Your Organization

When organizations offer family service projects, what benefits do they see? More than they originally imagined. Providing family projects:

Develops stronger relationships between families and the organization. When families participate in meaningful service opportunities, they feel drawn to your organization. They want to do more, and they build stronger ties to your organization. Families also are more apt to participate in other aspects of your organization. Some even become strong advocates and allies for your organization.

Helps keep valued employees. When workplaces provide family service opportunities, employees are more likely to stay with the company longer. In addition to retaining employees, companies that provide volunteer opportunities also find it easier to recruit employees. Parents are more content to work for companies that offer family service projects that everyone can get involved in, rather than only projects for adult individuals. Teachers who are involved with their schools' family service projects are more likely to continue in their jobs from year to year. Of the significant factors in reducing attrition, the one with the greatest effect is improving the teachers' relationship with parents and the broader community, researchers say. Well-organized family service projects at school can help.

Creates good public relations. Every time your organization does a family service project, people in the community notice. Offering family volunteer projects shows that your organization believes in helping others, making the community a better place, and providing ways to bring families together. Corporate volunteer managers who integrate families into their volunteer programs say their organizations receive more community exposure and visibility.

Builds skills. Working on a family service project builds skills in everyone involved. Service project leaders say that participants improve teamwork, develop better problem-solving skills, and learn to communicate better. Businesses point to additional skills gained through service, such as leadership skills, resource development skills, and political astuteness.

Makes it easy for families to get involved. Indirect family volunteer projects, like those in this book, make it easy for families to participate. When the service project is held at a familiar, convenient site, families who may have been reluctant to connect with a school or another organization feel more comfortable participating by "helping out" at a service project.

Attracts families you might not otherwise reach. Schools, organizations, and businesses all point to the power of family service to bring in a diversity of families. "The event brought out many of the more diverse members of our school, probably because giving resonates with every community," said parent Michelle Thom after a Horace Mann School family service project in St. Paul, Minnesota. "It was wonderful to see and work alongside some of the immigrant families, in particular, who may not choose to come to some of the other events. We also ran into neighbors who aren't Horace Mann attendees."

Attracts people of all ages. Family service projects are also one of the few activities where you can get people of all ages involved and wanting to come back for more. As an organization gets families involved, project organizers often see families take the path of deeper involvement—in their organization and in volunteering. Depending on your organization, you may want to expand the definition of family so that it includes all people. For example, in a congregation, there are often single or elderly people who enjoy service projects but would not attend if it were only for "families." Some groups call their projects "intergenerational service projects" or define family as "anyone of any age who has or had a family member—even if people live alone."

How Family Service Helps Families

Not only do organizations benefit when families serve, but so do the families that participate. Family volunteerism teaches the lessons of compassion, tolerance, and service in a hands-on way. When family members roll up their sleeves and participate in meaningful service projects, they quickly learn that they can make a difference in creating a better community—and a better world. When an organization reinforces values that families hold, it becomes more likely that individuals develop a strong sense of character.

According to the Points of Light Foundation, the benefits of volunteering as a family include:

- Providing quality family time when family members can become closer.
- Strengthening family communication.
- Offering ways for family members to be role models.
- Giving families the opportunity to make significant contributions to their communities.

Service project leaders have told many stories of how family service changes parents: getting them to step out of their usual role and to step into something bigger. One mother (who came to a family service project at a school to care for her grandchild while her teenage daughter volunteered) got involved with the service project and started coming back for more. Over time, she embraced not only service but also the power of education. She then starting working toward her GED.

Social service agencies see family service as a key way to increase families' sense of well-being, reduce their isolation, strengthen connections to the family, develop skills of individual family members, and also increase parenting skills. Parents who do service projects with their children say they do so in order to learn about their communities, to spend quality time together as a family, and to be positive role models for their kids.

Even though families are busy, nine out of 10 families who participated in a National Family Volunteer Day project said the project gave them time to be together and share positive values that they like to teach as a family. Meaningful family service projects add value to family time.

Most families become more involved in family service over time. They become committed to service and to the causes they promote.

How Family Service Helps Kids

Parents are concerned about the welfare of their children, and they want their kids to grow up to be caring, successful adults. Minneapolis-based Search Institute has conducted surveys on more than 3 million young people and identified 40 Developmental Assets that kids need in order to do well in life and avoid high-risk behaviors like alcohol use, illicit drug use, violence, and school problems.

Family service is a key strategy for building all of the 40 Developmental Assets. Family service provides a key way to support young people (which builds Developmental Assets 1–6). Family service empowers young people (which builds Developmental Assets 7–10). It provides clear boundaries and expectations (which builds Developmental Assets 11–16), and it gives a constructive way to spend time (which builds Developmental Assets 17–20).

In addition, family service promotes a commitment to learning (which builds Developmental Assets 21–25), instills positive values (which builds Developmental Assets 26–31), builds social competencies (which are Developmental Assets 32–35), and promotes a strong sense of identity (which builds Developmental Assets 36–40).

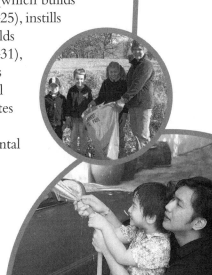

What's most striking, however, is not only how family service builds Developmental Assets but how Developmental

Assets encourage kids to serve. Search Institute researchers found that only 62 percent of young people with 10 or fewer Developmental Assets are likely to help others. Yet 96 percent of young people with 31 or more Developmental Assets report helping others one or more hours per week.

When you ask service-minded teenagers when they first volunteered, most say they started by age 14. Almost half start by age 12, according to a landmark study on family volunteerism (*Volunteering and Giving,* edited by Virginia Hodgkinson). When kids volunteer with their families, they're more likely to be involved in service throughout their lives. Two-thirds of adult volunteers say they began volunteering when they were young. Adults who began volunteering as a child or teenager are twice as likely to volunteer as adults who never volunteered when they were young.

Although many schools and organizations provide service projects for children and youth, young people are more likely to see the value of service when they do service projects with their families.

How Family Service Helps Communities

Communities benefit when families are used to volunteering. With family volunteers, community economic development can happen more quickly and more effectively. Although nonprofit organizations often spearhead efforts for community development, they rely heavily on volunteers to accomplish what needs to be done. And because family volunteers give not just their time but also their money, communities reap financial benefit as well.

This is also true when a disaster occurs. After the September 11 terrorist attacks, three out of four people surveyed said they responded by volunteering in some way. Some donated blood. Some donated their time to help the victims. Many gave money, food, or clothing. Organizations can help funnel this energy into a big impact. While one family can make a difference in helping out, imagine what good 100 families—or even 15—can do together.

Researchers have found that family service projects build close-knit families, and the greater number of highly functioning families a community has, the stronger the community becomes.

Most important, family service helps people in need. Ask families who donate their time to doing a work camp experience (such as repairing homes for the poor) or to serving a meal at a homeless shelter, and they will tell you their presence makes a difference. They see service recipients light up when they receive the help they need.

Indirect Service

The challenge, however, is that most families don't do this type of direct family service. It's scary to them. They are intimidated by the idea of interacting with recipients or they believe it takes more of a commitment than they can give.

That's why this book focuses on *indirect* family service projects: to keep the pressure low and attract families who would shy away from direct service. Indirect service projects are done at your organization's site or somewhere else, not at a recipient site where families would meet recipients face to face. Someone in your organization will have direct contact with the recipient organization, and that person can tell your families what an impact they've had. In the meantime, families will feel encouraged to do the good work that helps your organization, their children, their families, and their community. Once families get used to doing family service in small, easy, comfortable ways, they're more likely to take the next step and start doing family service directly for those in need.

We wrote this book to help you make family service easy, fun, inviting, and successful. For organizations that already offer family service, it's time to go deeper. For those that do not, it's time to begin.

We'd love to hear how your family service projects work. You can write to us with your stories or questions in care of our publisher:

Free Spirit Publishing
217 Fifth Avenue North, Suite 200
Minneapolis, MN 55401-1299

Or email us at help4kids@freespirit.com

Jenny Friedman, Ph.D., and Jolene Roehlkepartain

Introduction

Leading Successful Family Service Projects

Doing Good Together is a collection of group activities that help schools, organizations, and workplaces create successful family service projects. Through easy projects, interactive learning, and reflection, families see how they can make a difference, and they become closer to each other during the process. These family service projects help families understand the importance of caring and compassion, empowering them to make positive choices for themselves and have a positive impact on the lives of others.

The family service projects in this book are organized into chapters based on theme. They serve a wide range of recipients and offer many different benefits. They have been developed for use by schools, organizations (recreation programs, clubs, sports teams, government agencies, and congregations), and workplaces (corporations, small businesses, and nonprofits).

The projects in this book are designed to be used with families with preschool to 12th-grade children—and also with families who don't have children. Because of the broad audience, you may need to customize activities to fit your situation. Schools and organizations that already have service programs will find these projects particularly useful as they begin to explore and expand their programs to include families. Those that are just beginning will find the clear, step-by-step projects a great way to get started and create a successful family service program. Regardless of your experience, we recommend you read the entire introduction in order to best prepare yourself for organizing family service events.

All the handouts in this book are included as PDF documents on the CD-ROM. They can be customized and printed out.

Integrating Family Service into Your Organization

Since family service projects are concrete and easy to set up, many organizations jump right in. Yet it pays to slow down a bit and be intentional about your approach. If you want to integrate family service into your organization's mission and goals, it's often helpful to follow these six guidelines.

1. Share your family service vision with key people

People excited about family service have found that getting key personnel involved from the beginning helps ensure that their family service efforts are supported. If you're in a school, it's essential to get the support of administrators as well as teachers who are seen as leaders. If you're in an organization or business, connect with the leaders and movers and shakers.

Getting important allies on board from the beginning can greatly enhance your family service efforts. Many leaders have ideas about how to reach families, work within the current systems, and lend support.

2. Build a family service team

Your family service efforts will go much further if you build a family service team. This ensures that everything doesn't fall on the shoulders of one person, which could kill the entire effort if that person happens to leave or move (or get burned out).

In addition, team members bring different strengths to the table. It's often helpful to have committed parents who believe in family service; they often can get the word out to other parents, and they can provide a valuable perspective on how to attract busy families. People who are skilled in communications can help with promotions and publicity. You'll also need individuals who are creative, are great managers (to pull together people and materials for events), and have strong people skills.

3. Develop a vision for family service

Have your team dream about what an ideal family service effort would look like. Ask: "If visitors came from out of state and asked what we're doing for family service that's attracting so much attention, what would we say?"

This often is a good starting point. After discussion, consider creating a vision statement that is a clear written summary of your family service vision. Most organizations can do this in one to four sentences. Remember that a vision statement is different from a mission statement. A vision statement focuses on what you want, whereas a mission statement says how you get there.

Some family service vision statements include ideas like these:

- We believe every family can make a difference in our community through family service.
- The vision for our school is to engage families in meaningful service.
- We envision that families in our community foster caring, kindness, tolerance, and compassion by valuing what truly matters. Our families act on their values by doing meaningful family service.

4. Create awareness, energy, and commitment

You develop awareness, energy, and commitment for family service by helping people understand the idea and motivation behind family service.

The preface to this book contains a lot of information about why family service matters; use that information as a resource when working with families in your organization. It can help people understand why service is so important, and it can inspire them to act.

Provide lots of opportunities to serve. If you make the case for family service and then offer only one family service project, you may have trouble engaging families. But if you make a commitment to offer an annual family service project—or a quarterly family service project—then people will begin to see that it's important to act and keep making a difference.

Your publicity efforts often can create energy around your family service projects. People get excited when they hear about creative ways to make a difference. For example, in one community, a family service project was created for family members to do simple weavings that were then displayed in the foyer of the community's new food bank. The project became a symbol of how individual strengths are woven together to make a difference in a community.

5. Connect with other family service leaders

Who else in your community, school district, or area does family service? Or coordinates general volunteer projects? Get to know these people. Ask about their successful projects and what they've learned. Swap ideas. The best part about family service is that the possibilities are endless. Whenever there is a need, there's a creative way for families to serve. When you connect with others who are also doing what you're doing, you can often generate more energy and ideas than you could if you tried to do it all alone.

6. Make success easy—and ongoing

One of the best ways to motivate families is to provide low-risk opportunities where they have a really good experience and want to come back for more. Choose family service projects that are easy (don't require specific skills) and low cost, and that have immediate success. Most of the family service projects in this book meet these criteria, and will create a sense of energy among members of your organization and the families involved in service.

But getting families into your organization to do family service is only one step. You also want to encourage the step of having families do service on their own. Consider including family service projects that families can do at home in your newsletter or at your website, or creating a handout to send ideas home with families. Your efforts will have a long-term impact only if you support and strengthen families' commitment to family service in general.

Not all families will do family service on their own, but if you encourage them to do so—no matter where they are—and provide resources and ideas to make it easier, many will.

Keys to a Successful Family Service Project

We know when family service projects succeed. A lot of families come out to the project. A lot gets accomplished, and people want to do more.

But how do you get to these outcomes? We've discovered seven keys that family service projects need to succeed:

Key 1: Purpose

A successful family service project has a strong sense of purpose. Whether it's feeding the hungry, providing support to the sick, or beautifying the environment, a concrete, appealing purpose draws people in and makes a project worthwhile. Each of the 101 family service projects in this book begins with a purpose.

Key 2: Simplicity

When you're working with families who may have infants, preschoolers, and teenagers, the most successful projects will be ones that are simple—yet meaningful. When you have families together, you want to spend most of your time doing the family service project instead of trying to explain it. The 101 family service projects in this book aim to keep projects simple by providing simple material lists, simple steps before the project begins, and simple steps for doing the project.

Key 3: Creativity

Most family members are familiar with common service projects, such as picking up litter and raking lawns. After a while, such projects can become ho-hum, even though they are important. Infuse creativity into common projects and develop new projects that have an interesting twist. Many times what gets families talking are the creative projects, such as project 16: Nets by the Numbers, 31: Whisper Phones, 40: Quarter Rally, and 59: Operation Remember.

Look through the "Bonus Ideas" section of each project for ways to inject more creativity into the project. Develop your own ideas to make projects even more engaging. Enlist the help of a creative partner who could add another dimension to your family service project. Ask for ideas.

Key 4: Intergenerational appeal

Successful family service projects appeal to all families. In our society today, we tend to segregate family members by age. We send kids to school to attend classrooms where everyone is the same age. We send elders to "adult daycare" and young children to childcare. Very rarely are families offered opportunities to be together—and serve together.

A family service project that is intergenerational, providing meaningful ways for all family members to contribute together, can strengthen families as well as provide valuable service. Be sure to emphasize to your group that family members of any generation and age are welcome. The family service projects in this book are created to appeal to multigenerational families.

Key 5: Relationship building

Deepen relationships between family members and also between families at your family service events. Create ways for people to connect in meaningful ways. Many successful family service projects begin with a community-building game, such as those found in chapter 12. Some even have a conversation starter, such as "After you say your first name, talk about one low from your week and one high." The more you build relationships, the more likely families will come back for more.

Key 6: Reflection

Many students and schools are familiar with service learning, which is a learning strategy that integrates meaningful community service with self-reflection, self-discovery, and the acquisition of skills, values, and knowledge. When family members have the opportunity to reflect on the service project that they have just participated in, they integrate their experience with their thoughts and feelings. They think about what they've done and what they could do next. All the family service projects in this book include a number of reflection questions to ask families toward the end of your time together.

Key 7: A next step

Although you will encourage more participation and a higher rate of success if you make family service projects easy and simple, you also want to encourage families to continue doing service. Some organizations create a list of easy service projects families can do at home. In schools, you can even ask students to bring back the list with checkmarks indicating which projects their families did, then add a loop to a paper chain for each project completed. By building a "chain of caring," students will have a visual reminder of the family service they have done, and that can motivate

them to do more. You can hold follow-up meetings, send home a newsletter or handouts, or use your website to provide additional service ideas to your families. See Chapter 11: Projects Families Can Do on Their Own.

Doing a Project

Each of the projects in this book contains the following elements. Be sure to read the entire project before you begin.

Purpose

The purpose appears at the beginning of every family service project and provides a quick overview of the project. It succinctly states what the families will do, whom the service will benefit, and why this project matters.

Possible Recipients

This section helps you identify appropriate recipients for the service, such as a homeless shelter, a crisis nursery, or a food shelf. Most projects highlight local recipients as well as organizations with a broader reach, such as national and international groups. Be sure to contact the recipient group you choose before beginning your project. See page 6.

Time Requirement

This includes time needed to plan your project, prepare for it on the day of your event, and complete the project steps with families.

People

Most of the projects in this book appeal to a wide age range, so all families can get involved, though some require older children and teenagers while others may be more appealing to younger children. In the "People" section, you'll find guidelines regarding what age range is best for the project. And while you'll want to recruit volunteers from within your organization to help out with general tasks for most projects, the "People" section will let you know if there are any unusual or particularly important needs for volunteers. This section can also help you estimate your expected output.

Materials

This section lists all the materials you'll need to do the actual project as well as suggestions on where to find unusual materials. For most projects, you'll need to decide whether to provide all materials, buy materials and have families make a donation to cover the costs, or ask families to donate the materials. In many cases, a combination of these will be appropriate. Be sure to plan ahead.

Connecting Point

Help families understand the importance of the project with the "Connecting Point," which puts a finer focus on the "Purpose" by emphasizing a real-life, concrete connection between what families are doing and how the recipients will benefit from it.

Doing the Project

These are the steps you'll follow to plan, organize, and execute the project.

Debriefing the Project

A central part of successful family service projects involves "Debriefing the Project." When families can talk about and process their experience, they're more likely to make sense of what they did and see the value in it.

Some people aren't used to reflecting on experiences, which can make the time difficult at first. The more questions you can create for families to discuss, the easier it will be for them to debrief your family service project. Make sure you create ways for kids to talk. (If young children are tired by this point in your project, take a quick break for kids to stretch—or even run around the room if that's safe.) Adults can dominate conversation without realizing it. Asking, "What does each person at your table think about this project?" will help encourage everyone to participate.

The questions in "Debriefing the Project" begin by asking families concrete questions about their experience. The questions then ask families to reflect on their experience before talking about what they can do next. If a lot of families are present, it may be more effective to have families talk within small groups, such as at their tables. Then you can have a large-group discussion after families have had the time to go through the debriefing questions.

Debriefing questions are titled "Talking Points" in Chapter 11: Projects Families Can Do on Their Own.

Helpful Resources

Family members often get excited about the family service projects they're doing and may want to learn more about the social issue you're addressing. This section includes reading suggestions for young children and for teens. Consider incorporating these helpful resources directly into the project or distributing a list of resources that family members can look for on their own. Most of the books are recent and easy enough to get, but we've included a few older books that we consider classics. You can usually track these down through a library.

Bonus Ideas

Although you can do each family service project as it's presented in this book, sometimes you may want to adapt a project or add a creative twist to it. The bonus section gives you additional ideas on how to take a family service project further.

Handouts

Many projects include reproducible handouts that give directions, provide a list of possible donations, or serve as a sponsorship form (for example, for project 35: Family Read-a-Thon) for families. Handouts for each chapter are grouped together at the end of that chapter, so they're easy to find. They're also on the CD-ROM included with this book, so you can customize them and print them out.

Choosing a Project

This book includes 101 family service projects, most of which can be completed in one to two hours. Review the possibilities in light of your goals (what issue is important to your group). You may want to bring families together to do a single project, or perhaps you'd like to create five to ten "booths" or "stations," each of which offers a simple hands-on project that families can choose to participate in as they wish.

Most of the projects in this book are indirect family service projects. That means you don't see the recipients you're serving. The reason for this is simple: to create a low-risk, easy way for families to get involved in service. Even though visiting residents at a nursing home is a great family service project, it is intimidating to many families, especially those who are not used to family service. In addition, direct family service projects, where families work with the recipients, are more difficult to do well because they add a number of layers of complexity. For your convenience, chapter 10 offers direct family service projects for when your group is ready to take that step. Since the main goal with this book is to make family service easy and simple, indirect projects are what we have emphasized.

When you choose a project (or set of projects), consider carefully how much time will be required. Projects that involve collecting and assembling kits or various items, such as 13: School Kits, 20: Baby Kits, and 25: Toy Treasures, can end in a few minutes if you don't have other activities planned. With projects like this, you may want to spend more time on the "Connecting Point" and other education pieces you find (often, recipient organizations have lots of information at their websites). Or create two to five stations, each with a different family service project. For example, if you want to have a family service event to support our troops, consider setting up five stations with five different projects from this book. Finally, consider opening your event by playing one or more of the games suggested in chapter 12. This can add substance and fun to your project.

Also be aware of how much space each project will require. Making blankets, for example, involves a large amount of floor space. You can set up stations in one large room or scatter them around your school, organization, congregation, or community building.

The cost matters as well. Organizations with limited finances or those new to family service projects often choose low- and no-cost family service projects. These types of projects are much more accessible to all kinds of families—especially to those who may not be able to afford an "entrance fee" or a "service project donation fee."

Choosing a Charitable Organization

In your area, you likely have a number of charitable organizations that will happily receive your donations or service. Make your decision of which to serve based on the goals and enthusiasm of your group and the needs in your community. For example, one congregation learned that their local food shelf was in dire need of breakfast cereals. So they created a family service project of collecting breakfast cereals. This got families talking about nutrition, and many children talking about their favorite cereals and wanting to share them with those in need.

Before you do any family service project, always check with the possible recipients to talk about your project and any requirements they may have for receiving donations. Your project will be stronger and more meaningful if you learn in advance what kind of help recipients truly need and what requirements they have. This is particularly true for any military donations, because there are strict laws about what they can and cannot accept.

Many organizations that distribute kits and items to disadvantaged people have religious ties. When we mention these organizations, we are not promoting a religion but rather noticing solid organizations that are doing good. If your group has religious ties, consider seeing if your denomination or religious organization has a volunteer or relief arm that distributes items. If you're in a secular setting, check with government agencies to see if you can distribute items through them or through a local nonprofit.

Usually, once you contact an organization and meet their needs, you'll develop a relationship. Over time, you'll work together to create other family service projects that truly help the recipient organization's mission and needs. This relationship often inspires you—and the families who do these service projects—to want to do more.

Preparing for Your Project

Once you know what your recipient organization's needs are, it's time to start planning how you will execute your family service project. One of the first things you'll need to do is locate a space to host your event. If a space is available in your organization's building, you'll likely have to reserve

Six Questions to Ask the Recipient Organization

Call the organization you're interested in serving and find out whom you should work with to coordinate donations. Explain to that person that you would like to donate items through your family service project, and be clear that you're interested in donating items, not having families come to the organization to serve. Ask these questions:

1. Which items do you need? (If you're meeting in person, bring this book with you and show some of the projects you're interested in doing.)

2. Can you use everything we create? (For example, if you're creating place mats, estimate how many you'll make, such as 50, and ask if the organization will accept them all.)

3. Are there certain days or hours when it's best to bring the donations?

4. How would you like us to bring the donations? For example, do you want us to drop off donations all at once?

5. Can families drop off the donations? If so, can they bring their kids?

6. Can you give the volunteers who drop off the donation a short tour?

it well in advance. If you don't have available space, you will need to look into renting one.

Read carefully through the project or projects you've chosen, especially the "Doing the Project" steps, to begin planning your event. Each project has "Bonus Ideas" you will want to consider, and many have handouts you'll need to photocopy. Do you want to incorporate games (see chapter 12) or education materials from the recipient organization? It's never too early to begin accounting for the materials you'll need, as well. If you'll be asking for donations (for example, craft supplies or food items), identify possible donors and contact them. If you'll need to acquire things like tables and chairs, computers, projectors, garbage barrels, or recycling bins, start locating these items as soon as you can.

Create a sample of the item you will make during the service project. This not only will show families how the finished product looks but also help you prepare for questions families may have when they're doing the project, since you will have gained expertise in doing the project. This is even more important for projects that require assembly or some type of creation.

Create a budget

Consider the cost of materials, food, and space rental (if applicable). Decide which items can be donated. Some organizations are skilled at getting donated items. Others find it easier to have individual families pay a fee to cover the costs. Both methods have their strengths and weaknesses, and some organizations have found that having a mix of the two can be effective.

See if you have families (or even members of your organization) who have ties to companies that may be willing to donate. For example, one parent worked for a corporation that manufactures breakfast foods. When the parent asked about a donation, the corporation was happy to donate all the breakfast foods required to complete the family service project. All the parent had to do was ask.

Money can become an obstacle for families if you're not careful. Many families are inundated with requests and fundraisers. Closely monitor how much you require families to contribute to a family service project. You'll attract more attendees if the cost is low—or nonexistent. A few of the activities in this book can be done at no cost. Check out projects 51: 100 Steps to Peace and 55: Paper Peace Quilt.

Choose a strategic date

When will you hold your event? Be sure to consider things such as holidays, school schedules, and busy times of the year. Many families travel during the summer, so attendance rates can be lower then, although some families are looking for activities to do with their kids during the months away from school. For many families, the months of September and May are already loaded with back-to-school and end-of-school activities. During the school year, schools often will offer a family service project that coincides with parent-teacher conferences or open houses, since a family service project often can boost attendance for these events.

The winter holidays can be a tricky time. For some families, the holidays are already too busy, and they're not interested in adding one more activity to their jammed calendars. But other families are looking for family service projects during this time because they want their kids to focus more on giving rather than on getting. So experiment with the holidays and see what works for your organization.

It's important to set a date early on and get the word out about the date. Although some families are loose about their schedules, some are highly scheduled. Busy families often are interested in family service projects, but they won't be able to come if they find out about your project only a few days in advance. Take a double approach to getting the word out: Publicize the event early and then again shortly before your project. That way you're more likely to attract highly scheduled families *and* families who decide to do activities at the last minute.

Find volunteers

Besides the families who volunteer to participate, you will need volunteers to help make your event run smoothly. Consider asking members of your organization to chip in by focusing on tasks in the following five areas:

- **Setup and cleanup volunteers** will gather all your materials, set up the area for your project, and clean it up.
- **Donation solicitors** will approach businesses (and families who like to give) for donations of supplies and materials.
- **Promotional volunteers** will get the word out about your project and take photos during the event for publicity.
- **Greeters** will be at the doors to welcome families and direct them to your event.
- **Project leaders** will lead and run your service project during the event.

You can also recruit families for these roles. You can often find families by tapping into your employee or membership base or by connecting with your school's parent-teacher organization, such as the PTA, PTO, or PTSO. Family volunteers, in addition to your organizational volunteers, can be critical to your success.

Don't overlook the leadership of older kids and teens. For example, in one K–5 school, the fifth graders were asked to lead family service projects during an event that included a number of different family service stations. The younger kids were excited to spend time with these older kids, and the older kids were proud to show that they could teach families how to do a family service project. Consider asking high school students to help. Many are looking for volunteer opportunities to fulfill class requirements, to bolster college applications, and just because they enjoy it.

You may not need a large team of volunteers to pull this off. Some organizations have one or two volunteers who do it all. Others recruit families, so you have both parents and children helping out. It all depends on how large of an event you're planning.

Recruit families for your service project

Recruit families for your service project by getting the word out through your website, email, newsletters, flyers, and other promotional materials. Recruitment works best when you do it often and in as many different ways as possible. Start as soon as you set the date for your project, and look for promotional outlets beyond the obvious ones just named, including marquees, bulletin boards, and perhaps local media, which often look for stories about families doing good things in the community. Media coverage can get the word out to families you wouldn't be able to reach through your inhouse methods.

Don't underestimate the power of word of mouth. When families get excited about something, they tell other families about it. Even though families are busy, they're always on the lookout for meaningful activities that bring out the best in their family members—and also bring their family together. Personal invitations are particularly powerful. Nothing is more effective than someone personally asking a family to attend and mentioning how nice it would be to see the family there. Some organizations even set up a phone tree to get the word out.

Often, a powerful way to recruit families is by getting kids energized. At one school, volunteers came to classrooms and read picture books about hunger in the days before a family service project of working at a community kitchen. Volunteers then helped the children make invitations on paper plates to take home to their parents. (The paper plates said, "Help us feed hungry people" and listed the date, time, and place of the family service project.) When the kids got excited, they got their parents motivated to attend, and more families came than what organizers had expected.

If you can, focus your recruitment efforts on the suggested age range of the project you're doing. If you want to attract families with pre-schoolers, reach out to those families. If you want families who have high school students, find ways to recruit these families.

Link your project to working systems

Instead of starting from scratch, see how family service can fit with systems that are already working. For example, does your organization already have a parents' night? Is there a way to include family service in that? A number of colleges and universities have discovered that parent weekends are a perfect opportunity to add a family service project. Or does your organization already offer service projects for kids to do? Is there a way to expand them to include families? Integrating family service into existing systems is a great way to minimize extra efforts and take advantage of what's already working for you.

Create ways to get families talking

It's important that your event begin conversations between parents and children about social issues and the value of giving and service. Before the event, consider having an assembly or gathering to discuss the issues, show videos, or have a speaker make a presentation about the difference that everyone's participation will make. Consider setting out table tents with reflection questions written on them. Or make time during the event for small groups of families to talk about the issues you're addressing. Consider having a guest speaker. If you're making sandwiches for a homeless shelter, for example, a person who was formerly homeless or a shelter worker could be on hand to talk about how important your service project is and to answer anyone's questions.

Discussion after the event is equally valuable. An easy way to get conversations started is by having families evaluate the event. As families fill out the evaluation form, they typically discuss how the project went for them and what they enjoyed. You can also plan to celebrate the success of your event when it's over, giving families the opportunity to reflect on what they accomplished. What did they like about the event? What could make it more powerful? Getting family members talking will cement their experience and often make it more likely that they'll want to do more.

Use handouts

Families often find it helpful to receive a handout that gives them a list of resources—or gives them ideas of how else they can serve together as a family. Throughout this book, you'll find ready-to-use handouts to photocopy (or print out from the CD-ROM) and distribute. You can also create your own. Consider handouts that describe the family service project, have a list of reflection questions, list additional volunteer opportunities, provide book suggestions, or give more in-depth information about a social issue or a specific charitable organization.

Some of the handouts in this book are intended to be distributed before the event. Others are used during the event, while some can be given at the end of the event. Make sure you have read the project guidelines and you know how to use the handouts in the most effective way possible. Plan ahead: Remember to make copies before your event so your handouts are ready to go.

Consider offering refreshments

Food is often a significant attraction for families and can make your event feel more festive. Ask for donations from families or from local businesses. If you decide to offer food, consider making it free of charge, or use funds raised from food sales to help pay for the event or as a donation to charity. You will need to decide whether you'll offer snacks (such as cookies and bars, popcorn, sno-cones) or a meal (submarine sandwiches, pizza, hot dogs, and so on). If your event occurs around dinner or lunch, offering more substantial fare can be a big draw for families. Whatever you decide, you'll need to plan for obtaining the food, serving it, and cleaning up. Also, plan whether you intend families to eat before, during, or after the project.

Record your event

If possible, have a photographer and/or videographer come to the event. (Think of a high school student, parent, or other community member who might volunteer for this task.) Families enjoy seeing photos of their activities. Plan a slide show or video as part of your post-event celebration. Or you might email photos to the participants along with a thank you, or post photos in your newsletter or at your website.

Executing the Project

After you've done all the necessary preparations, the big day finally arrives: It's time to do the project or projects you've chosen. Follow these steps.

Set up your space

Before the event, set up your space so it's comfortable, organized, and welcoming to families. Set up tables and chairs so families have places to sit and do the project. Gather all your materials. Make sure you have garbage and recycling bins. If you need items such as projectors, computers, or laminators, make sure they're in working order. If you plan to offer refreshments, gather them beforehand. Also know where restrooms and exits are so that you can direct families to these places when needed.

Set up a sign-in table, so families can sign in with their names and email addresses. Afterward, you can send a thank-you note or photos from the event. Some organizations even create a website (or use part of their website) to post photos from their family service events.

Create a warm, caring atmosphere

Family members notice right away when they've entered a room where they are welcome. People greet them and say how glad they are to see them. They're directed to where they need to start. Greeters help create a warm, caring atmosphere, an essential component of a successful family service project. Think about what else you can do to make the atmosphere relaxed, comfortable, caring, and warm. Consider providing nametags.

Introduce the project

Welcome families and introduce them to the service project. For each project in this book, you can refer to the "Purpose" and the "Connecting Point" sections to guide you.

Feel free to also talk about the recipients. Let families know how much what they're doing matters. Some of the websites listed under the "Possible Recipients" sections have stories of individual recipients that you can print out and discuss. If you're working with a local organization, talk to your contact at that organization in advance for information you can share with the group.

Once you've introduced the project, give directions for doing it. Encourage families to ask for help when needed. (Do you want them to raise their hand or seek out certain volunteers?) Talk about what they do when they've finished the project, such as putting the completed lunch bags in a box at the front of the room. Explain what will happen after the event, such as a volunteer delivering all the donations to the organization by a certain time.

Do the steps

Have your families begin the project by going through the steps described in the "Doing the Project" section of each project. As they work, walk around the room and talk with people. Have your other volunteers do this as well. This makes it easier for families to ask questions, and it also creates a warm atmosphere. Some organizations station a volunteer at various workstations or tables so they're doing the projects side by side with the families. What's important is to figure out ways to be with families and help them feel like you're all working together. Be sure to debrief the project using the debriefing questions included in each project (see page 5).

Evaluating and Celebrating the Project

It is always a good idea to evaluate any family volunteer event. You may use evaluation to determine which projects were favorites and which events stimulated the most discussion within families and encouraged them to pursue other service opportunities. Evaluation results can also help inform your next event. While debriefing helps families get the most out of projects, evaluating helps you improve your projects in the future.

A simple way to evaluate is to provide an evaluation questionnaire for participants to fill out. You could create your own form or use the one on page 12 of this book (and also on the CD-ROM). If you want to create a quick, short evaluation, consider asking three questions:

1. How would you rate your family's experience during this family service project? Circle one: Great. Okay. Disappointing.

2. What was the best part of this family service project?

3. What suggestions do you have to improve this family service project?

Alternatively, have a volunteer circulate among families and interview them toward the end of the event. This can be especially valuable if you have a lot of families who don't have high literacy skills or who speak English as a second language.

It's important to hear from everyone—from your youngest participants to your oldest ones. Family members are often more likely to take the time to fill out an evaluation if you give them a free coupon for ice cream, for example, or have them add a picture of a hand (or heart) to the wall with their name on it to show that they've made a difference. You could also email an evaluation form to participants later on, although your response rate will probably be much lower. Once families leave, it can be harder to get them to respond to emails and surveys.

It's also a good idea to evaluate the event with the volunteers from your organization. Ask questions such as:

- Did the event fulfill its goals and objectives? Why or why not?

- What worked?

- What needs fine-tuning?

- How well attended was the event?

- What was the feedback from participants?

- What can improve an event like this one for next time?

Celebrate your success

It's important to celebrate your successes and thank everyone who contributed. Consider holding an assembly or special service to announce the results of your family service project not long after the event. Try to celebrate within a few days to a month afterward, depending on your organization. For example, if you're in a school or business that meets daily during the workweek, you can usually celebrate within a few days or a few weeks. If your organization meets monthly or only a few times a month, then you can celebrate a bit later after the event.

Show slides of the event. Have the service recipients talk about its impact. Send photos to everyone who participated, along with a thank-you note for their help. Make a visual display, such as having family members write their names on paper hearts and displaying them on a wall with a sign that says, "Together, we can make a difference." Write a story for your organization's newsletter, website, or other outlet. Think about publicity opportunities in school district publications and in your local media.

The Morris County, New Jersey, chapter of Jack and Jill of America celebrates its annual family service project by posting the accomplishments at the organization's website. Every year, they do a family service project to help homeless shelters in Morris County, renovating children's rooms, donating furniture, providing children's books, and hosting parties for the shelter's child residents. This project has grown by developing a project for the family's teenagers who plan the menu, shop, cook, and serve breakfast once a month for the residents.

Family Service Project Evaluation Form

Name of family service project: _____ Today's date: _____

For each statement, please check one response:

	Yes, Absolutely	Somewhat	Not So Much	Not Applicable
1. The project was interesting.				
2. The project was well organized.				
3. The project engaged family members of all ages present.				
4. The project took the right amount of time.				
5. The handout was helpful.				
6. The leader knew a lot about the topic.				
7. The leader covered the project clearly.				
8. The leader responded well to questions.				
9. I feel like I made a difference through this project.				
10. I want to do another family service project.				

What did you like best about this project?

What could be improved?

Overall, how would you rate this family service project? (Check one box.)

❏ Excellent   ❏ Good   ❏ Fair   ❏ Poor

Thank you for your feedback! Your opinion will help make future family service projects even better.

Enhancing Your Family Service Program

Once you get started doing family service projects, you'll wonder what else you can do. There are many possibilities, and you can create deeper, more meaningful events by expanding your perspective. Start by making any improvements that you identify through evaluations. Be receptive to suggestions from the families that volunteer, because they are the ones who can really improve your program.

Then, consider the following ideas:

Provide creative touches that capture people's attention

Creative touches make a difference. If you have a lot of young children, for example, consider adding paper "tablecloths" to the table. When the children get restless, have them draw pictures on the paper with washable markers or crayons. Or consider having a basket of plastic eggs with short messages inside. Each family service project in this book includes a "Bonus Ideas" section that can jump-start your creativity and get you thinking in new ways.

Create meaningful conversation starters for participants

Although every family service project in this book has reflection questions, you can go deeper than that. Create conversation starters that help family members get to know each other better—and also to get to know some of the other participants. You can put the conversation starters on individual pieces of paper and place them in a bowl in the middle of each table. Or you can make paper fortune tellers and have questions inside.

Consider asking questions, such as these:

- Where did you spend your childhood?
- What's your favorite book or magazine? Why?
- What gets you excited about life?
- Why is family service important to you?
- What is the most memorable trip you've ever taken?
- What do you wish you had more time to do?
- What is your favorite activity to do with your family?
- What has been one of the biggest surprises in your life so far?
- Are you a morning person or a night owl?
- What is the one social issue you're most concerned about? Why?
- What is your favorite music? Why?
- What do you like best about your job/school/ volunteer activities? Why?
- What makes you laugh?
- How would the world change if every family got involved in family service?

Showcase your results

Find ways to showcase your results. Families like to see that what they do matters. Post the number of healthcare kits you made. Make a paper display on the wall of a gigantic sandwich (if you made sandwiches) and ask each person involved to add a colorful piece of cheese, tomato, or lettuce, to make a super-sized sandwich.

Many recipient organizations' websites feature stories, photos, or videos of recipients telling how much donations help them. These personal reflections help families feel more connected to the recipients—even if they've never met them.

Besides publicizing your success, recognize the families who are involved. Take photos and make a Family Service Hall of Fame wall: Create a wall of red construction paper hearts that says "100 Reasons We Do Family Service Projects" and then have each family write their reason on a heart and include a photo.

Recognize families' contributions outside your organization

As you get to know families, find out if they're doing family service at home. A number of them are. When you learn about what they're doing, recognize their efforts. For example, the Doing Good Together website (www.doinggoodtogether.org) features stories of what families are doing. Other organizations do the same, and if your organization has a website, so can you. You may also recognize family work through a newsletter, bulletin board or wall display, or by drawing attention to them at your service event.

What's important is to share stories. By telling stories, you not only recognize families doing good together, but you also inspire other families to become creative and think of ways they can help out.

For example, the Layton family of Payson, Utah, created a "jump-a-thon" for their neighborhood kids to get into the spirit of giving. Along with their four children, the Laytons—kids included—chose two organizations to receive the proceeds: the Utah Foster Care Foundation and the Make a Child Smile Foundation. The day after Thanksgiving, Mr. Layton rigged a tarp over the family's large backyard trampoline (for fear it was going to rain). Starting at 7 a.m., 35 kids and three adults took turns jumping in the "jumping cave" for 12 hours. The participating jumpers had collected pledges in advance, and when the event was over, they had raised $566.

Stories like these show that there are endless possibilities for doing service together as families. They also reveal the great ideas people can dream up by starting out with the question "What if . . . ?"

Introduce families to a wide range of social issues

Sadly, our world is filled with problems, pain, and great need. The family service projects in this book cover a wide range of social issues. You'll find projects from easing poverty to helping people who are sick. Within each of these general categories is a plethora of specific social issues, such as cancer, endangered animals, support for troops, and more. As you plan your family service projects, keep these various social issues in mind and help expand people's thinking about them by providing projects involving a wide range of issues.

Start a book club

Many people enjoy book clubs, but most book clubs are segregated by age and gender. What if you started a family service book club? You may want to have one that's geared for families with young children and another that's geared for families with teenagers; you can dig into a lot of books and social issues through this format. All of the 101 family service projects in this book contain recommendations for a book for younger children and a book for teenagers. Consider creating book clubs based on these books. Or even do a one-time book club for which everyone reads one of the books.

Book clubs are a great way to look more deeply at social issues and tap into another side of family members. As participants discuss a book about a social issue, such as homelessness or cancer, not only do they learn more about the social issue, but they inevitably face these questions: What can we do about this? How can we tell others about this situation? How can we make a difference?

Notice what works

Build on your successes. Some projects draw more families than others. Find out why. Sometimes it's the project. Sometimes it's the timing. Once you learn why something is working, keep building on that. You don't want to bore families by repeating things over and over, but you can create different adaptations on what works.

Keep positive

Working on social issues doesn't need to feel heavy or morose. To stay upbeat, focus on how you're making a difference. It's true that your handmade cards will not cure a child of cancer, but they will lift a child's spirits. Your sandwiches will not end hunger, but they will feed a number of people who will appreciate what you do.

Empower families to notice that our small actions count. When we do good together, we can help make our world a better place and make a difference in ways that truly matter.

Chapter 1
Projects to Provide Friendship and Comfort

Everyone likes to feel wanted and connected. Whether an elderly person is lonely, a child feels out of place at a new school, or an adult is going through a rough time because of a layoff, these family service projects remind people that they're cared for—and that they matter.

① Blanket the World

Purpose

Through blankets created by family volunteers, help provide security, warmth, and comfort to children who have been traumatized, are seriously ill, or are in need of care.

Possible Recipients

- Local options: a homeless shelter, a domestic-abuse shelter, a children's hospital, or a crisis nursery
- Other options: Project Linus (www.projectlinus.org) or Binky Patrol (www.binkypatrol.org)

Time Requirement

Planning time before the project: one to three hours. Gathering materials: one to two hours. Setup time on the day of your project: one to two hours. Project time: one to two hours.

People

This project is ideal for families with children between the ages of 5 and 18. Expect each family to make one blanket during the one-hour event.

Materials

- 2 pieces of fleece (1.5 yards each) for each family
- 1 pair of fabric scissors for each family
- 1 roll of masking tape for about every three families
- 1 tape measure, yardstick, or ruler for each family or two
- Optional: About 3 times as many copies of the "Make a Blanket for a Child in Need" handout (page 31) as the number of families you hope to attract

The fabric and fabric scissors are available at fabric stores such as Jo-Ann Fabrics & Crafts and Hancock Fabrics.

Connecting Point

Ask participants to imagine a blanket or stuffed animal that means a lot to them. Explain that there are children who are scared, worried, insecure, sad, or lonely because their parents might be serving overseas, their home has been damaged, or they are sick. A new blanket would be a warm and comforting surprise to these children.

Doing the Project

Before your event, publicize it by distributing the "Make a Blanket for a Child in Need" handout to families.

Make a sample blanket so you know how it's put together and to show as an example.

1. Place the two squares of fleece on top of each other back to back. This forms your blanket.
2. Trim the edges if the two fabric pieces aren't even with each other.
3. On one side of the blanket only, lay a strip of masking tape along all four edges, three inches in. The masking tape serves as a guide in cutting the corners and fringe.
4. Cut a 3" x 3" square from each corner outside the strips of masking tape. (Cut through both layers of the blanket.)

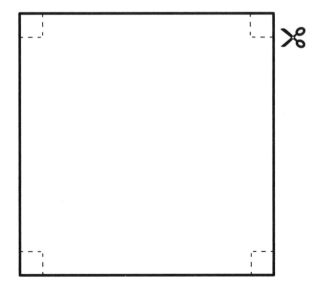

5. Cut parallel strips of fringe (about 1 inch wide each) into each of the four sides, stopping at the masking tape. Then remove the masking tape.

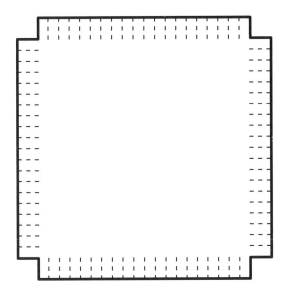

6. Tie each piece of top layer fringe to its corresponding bottom layer fringe. Tie a double knot so they're secure, but make sure the knots are not too tight against the body of the blanket or else the blanket forms a "bowl." Proceed around the entire blanket until all fringes are tied.

Debriefing the Project

- What was your experience in making the blanket?
- What was it like to make something for someone you've never met?
- Do you have a special blanket or stuffed animal? What else makes you feel safe and comforted?
- Why is it important to make blankets for children who are sick, sad, or afraid?
- What else can we do to help children?

Helpful Resources

- For children: *Geraldine's Blanket* by Holly Keller (Greenwillow Books, 1988), a story about how attached Geraldine becomes to her blanket.

- For teens: *Teen Knitting Club: Chill Out and Knit* by Jennifer Wenger, Carol Abrams, and Maureen Lasher (Artisan, 2004). This book discusses materials, stitches, and techniques, and includes helpful charts and illustrations to help you make everything from the basic hat to the poncho.

Bonus Ideas

- Ask attendees to come in their pajamas.
- Consider making blankets of different sizes. For families with younger kids, you can make smaller blankets and donate them to a maternity ward for newborns. (Project Linus and Binky Patrol also will distribute them to babies if you follow their guidelines.) For families with older kids, larger blankets can be fun to work on all together. You can find different sizes by searching at www.binkypatrol.org.
- If you have access to a computer or video player, watch a short story about Project Linus at www.msnbc.msn.com/id/16711082/.
- Consider tying a tag onto each blanket with a piece of ribbon. (Use squares of construction paper or colored cover stock paper.) On each tag, write something like, "This blanket was made especially for you by the families of _____ (name of school, organization, or business)." Have each person who works on the blanket sign his or her first name on the card.
- If you're organizing an event mainly for young children and their families (such as through a preschool), have volunteers prep the fabric ahead of time so families are only doing the tying, not the measuring and cutting. This requires more volunteer time upfront, but it makes it easier for families with young children to participate.
- Fleece fabric regularly goes on sale at fabric stores. Take advantage of those sales.
- Find more blanket patterns by going to the Project Linus website and clicking on "patterns/links."

② Place Mats to Go

Purpose

Make mealtime even more meaningful for seniors who receive Meals on Wheels by providing colorful place mats with uplifting messages.

Possible Recipients

- Local options: any social service agency that provides meals for homebound residents
- Other options: Meals on Wheels Association of America (www.mowaa.org lists local Meals on Wheels programs)

Time Requirement

Planning time before the project: one to two hours. Gathering materials: one hour. Setup time on the day of your project: 30 minutes to an hour. Project time: 30 minutes.

People

This project is ideal for families with children between the ages of 3 and 12. Expect each family to make one or two place mats during the 30-minute event.

Materials

- 8½" x 11" construction paper in many colors (about 2 sheets for each attendee); or 2 blank paper place mats for each attendee
- 1 pair of scissors for each family
- 5 markers for each family
- Decorating materials such as magazines and gardening catalogs from which pictures can be cut, paper samples, and stickers (enough for each family)
- 1 glue stick for each family
- Clear contact paper or laminating materials for each family

Paper place mats can be purchased at party-good stores; other supplies are available at craft stores such as Michael's or Jo-Ann Fabrics & Crafts.

Connecting Point

Talk about how lonely people can become when they are sick or homebound: A person who delivers a meal may be their only human contact. Your project can remind people who are homebound that someone else cares.

Doing the Project

Before your event, make a sample place mat so that you know how it's put together and to show as an example.

1. Have each family choose one piece of colored construction paper to be the place mat background. Give families the option of working on one place mat together or having each family member make one.
2. Have families decorate place mats with their own artwork, clipped images from catalogs and magazines, positive messages, and cutout figures such as hearts, flowers, or other shapes.
3. Use clear contact paper or laminate finished place mats to make them durable.

Debriefing the Project

- What did you experience as you made your place mat?
- Why is making a place mat a good service project?
- How do you think the seniors who receive your place mat will feel when they see what you've made?
- Sometimes people who are homebound get lonely. When have you felt lonely? What makes you feel better when you're lonely?
- What else can we do to help people who feel isolated?

Helpful Resources

- For children: *The Rainbow Fish* by Marcus Pfister (Scholastic, 2000), a tale about the beauty people hold inside.

- For teens: *The Power of Kindness: The Unexpected Benefits of Leading a Compassionate Life* by Piero Ferrucci (Tarcher, 2006), a book that explores this simple but profound subject.

Bonus Ideas

- Sometimes a local Meals on Wheels representative is willing to provide a list of first names so families can make personalized place mats for recipients.
- If you're working mainly with families who have young children (such as through a

preschool or childcare center), have pictures already cut out of magazines and gardening catalogs so children don't have to do the cutting. You can either have volunteers do this in advance or ask the parents to do the cutting during the project.

- Meals on Wheels programs also often want decorated brown or white paper lunch bags. Check with a local representative.
- Have families make matching coasters or a greeting card for the recipient as well.

3 Friendship Boxes

Purpose

Cheer up a child going through a stressful transition by providing a box of toys and prizes.

Possible Recipients

- Local options: a local homeless shelter or domestic-abuse shelter that caters to families with children
- Other options: the Red Cross Friendship Box program through a local Red Cross chapter. Visit the American Red Cross at www.redcross.org and enter your zip code under "Your local Red Cross." Then contact a local Red Cross to find out if they have a Friendship Box program.

Time Requirement

Planning time before the project: one to two hours. Gathering materials: one hour. Setup time on the day of your project: 30 minutes to an hour. Project time: 30 minutes.

People

This project is ideal for families with children between the ages of 3 and 18. Expect each family to make one or two friendship boxes during the 30-minute event.

Materials

- An empty shoe box for each family, plus one for a sample
- Wrapping paper or contact paper for each box
- 1 glue stick for each family if using wrapping paper
- 1 ream of 8½" x 11" white paper
- 5 markers of different colors for each family
- Variety of small toys and similar items to fill the boxes: unused toys from fast-food meals, school supplies, stickers, small stuffed animals, small notepads, containers of play dough, card games, small puzzle books, and so on
- Optional: 1 or more copies of "The Power of Friendship" handout (page 32) per family

Ask families to collect and donate the small items to put in the boxes, or ask for a financial donation and buy them yourself. Inexpensive items to fill the boxes can be purchased through a local dollar store or through Oriental Trading (www.orientaltrading.com). The rest of the materials are available at discount stores, such as Target, Kmart, and Walmart.

Connecting Point

Ask participants what items they own that remind them of their friends. Explain how children who live in homeless or domestic-abuse shelters may not have many friends—and they rarely have a place to store their valuables.

Doing the Project

1. Before your event, publicize the project with families and ask them to collect and bring small toys and other items.

2. Make a sample friendship box so you know how it's put together and to show as an example.

3. Decorate the outside of the shoe box with wrapping paper or contact paper.

4. Make a card with a positive message, using the white paper and markers.

5. Fill the friendship boxes with the handmade cards and the items families brought.

6. If you wish to distribute the handout "The Power of Friendship," do so now and have families complete it. If you like, ask families to share answers with the group.

Debriefing the Project

- Why do you think families become homeless?

- Why would it be hard to live in a homeless shelter instead of your own home?

- Why is it important to be concerned about children living in shelters?

- What else can we do to help children living in shelters?

Helpful Resources

- For children: *Fly Away Home* by Eve Bunting (Sandpiper, 1993), a story about a homeless boy and his father trying to find a place to live in a busy airport.

- For teens: *Rachel and Her Children: Homeless Families in America* by Jonathan Kozol (Three Rivers Press, 2006), a true story based on interviews with the homeless.

Bonus Ideas

- Instead of having families bring supplies, encourage them to make a five-dollar donation to participate and have all the supplies available. If you have any leftover donations, give that money along with your friendship boxes to the organization you're serving.

- Encourage families to write four or five short notes to insert in their friendship boxes.

- If volunteers are providing all the items to place into the friendship boxes, set up assembly-line piles of each type of item together (such as all the crayons in one pile and all the stuffed animals in another pile, and so on). Have families decide on a certain number of items (such as 10) to put into their boxes, then choose from the piles.

Helping Hands Notepaper

Purpose

Make notepads in the shape of children's hands to cheer up people who are sick or elderly.

Possible Recipients

- A local nursing home, senior residence, or hospital

Time Requirement

Planning time before the project: one to two hours. Gathering materials: 30 minutes to an hour. Setup time on the day of your project: 30 minutes to an hour. Project time: 30 minutes.

People

This project is ideal for families with children between the ages of 3 and 12. Expect each family to make one notepad during the 30-minute event.

Materials

- Lots of 8½" x 11" white paper (at least five sheets per family)
- 8½" x 11" construction paper in various light colors, two for each family
- 5 washable markers in different colors for each family
- 1 pair of scissors for each family
- 1 pencil for each family
- 1 single hole puncher for every two to three families
- 3 to 4 balls of yarn in various colors

Yarn is available at fabric stores such as Jo-Ann Fabrics & Crafts or Hancock Fabrics. All other materials can be purchased at discount stores such as Target, Kmart, or Walmart.

Connecting Point

Ask participants if they have ever been lonely. Talk about what those feelings are like. Explain that people in nursing homes, senior centers, or hospitals may sometimes feel lonely and that we can show them we care by creating helping hands.

Doing the Project

1. Before your event, make a sample notepad so you know how it's put together and to show as an example.

2. Give each family two pieces of colored construction paper and have them fold one piece in half.

3. Children place one hand on the folded construction paper while adults help them draw around the hand with a pencil, leaving extra room at the wrist where the paper will be tied together with yarn.

4. Place one piece of folded white paper under the construction paper and cut out the hand so that four pieces are made: two on the colored construction paper and two on the white paper.

5. Children write "Your Helping Hand Notepad" on one of the construction-paper hands (for the front cover) and decorate the other hand (which will be used as the back cover, so make sure the hands line up when assembled and the decoration is facing the back). Encourage children to sign their first names and write a message of care on the back cover.

6. Cut out at least 10 hands (you can cut multiples at a time) in white paper.

7. Stack all the cutout white paper hands between the construction-paper hand front cover and back cover so the shapes line up. Punch two holes about 2 inches apart in the wrist portion, and then cut a piece of yarn to tie the papers together and form a bow on the wrist of the front cover.

Debriefing the Project

- When someone receives the helping hand notepad you made, how do you think he or she will feel? How do you feel when you receive a special gift?

- Why do you think someone who has never met you would like a helping hand notepad that you made?

- You helped someone today by making a notepad to donate. There are times when *you've* probably needed help, too. Name a time when someone has helped you.

- How else can you be a helping hand for someone?

Helpful Resources

- For children: *Miss Tizzy* by Libba Moore Gray (Aladdin, 1998), a heartwarming story about neighborhood children returning the devotion of the eccentric Miss Tizzy when she becomes ill.

- For teens: *The Friends* by Kazumi Yumoto, translated by Cath Hirano (Farrar, Straus and Giroux, 2005) about three Japanese boys befriending a wise, old man.

Bonus Ideas

- See if anyone would like to create "a step in the right direction" notepads by taking off their socks and shoes and drawing the outline of their foot.

- Have families fold an 8½" x 11" piece of white paper in half and draw an outline of their child's hand with the pinkie finger side at the fold so that when you cut out the hand, it will open up to two connected hands. Use this to create a helping hands card to accompany the helping hands notepad.

- Consider combining this service project with another complementary project, such as 8: Craft Packets (page 27).

(5) Bird Buddies

Purpose

Attract birds to places where people who rarely get out can enjoy watching them.

Possible Recipients

- A local nursing home, senior center, or homeless shelter

Time Requirement

Planning time before the project: one to two hours. Gathering materials: one hour. Setup time on the day of your project: 30 minutes to an hour. Project time: one hour.

People

This project is ideal for families with children between the ages of 5 and 18. Each family will make one bird feeder during the one-hour event, so if you'd like to donate 25 bird feeders, you'll need 25 families.

Materials

- 1 empty plastic 2-liter soda pop bottle per family

- 1 12-inch dowel or sturdy twig per family

- 3-foot piece of yarn or string for each family

- 1 pair of scissors for each family

- 1 roll of masking tape for every two to three families

- 4 cups of birdseed for each family
- 3 permanent markers in various colors for each family

Dowels are available at craft stores such as Michael's or Jo-Ann Fabrics & Crafts.

Connecting Point

Ask participants if anyone has a bird feeder and what they think of them. Talk about how some people are either homebound or live in places where the main way they get out is by looking out the window. Explain how a bird feeder can bring the activity of the birds to them.

Doing the Project

1. Before your event, make a sample bird feeder so you know how it's put together and to show as an example.

2. Instruct adults to use the scissors to poke a hole in the side of their plastic bottle about 2 inches from the bottom. Then have them poke another hole directly across from the first hole and insert the dowel or stick through both holes. It should rest evenly and extend out from both sides.

3. Poke a few more holes about 2 to 3 inches above the first hole. Birds will stand on the stick below and reach into these holes to get birdseed. (Make sure the holes are not too high or too large. It's better to have fewer holes farther apart, otherwise birds will only use one of the holes.)

4. Place masking tape over the holes and then poke holes in them. The masking tape helps to protect the birds from rough edges.

5. With the supervision of adults, have children color designs with the permanent marker onto the top portion of the bottle. Make sure the bottle remains uncolored near where the birds will peck for food.

6. Tie yarn or string to the top of the bottle and form a loop so it can be used to hang the bird feeder.

7. Fill the bird feeders with birdseed and screw the cap on to keep the seed dry.

Debriefing the Project

- What words come to mind when you think of senior citizens or people who are elderly? What makes you think of those words?

- How often do you spend time with elderly people? When?

- What do seniors have to offer us? (For example, their lifelong wisdom, their experience, their mentoring, their stories)

- Why is it important to feed the birds—for the birds and also for people?

- How else can we bring people and animals together?

Helpful Resources

- For children: *Counting Is for the Birds* by Frank Mazzola Jr. (Charlesbridge Publishing, 1997), a counting book about different types of birds arriving at a bird feeder.

- For teens: *The Audubon Backyard Birdwatcher: Birdfeeders and Bird Gardens* by Robert Burton and Stephen Kress (Thunder Bay Press, 2002), a book on how to attract different types of birds through food, water, shelter, and flowers.

Bonus Ideas

- Tie a piece of string or yarn around a pinecone so it can be hung. Coat the pinecone with peanut butter and roll it in birdseed. Then hang it up outside from a tree branch.

- Tie string around the neck of an open baby food jar. Fill up the jar with orange juice and hang it from a tree. This will attract orioles.

6 Rock-a-Thon Revolution

Purpose

Raise money for children in poverty while rocking in rocking chairs.

Possible Recipients

- Any local cause that needs funds for families with young children, such as a crisis nursery, a family homeless shelter, or a domestic-abuse shelter for families

Time Requirement

Planning time before the project: one to two hours. Gathering materials: one hour. Setup time on the day of your project: one hour. Project time: one to six hours, depending on how many families are rocking and how many hours they pledge to rock (you can raise the same amount of money in fewer hours with more families rocking at the same time).

People

This project is ideal for families with children between the ages of 3 and 18. If your group has lots of younger children, you may need to accommodate them by having families rock in short shifts, providing activities for the young kids when they're not rocking, or having a shorter event.

Materials

- 1 rocking chair per family
- 1 copy of the "Rock-a-Thon Donation Sheet" handout (page 33) per family
- Things to do while rocking, such as reading picture books aloud, playing music, or doing some other type of activity

Consider borrowing rocking chairs from individual volunteers or childcare centers.

Connecting Point

In the United States, one out of six children lives in poverty, says the National Center for Children in Poverty. According to the *Toronto Star,* one in nine Canadian children lives in poverty. Even for families that have more money, having young children puts an economic strain on the family because of the need for clothing, food, diapers, educational toys, and shelter.

Doing the Project

1. Ask families to pledge to rock a certain number of hours during your event.
2. Have families collect donations before the event using the Rock-a-Thon Donation Sheet. They can ask donors for flat donations and collect them immediately so they don't have to go back to collect funds after the event.
3. Set up the area where you will have the family service project. You'll need lots of space to set up a rocking chair for each family you're expecting.
4. During the event, have activities to do while people rock. Read picture books aloud, play music (and have people rock to the beat), or do something else. Since each family will have only one rocking chair, family members can take turns rocking while the others read aloud picture books. Or have families sign up for shifts so that everyone in the family can rock at the same time.

Debriefing the Project

- What did you think of rocking to raise money?
- How do you think the money we raised will be used by _____ (name of organization you're donating the money to)?
- Why is it important to raise money for good causes?
- How else can we help a good cause?

Helpful Resources

- For children: *The Old Red Rocking Chair* by Phyllis Root (Arcade Publishing, 1992), a story about an old rocking chair that gets thrown out and develops a new lease on life.

- For teens: *Nickel and Dimed: On (Not) Getting By in America* by Barbara Ehrenreich (Henry Holt, 2008) tells of how difficult it is for the working poor to make it in our country.

Bonus Ideas

- Instead of having families collect donations, have them each contribute to participate. Or in addition to monetary donation, encourage families to bring store-bought diapers, formula, baby food, baby clothes, and other necessities that your recipient organization needs.

- To add interest to the rocking, have times where you rock quietly then loudly, fast then slow, while everyone sings (or hums) a song together, or makes up a story about the rocking chair that he or she is in.

- Recruit local talent to volunteer to entertain the volunteers while they rock, such as jugglers, musicians, and gymnasts. (Check with a local middle school and high school for possibilities.) This may be a great way to publicize the event and get more families to rock.

- Consider having teams (made up of one family or a couple of families together) try to keep each rocking chair going for a number of hours. This added competition can make it fun for kids to ensure that the chair never stops rocking.

7 Personalized Coloring Books

Purpose

Give children something meaningful to do while waiting in an emergency room with handmade coloring books.

Possible Recipients

- A local hospital emergency room

Time Requirement

Planning time before the project: one to three hours. Gathering materials: one to two hours. Setup time on the day of your project: one to two hours. Project time: one to two hours.

People

This project is ideal for families with children between the ages of 8 and 18. During the one- or two-hour event, four or five families will collaborate to make a coloring book, so if you'd like to donate five coloring books, you'll need about 25 families. If you have access to a photocopier, you can make a lot more.

Materials

- Lots of 8½" x 11" white paper (about 10 sheets for each family)
- 8½" x 11" tracing paper (about 5 sheets for each family)
- 1 black thin-line marker and 1 black pen per person
- Coloring books (new or used) and other images for tracing
- 1 stapler for every two to three families
- Heavyweight colored paper, such as 65-pound paper, about 4 sheets for each family
- Access to a photocopy machine if people use tracing paper or if you wish to make a lot more coloring books

Heavyweight colored paper and tracing paper are available at office-supply stores such as Office Max or Office Depot.

Connecting Point

Almost half of all emergency room patients are children, and the average patient waits for three hours to receive care. Emergency rooms can be chaotic, frightening, and boring, but personalized coloring books can help soothe children and give them something meaningful to do while they wait for medical care.

Doing the Project

1. Before your event, make a sample coloring book so you know how it's put together and to show as an example.

2. Give each person a piece of 8½" x 11" white paper and a black pen or marker. Encourage them to draw an outline of a picture (that takes up almost the entire page) that will be included in a coloring book. People who feel uncomfortable with freehand drawing can trace an image from a coloring book (or other source) with tracing paper and add some extra details to make the picture unique.

3. Encourage individuals to make more than one picture.

4. Families that enjoy drawing by hand can make coloring book covers by drawing a picture on the heavyweight paper.

5. Photocopy any of the pages that have been drawn on tracing paper so every drawing appears on 8½" x 11" white paper to make it easier for the recipients to color.

6. If you have only a few families present and you have access to a photocopier, consider making multiple copies of people's drawings so you can create even more coloring books.

7. Have families form groups in which they combine their pictures into coloring books with one coloring book cover, 20 inside pages, and a blank piece of heavyweight paper for the back. Bind the coloring book by stapling the left side.

Debriefing the Project

- When a child who is sick or afraid uses the coloring book you made, how do you think he or she will feel?

- Why is it important to express our creativity?

- What other ways could we use creativity in service projects?

Helpful Resources

- For children: *At the Hospital* by Melanie Joyce (Weekly Reader Books, 2008), a story about Arthur, who falls off his bike, and his friend Fred, who goes with him to the hospital for care.

- For teens: *Emergency Room* by Caroline B. Cooney (Scholastic, 1997), a fictional account about two 18-year-old volunteers in the emergency room and what they face in the fastest-moving room in the hospital.

Bonus Ideas

- Encourage families to sign their names on the back covers of the coloring books and make positive messages, such as "Caring people are thinking of you" or "Don't be afraid. People are sending good wishes your way."

- Get cardboard tubes and place one coloring book and a few crayons into each tube. Then decorate the cardboard tube (or wrap it in wrapping paper).

- If you know of a talented artist (child, teenager, or adult), ask him or her to draw outlines of the children (or families) present. Or find a group of students from an art class to do this. Then create a coloring book of your community. Instead of donating the coloring books, sell them. Families will often be happy to buy coloring books that include pictures of their children to give to family and friends. Then use the donations raised to fund a worthy cause.

(8) Craft Packets

Purpose

Create craft packets for bedridden or hospitalized children.

Possible Recipients

- A local hospital, pediatrics clinic, or school that would know of bedridden or sick children

Time Requirement

Planning time before the project: one to two hours. Gathering materials: one hour. Setup time on the day of your project: 30 minutes to an hour. Project time: 15 minutes.

People

This project is ideal for families with children between the ages of 3 and 18. Expect each family to assemble one craft packet in 15 minutes or less, so you can plan to make two or three times as many packets as families, even during a short event (30 to 45 minutes).

Materials

- 1 gallon-size sealable plastic bag for each kit
- Art supplies to include in craft kits, such as pipe cleaners, small sketchbooks (or notepads), washable markers, stickers, glitter glue sticks, colored pencils, and crayons
- 5 sheets of 8½" x 11" paper (in various light colors) for each family
- 5 washable markers in various colors for each family
- 1 glitter glue stick for each family
- Stickers (optional)
- Optional: Copies of the "Creativity and Service Projects" handout (page 34), twice as many as the number of people you plan to recruit

Connecting Point

Ask participants if they have ever experienced—or know someone who has experienced—being bedridden for a period of time due to illness or an accident. Have the individuals briefly tell their stories. If no one has a story, tell about how pediatric cancer wards at hospitals are often full of patients who are bedridden.

Doing the Project

1. Before your event, make a sample craft packet so you know how it's put together and to show as an example.
2. Separate the art supplies for the craft kits into piles and stations. For example, place all the pipe cleaners together in one area and remove all the washable markers from their boxes and make a pile. Do this for each art supply.
3. Give each family one plastic bag. Have them line up and take a certain number of each craft item to place in their bag, depending on the amount of craft supplies that you have.
4. Encourage each family to make a card with a positive message on the outside using colored markers. On the inside, have families write, "You still sparkle!" with glitter pens or glitter glue sticks before signing their names in colored markers. Give time for the glitter glue to dry before closing the cards. Once the cards are dry, place one inside each bag and seal the bag.
5. Families may decorate their bags with stickers.
6. Families can repeat the process to make more kits as time allows.
7. Optional: Distribute the "Creativity and Service Projects" handout to each person. Give people time to complete the handout.

Debriefing the Project

- What did you think of creating craft packets for kids who are sick?
- How does being creative help a person feel better?
- What do you think it would be like to be stuck in bed for one day? Two days? A week? A month?
- Sometimes it can be uncomfortable, even frightening, to be around a person who is sick—or to visit a hospital. Why is that? What can we do about that?

- What would you make if you got this craft kit while you were in the hospital?
- How can we help sick people feel better? What cheers you up when you're feeling ill?
- Do you know anyone who is sick who could use some cheering up? What could you do for him or her?

Helpful Resources

- For children: *Franklin Goes to the Hospital* by Paulette Bourgeois (Scholastic, 2000), a story about Franklin going to the hospital to get his cracked shell fixed.
- For teens: *One True Thing* by Anna Quindlen (Random House, 2006), a story about a high achiever who quits her job to care for her mother with cancer.

Bonus Ideas

- Suggest families bring one new store-bought craft kit, such as watercolor painting kits, beeswax sheets for candle making, black-velvet pictures to color, story stickers, coloring books with crayons, play dough, puffy paints, sketch books with colored pencils, beading kits, DoodleArt posters, friendship bracelet kits, sand art, stamping, or sketch books with glitter pens or glitter glue. Then have them create a card as the service project to give along with the craft kit.
- Encourage families to make Helping Hands Notepaper (project 4) for each hospitalized child to receive in addition to the craft kit.

9 Share a Song or Two

Purpose

Brighten a lonely person's day with music you create.

Possible Recipients

- A local nursing home, homebound residents (you can often get names from local places of worship), a local Meals on Wheels, or a military service base

Time Requirement

Planning time before the project: one to two hours. Gathering materials: one hour. Setup time on the day of your project: 30 minutes to an hour. Project time: one to two hours.

People

This project is ideal for families with children between the ages of 3 and 10, but you can do it with families with older kids, too, if the entire family enjoys singing—including the older kids.

Well before your event, consider forming a task force of interested families who can provide input into the music selections and help you track down lyrics. You may also want to recruit a technically savvy volunteer to help with recording and duplicating CDs.

Materials

- 1 digital recorder to make CDs
- Recordable CDs with cases
- Lyrics to songs that families will know and enjoy singing, such as holiday songs (if you plan to give these away for the holidays), simple patriotic songs (if you're sending the recordings to the troops), simple hymns (if you're a congregation giving these away to homebound congregational members), or simple well-known songs such as "If You're Happy and You Know It," "Down by the Bay," "BINGO," "Pop! Goes the Weasel," and "Row, Row, Row Your Boat." You can often find the lyrics to these songs by searching on the Internet. Be aware of copyrighted musical

material: It's illegal to copy and distribute lyrics to copyrighted songs. However, a number of older songs for children are copyright free and you may print them out for people to use.

Connecting Point

Ask participants how often they listen to music and why. Explain that music can stir positive emotions in people who feel isolated or lonely. For example, many older people are disconnected from society because of health reasons, and many soldiers may be isolated from their families while stationed away from home. A musical recording can brighten their day and show them that many people are thinking of them.

Doing the Project

1. Before your event, if you would like assistance, find a technically savvy person who has a digital recorder and can record the group and make copies on CD.

2. Choose 10 to 12 songs for families to sing, and find the lyrics to the songs so you can make them available on the day of your event.

3. Have families practice singing the songs. Consider adding variety by doing rounds, having an occasional solo or duet, or having the group accompanied by a special instrument such as a flute, guitar, or piano.

4. Make a recording of the songs.

5. Make copies—or have your technically savvy volunteer make copies—of the recording on

CD so you can donate the CDs to your recipients. Talk to your recipient organization about how many copies they can use.

Debriefing the Project

- What's your favorite song? How do you feel when you listen to it?
- Why do you think so many people enjoy listening to music?
- How else can we use music to brighten someone's day?

Helpful Resources

- For children: *Sing, Pierrot, Sing: A Picture Book in Mime* by Tomie dePaola (Harcourt, 1987), a wordless storybook about the mime Pierrot and the children who want him to sing.
- For teens: *The Artist's Way* by Julia Cameron (Jeremy P. Tarcher, 2002) a guide to help teenagers tap into the creativity inside of them.

Bonus Ideas

- Consider getting families with teenagers who enjoy singing to create a recording. Empower these families by having them choose the music and create a rehearsal schedule before the recording.
- Have families decorate the CD cases and make cards for the recipients.
- If you have a projector, consider projecting the lyrics onto a screen or wall so that everyone can see them.

(10) Playful Pen Pals

Purpose

Make a friend by becoming a pen pal to someone who is hospitalized or homebound.

Possible Recipients

- A local nursing home, homebound residents (you can often get names from a

local congregation), or children in the hospital

Time Requirement

Planning time before the project: one to three hours. Gathering materials: one hour. Setup time on the day of your project: 30 minutes to an hour. Project time: one hour.

People

This project is ideal for families with children between the ages of 8 and 18. Expect each family to write to one pen pal during the half-hour to one-hour event.

Materials

- 8½" x 11" white paper (or stationery) for each family
- Pens and washable markers for each family
- 1 envelope for each family
- 1 first-class stamp for each family
- 1 copy of the "Pen Pal Writing Topics" handout (page 35) for each family
- Optional: Stickers

Connecting Point

Many nursing home residents (or homebound people) often feel lonely and bored. A highlight of their day may be when the mail comes. Their day brightens when they get a personal note from someone.

Doing the Project

1. Match up each family with one individual recipient. If you have more families than individuals, have two families write to one recipient. If you have more recipients than families, see if any families would be interested in having more than one pen pal.

2. Distribute the handout "Pen Pal Writing Topics." Talk about the handout so families know what to include in their letters.

3. Have families write a letter to the person. Encourage them to tell about how they spend their day, what hobbies they have, what activities they enjoy, and some of their favorites (such as favorite food, TV shows, or collections). Explain that the more details they can give (without violating their privacy), the more interesting the letter will be.

4. Have families decorate the letter as they wish with stickers, drawings, and so on.

5. Ask families to consider whether they want this to be a one-time event or if they would like to invite their pen pal to correspond with them. (Note, however, that not every recipient will respond to this invitation.) If families want to encourage contact, have them put their home return address on the envelope. (Otherwise, have them use the address of your organization.) Collect all the letters and mail them.

6. Consider setting another date in a month for the group to get together and write another letter. (Also encourage people to send letters from home if they wish, as well.)

Debriefing the Project

- How easy was it to write a letter?
- What did you write about? Why?
- Why do you think personal mail is important to people who are older or sick?
- How do you feel when you get mail?
- Who else could use some cheering up? What could we do for him or her?

Helpful Resources

- For children: *A Pen Pal for Max* by Gloria Rand (Henry Holt, 2005), a story about a pen-pal friendship between a 10-year-old boy from Chile and a girl in the United States.
- For teens: *Foreign Correspondence: A Pen Pal's Journey from Down Under to All Over* by Geraldine Brooks (Anchor Books, 1999), which tells of the relationships the author built with many pen pals around the world.

Bonus Ideas

- Have a digital camera or cell phone camera (with a photo printer) handy and take pictures of each family to include with the letters.
- Encourage families to draw a picture for their pen pal to include in the mailing.
- Ask the recipient organization if residents can receive email. If so, provide an email option to your group. Some people enjoy getting email as much as mailed letters.

Make a Blanket for a Child in Need

Using polar fleece fabric, children and parents will work together to create cozy blankets that will be donated to children in need. A number of organizations provide care and comfort to children who are seriously ill or otherwise in need through the gifts of handmade blankets created by volunteers like you. For more information, visit www.projectlinus.org or www.binkypatrol.org.

We'll all feel a sense of accomplishment as we cut fleece and tie knots to create beautiful, cozy masterpieces. Join us for this warm experience.

Date: _____

Time: _____

Place: _____

Please bring:

- Two pieces of polar fleece, each piece measuring 1.5 yards square. (Try to coordinate the two pieces of fabric, as they will be placed back to back to create both sides of the blanket. Many families buy one solid color piece and one matching patterned piece. We have found that children love to choose the fleece prints. It gets them involved and excited!) No sewing is involved. If you have more than one child, they can work together or create separate blankets.

- Fabric scissors (or rotary cutter), if you have them

- Masking tape

- Tape measure, yardstick, or ruler

Please RSVP by _____
                                                            (date)

to _____.
        (project coordinator)

The Power of Friendship

Friends give our lives meaning. They listen to us and make life fun. Answer the questions below about what friendship means to you.

Name a friend you enjoy a lot.

Why do you like this friend so much?

What has a friend given you that meant a lot to you?

When have you missed your friend?

What can you do to be a good friend?

Rock-a-Thon Donation Sheet

Our family is participating in a Rock-a-Thon (yes, we're rocking in rocking chairs) to raise money for children in poverty through _____,
(name of organization)
a worthy cause that needs our support.

Our family plans to rock for _____ minutes on _____.
(date)

Your support is important, and every donation makes a difference.

Donor's Name	Donation Amount
1. _____	$ _____
2. _____	$ _____
3. _____	$ _____
4. _____	$ _____
5. _____	$ _____
6. _____	$ _____
7. _____	$ _____
8. _____	$ _____
9. _____	$ _____
10. _____	$ _____
Total:	$ _____

All donations are tax deductible. Make checks payable to _____.
Thanks for your support!

Creativity and Service Projects

Effective service projects are more than just pitching in to get the work done. They're also about creativity—your creativity. Answer the questions about creativity below.

What do you enjoy creating most?
(Consider painting, drawing, writing, theater, video, photography, music, and more.)

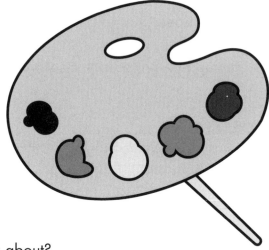

When you use your imagination, what do you think about?

How can you use your creativity more in service projects?

How can people's creativity make our community a better place?

Pen Pal Writing Topics

Not sure what to say in your letter? Consider these ideas:

Topics to Write About

How you spend your day (school, work, volunteering, raising a family, and so on)

The clubs and activities you participate in (and why)

Your hobbies

Your collections

Your pets

Your favorite TV shows and movies (and why)

Your favorite music

The places you've traveled to

Your favorite family activities

The latest book you read and why you liked it

Your favorite foods

What gets you excited (and why)

Topics to Avoid

Your problems

Your worries

Your achievements

Politics

Religion

Controversial subjects

Remember to . . .

Ask questions

Make the letter an invitation for a conversation

Chapter 2
Projects to Help Ease Poverty

Many people struggle to pay for the
essentials, such as housing, food, and clothing.
The family service projects in this chapter
help ease the burden of poverty by supplying
those in need with necessities and the knowledge
that others care about them.

Super Sandwiches

Purpose

Make sandwiches for people who pick up lunch at a nearby shelter.

Possible Recipients

- A local homeless shelter, domestic-abuse shelter, community kitchen, or some other type of shelter

Time Requirement

Planning time before the project: one to two hours. Gathering materials: one hour. Setup time on the day of your project: 30 minutes to an hour. Project time: one hour.

People

This project is ideal for families with children between the ages of 5 and 18. Expect each participant to make and package about 20 sandwiches during the one-hour event, so 10 people can donate 200 sandwiches.

Materials

- Enough bread to make 200 sandwiches
- Sandwich meat and cheese (or nut butter and jelly) for 200 sandwiches
- 2 butter knives for each family if you're making nut butter and jelly sandwiches
- 200 quart-size, zip-top freezer bags
- 1 pair of disposable gloves for each person
- 4 to 5 spray bottles of antibacterial cleaning solution
- Lots of paper towels or paper napkins
- 20 twist ties
- 220 sticky labels
- 1 pen for each family
- Access to restrooms with soap and water

Check with the shelter or community kitchen first to find out the requirements for sandwiches. Many accept meat and cheese sandwiches without condiments that they then freeze.

Some want two slices of meat; others say one. Others prefer only peanut butter and other nut butters with jelly. If you do use meat and cheese, consider using sliced salami or bologna slices because they are less expensive than other meats and so you don't have to cut. Many grocery stores are willing to donate the food for causes like this.

Connecting Point

Ask participants to imagine what it would be like not to have lunch. Explain that there are adults, teenagers, and children who are fed because of the generosity of volunteers. A handmade sandwich, made with loving care, not only feeds people's bodies but also gives them the knowledge that others care about them.

Doing the Project

1. Before families arrive, sanitize the tables with antibacterial cleaning solution (or have families help with this step as they arrive). Have paper towels or paper napkins available for families to use to make the sandwiches on.

2. Have family members wash their hands thoroughly with soap and water and put on disposable gloves.

3. Create working tables with about six people each. Have two or three families work together.

4. Give each table enough ingredients for making sandwiches. Make sure that only adults (and children 10 and older) have access to and use the knives. Keep the plastic bags that the bread comes in to use later in the project.

5. Assemble the sandwiches.

6. Place each finished sandwich in a quart-size freezer bag. If the shelter wants the sandwiches labeled, place a label on each sandwich bag.

7. Store the bags in a freezer or place where the shelter requested before delivery. Many ask that you put the sandwiches back in the bread bags and close with a twist tie. (You can usually fit about 10 sandwiches in one bread bag; keep

the same kind of sandwiches together in each bag.) Then place a label on the bag indicating the type of sandwich.

Debriefing the Project

- What surprised you as you put together the sandwiches?
- What was it like to make a bunch of sandwiches for someone else?
- When has someone made a meal for you? How did you feel about that?
- Why is it important to feed those who are hungry?
- What else can we do to help hungry people?

Helpful Resources

- For children: *The Lady in the Box* by Ann McGovern (Turtle Books, 1997), a book about two children helping a homeless woman by providing food and clothing.
- For teens: *A Kids' Guide to Hunger & Homelessness* by Cathryn Berger Kaye (Free Spirit Publishing, 2007), a practical book that shows kids the causes and effects of hunger and homelessness, what other people have done and are doing to help, how to determine what their community needs, and how to develop a service project to meet those needs.

Bonus Ideas

- Consider downloading the free hunger activity guide created by the Atlanta Community Food Bank, at www.acfb.org. Click on "Hunger 101" then "Curricula." *Hunger 101—A Guide and Activity Workbook* has many activities, games, fact sheets, and quotations you can use to supplement your event.
- Ask the shelter if you can enclose a card with each sandwich. If the shelter says yes, make a card about the size of a gift card (that lies flat). Have families write a short "thinking of you today" note and sign their first names. Recipients are often touched that strangers are thinking of them—and providing sandwiches—and they may feel less alone in their struggles. You could also write this message on a label that sticks on the outside of each sandwich bag.
- Instead of having families stay at one working table, consider creating three stations for them to go through. At the first station, have them decorate labels to stick on the bags (with greetings to the recipient) or create cards. At the second station, have them make the sandwich and place it into the zip-top bag, then take it to the third station, where a volunteer collects the sandwiches and packs them into an empty bread bag (or larger container) and labels it with the number and type of sandwich.

(12) Birthday Bags

Purpose

Create birthday bags for children who live in shelters and often don't get the chance to celebrate their birthdays because of the hard times their family is having.

Possible Recipients

- Local options: a homeless shelter, domestic-abuse shelter, community kitchen, food shelf, or some other type of shelter

- Other options: Cheerful Givers at www.cheerfulgivers.org

Time Requirement

Planning time before the project: one to two hours. Gathering materials: one hour. Setup time on the day of your project: 30 minutes to an hour. Project time: one hour.

People

This project is ideal for families with children between the ages of 3 and 18. Expect each family to make one birthday bag during the one-hour event.

Materials

- Enough copies of the "Birthday Bag Bash" handout (page 53) to publicize your event with families who might attend
- 10 small toys for each birthday bag (see the handout)
- 1 paper gift bag per family to hold about 10 small toys
- 60-pound, white card stock (8½" x 11"), cut in half to make birthday cards (one half sheet for each family)
- 1 envelope per family to hold the birthday card
- 5 markers in various colors for each family
- Decorating materials (such as catalogs and magazines, inexpensive wrapping paper, colored construction paper, and stickers)
- 1 glue stick for each family
- 1 pair of scissors for each family

  Families will donate the small toys.

Connecting Point

Talk about how hard it would be to have a birthday when you live in a shelter—parents feel embarrassed about not being able to afford presents, and kids wish their day could be special. A birthday bag will make a birthday at a shelter a much happier day.

Doing the Project

1. Before the project, distribute copies of the "Birthday Bag Bash" handout to families you hope to attract to your event. The handout includes ideas of where families can get inexpensive birthday items and encourages families to bring at least 10 small items. It often works best when a family brings 10 of the same item to share at the event.

2. Make a sample birthday bag to show as an example.

3. On the day of your event, set up families at tables. If families bring many of the same item, create combined piles of these items (all the puzzles together, all the stuffed animals together, and so on).

4. If your recipient organization will accept decorated bags, give each family a gift bag to decorate with the markers and decorating materials. (Check with the receiving agency about this ahead of time. Many will not accept bags decorated by children if an adult at the recipient organization plans to give the bag to his or her child. A child receiving a bag made by a child will know right away that the bag isn't from the parent.)

5. Have each family make a birthday card but not sign it. (The recipient parent will sign the card.) Encourage family members to be upbeat and sincere. Have them place the card in an envelope and write "Happy Birthday" or "It's Your Birthday!" on the envelope.

6. Next, fill each bag with 10 different items. If items are separated into piles of like items, you can have families form an assembly line. Have them place the card on top of the toys in the bag.

7. Place all the birthday bags in one area and count them. Talk about how many children will now have a happier birthday, thanks to their efforts.

Debriefing the Project

- What did you experience when you went shopping for the toys?
- What did you think about as you decorated the birthday bag and the birthday card?
- How do you think the child who receives your birthday bag will feel when he or she receives it? Why?
- What makes you feel good on your birthday? Why?
- What else can we do for children in shelters on their birthday?

Helpful Resources

- For children: *A Glove of Their Own* by Debbie Moldovan, Keri Conkling, and Lisa Funari-Willever (Franklin Mason Press, 2008), a tale about kids who love baseball and how they help those in need get "a glove of their own." This book is part of a much larger movement—the "play it forward" movement—to raise awareness, funds, and equipment for children who would otherwise go without.

- For teens: *Bud, Not Buddy* by Christopher Paul Curtis (Laurel-Leaf, 2004), winner of a Newberry Award and Coretta Scott King Award that tells the story of Bud, an African-American boy in Depression-era Michigan who is moved between foster homes until he begins a journey to find his real father.

Bonus Ideas

- Collect other birthday decorations to give to the shelter, such as crepe paper streamers, a birthday banner, and balloons.

- Consider asking individuals to bring in gently used gift bags to donate.

- Some organizations like to receive a cake mix, a can of frosting, and a box of birthday candles with the gift bags.

- Enter the results of your event on the Cheerful Givers website at www.cheerfulgivers.org. Click on "Get involved" and then "Record volunteer event."

(13) School Kits

Purpose

Give school supplies to children in shelters, refugee camps, and schools with few resources.

Possible Recipients

- Local options: a public school district, homeless shelter, domestic-abuse shelter, or some other type of social agency

- Other options: Church World Service at www.churchworldservice.org; click on "Kits," then "School Kit"

Time Requirement

Planning time before the project: one to two hours. Gathering materials: one hour. Setup time on the day of your project: 30 minutes to an hour. Project time: 30 minutes.

People

This project is ideal for families with children between the ages of 5 and 18. Expect each family to make one school kit during the 30-minute event.

Materials

- Enough school supplies to fill all the kits you want to make. (These will vary by recipient agency, so ask the agency for a list of recommended items. The website for Church World Service lists specific supplies for its school kit: blunt scissors, three 70-page spiral or tape-bound pads of paper, one 12-inch ruler, one hand-held pencil sharpener, one large eraser, six new pencils with erasers, one box of 24 crayons, and one cotton cloth bag to place the supplies in. The website has a free pattern and directions for making a bag.)

- 1 grocery store paper shopping bag with handles for each family (unless you're creating this for Church World Service, which requires cloth bags)

Connecting Point

Ask kids which school supplies they need in school. Ask who buys these items for them. Talk about what would happen if the person who usually buys their school supplies could not afford these items. Explain how there are millions of children around the world who cannot afford school supplies.

Doing the Project

1. Well before your event, decide which agency you will work with and get the list of school supplies from them. Consider making copies of the list to distribute to families.

2. Decide how you want families to help with school supplies. You could have a signup sheet for families to sign up to purchase five to 10 of the same school-supply item, purchase a complete kit, or give a financial donation (in which case you or another volunteer would do the shopping for kit items).

3. Make a sample school kit to show as an example.

4. On the day of your event, create a working station for each kit item. Have families place the items they wish to donate at the appropriate stations.

5. Give each family a cloth or paper bag with handles. Have them place one item from each station into the bag.

6. Place all the finished bags in one area for delivery.

Debriefing the Project

- What was your experience in creating school-supply kits?
- Why are school supplies so important?
- Why is it important for all kids to get a good education?
- What else can we do to help children who need school supplies?

Helpful Resources

- For children: *Gettin' Through Thursday* by Melrose Cooper (Lee & Low Books, 2000), a story about Andre, who is proud to show off his great report card on Thursday, but is disappointed because he can't get anything special for doing well until his mom gets paid on Friday.

- For teens: *There Are No Children Here: The Story of Two Boys Growing Up in the Other America* by Alex Kotlowitz (Anchor Books, 1992), the true story of brothers Lafeyette and Pharoah Rivers, ages 11 and 9 at the start, who have had to learn to survive in their violence-ridden Chicago neighborhood.

Bonus Ideas

- In mid- to late-summer, many stores have large discounts on specific school supplies. See if you can find volunteers who are willing to buy large quantities of these items on sale so you can make more school-supply kits than you otherwise would.

- See if your recipient agency would be interested in receiving school kits in the middle of the school year. Most want them at the beginning of the school year, but many students begin to run out of supplies as the school year goes on.

- Consider creating cards or labels to add to the kits (if the agency allows for personalization).

- Place the items in inexpensive canvas totes that can be ordered from www.tansclub.com (search for "cotton tote bags") or www.cheaptotes.com (search for "canvas tote bag"). If the recipient agency is open to it, decorate the bags. Families can decorate the totes using such things as fabric markers or paints, stencils, lace, fringe, pom-poms, or ribbons.

(14) Packaging Food for the Hungry

Purpose

Package food for starving and malnourished people around the world.

Possible Recipients

- Local options: international relief centers in your area that do food packaging to send overseas, such as Feed My Starving Children (www.fmsc.org), a Minnesota-based company
- Other options: Kids Against Hunger (kidsagainsthunger.org) has 80 food-packaging satellites in the United States and one in Canada

Time Requirement

Planning time before the project: one to three hours. Gathering materials: none. Setup time on the day of your project: none. Project time: one to two hours.

Note: This project is generally conducted on-site at the relief center you work with, but check with the organization to see if the project can be done at your location.

People

This project is ideal for families with children between the ages of 8 and 18. Each family can make many food packages during the one- to two-hour event.

Materials

- Recipient agencies will have all the ingredients ready (such as rice, soy, dehydrated vegetables, and special vitamin powder), along with the bags for your family volunteers to put together. Ask families to make a monetary donation for your event to help pay for the food.

Connecting Point

Ask participants if they have ever been to a developing country or have ever seen malnourished people, perhaps on TV. Have volunteers briefly tell their stories and reactions. Explain that many people in the world do not have adequate food, and many people starve every day. Relief organizations are working hard to get nutritious food to malnourished people.

Doing the Project

1. Well before your event, call the organization you wish to serve and ask about the process for setting a date for your family volunteers to package food.

2. If you will conduct your project at the relief center, it can be helpful for one of your leaders to volunteer there prior to this event. This often gets the volunteer excited about the project, and the volunteer can then prepare the group for what to expect. Some families may be hesitant to volunteer at a site other than your building unless there's someone in your organization who can reassure them that this is a great project to do.

3. On the day of your event, greet families as they arrive at your site. Travel together to the organization where you will be assembling the food packages.

4. Be prepared for an intensive, factory-line work experience. The goal is to put together as many food bags as possible. It's often helpful for volunteers to take short breaks and rotate the type of work to keep the event interesting.

5. Carefully follow the instructions of the leaders at the agency. They've done many of these events, and they know exactly what they want your volunteers to do.

6. After your group finishes, have everyone meet together in another area of the building (or back at your location) so you can debrief the project. Otherwise, families usually disperse and you don't have time to help them process what they experienced or get feedback.

Debriefing the Project

- What was your experience in creating these food bags?
- Would you do this type of project again? Why or why not?
- How do you feel when you're hungry?
- Why is it important to feed people who are hungry on the other side of the world?
- How do you keep starving people in your mind when it's easy to forget about them because you don't see them every day?
- How else can we help people who are hungry and malnourished?

Helpful Resources

- For children: *Tight Times* by Barbara Shook Hazen (Puffin Books, 1983), a story that shows how difficult life can get when a family is short on finances.
- For teens: *Soulmates: A Novel to End World Hunger* by John Henry Ballard, (World Citizens, 1998) about a teenager's class sponsoring a child in India and taking an eye-opening trip to that country.

Bonus Ideas

- Check with a local community kitchen to see if interested families could volunteer to serve one meal there.
- Have families who get excited about this type of project research other relief agencies in your area that offer similar volunteer opportunities.
- Ask the relief organization if there are other ways that families can volunteer to help out.
- Encourage families to visit Free Rice, a non-profit website run by the United Nations World Food Program, at www.freerice.com, and play the free, educational game. It's a fun way to learn about hunger—and help with hunger-relief efforts while playing.
- See if the organization will come to your location. Sometimes Kids Against Hunger and Feed My Starving Children will do this if your organization pays for all the donated food.

15 Winter-Wear Clotheslines

Purpose

Gather warm outdoor clothing to donate to people who are poor and homeless.

Possible Recipients

- Local options: a homeless shelter, domestic-abuse shelter, or some other type of shelter
- Other options: One Warm Coat (www.onewarmcoat.org)

Time Requirement

Planning time before the project: one to two hours. Gathering materials: one hour. Setup time on the day of your project: 30 minutes to an hour. Project time: 15 minutes.

People

This project is ideal for families with children between the ages of 3 and 18. Expect each family to bring in one winter donation for your 15-minute event.

Materials

- 1 clothesline
- Many clothespins (at least 2 per donated item)
- A place to secure and display the clothesline
- A decorated 11" x 17" sign with "Winter-Wear Clothesline" or "Mitten Clothesline" written on it

- Publicity that encourages families to bring mittens, scarves, winter caps, and other winter accessories to donate, being mindful that recipients could be children, teenagers, or adults and male or female

Ask families to donate the winter wear and lend the clothesline and clothespins for your event. Some groups set up a donation box for people to drop off donations for the event in advance. This is helpful because some people can donate items but are unable to attend your event.

Connecting Point

Ask participants if anyone has ever lost a mitten or warm hat during the winter months and needed to go without. What was that experience like? Explain that some people cannot afford winter wear. This project gives people with few resources the chance to stay warm in winter.

Doing the Project

Consider combining this short project with another 15- or 30-minute project from this book.

1. Before your event, decide how you will gather clothing donations and who will be in charge of this step. Will you approach local businesses for donations (either for clothing or for funding)? Will you put out a collection box for an extended period or ask families to bring items to the event itself? Encourage families to bring at least one pair of new winter mittens—but more than that if they can. Some project organizers purchase all the items needed themselves and ask families to donate a fee to participate.

2. The day of your event, hang up the clothesline in advance and test it by hanging winter items on it. Make sure it's strong enough so it doesn't sag or snap when you get lots of items placed on it.

3. If you live in a cold climate, have families talk about how mittens, scarves, winter caps, and winter coats keep them warm. If you live in a warm climate, consider showing photos of people bundled up in the snow.

4. Have families take turns securing their donated items onto the clothesline with clothespins. If

you have a lot of families and more donations than will fit on the clothesline, find another way to display all the donations.

5. Gather around the clothesline and talk about how many people will be warm this winter because of the donations. Keep the clothesline displayed for a number of days (or a week) so people can see what was donated.

Debriefing the Project

- What did you think of what you brought and how it added to the total of mittens, scarves, and hats donated?

- If you never owned a pair of mittens in the winter, how would you feel when someone gave you a pair to keep? Why?

- What difference does it make to see all the donations displayed on a clothesline rather than just put into bags?

- Why is it important to help keep people warm during the winter?

- How else can we help people in need during the winter months?

Helpful Resources

- For children: *Swimmy* by Leo Lionni (Dragonfly Books, 1973), a Caldecott Honor Book about a brave fish who teaches his friends that with a little ingenuity and teamwork they can overcome any danger.

- For teens: *Chicken Soup for the Volunteer's Soul: Stories to Celebrate the Spirit of Courage, Caring and Community* by Jack Canfield, Mark Victor Hansen, and others (Health Communications, Inc., 2002), a book full of true short stories that celebrate caring and community.

Bonus Ideas

- Some schools and congregations use an evergreen tree around the winter holidays to display the donated winter wear.

- Consider collecting winter wear over a period of time (such as a month) and add new items to the clothesline as they're donated so people can see the collection grow. Then have an event to mark the end of the donation drive where people bring in more mittens and everyone can celebrate what has been collected.

- If the recipient agency allows for personalization of donated items, consider having families write cheery notes and pin them on the donated items.

- For more ideas, download the free tools at One Warm Coat (www.onewarmcoat.org). Click on "Tools + Resources" and consider downloading the free guidebook, press release, and flyer.

16 Nets by the Numbers

Purpose

To raise funds to purchase bed nets so fewer people die from malaria.

Possible Recipients

- Local options: any local agency that does international work in trying to stamp out malaria in Africa and other developing countries, such as a denominational mission office that your church, synagogue, or mosque would know about
- Other options: Nothing But Nets at www.nothingbutnets.net

Time Requirement

Planning time before the project: one to three hours. Gathering materials: one to two hours. Setup time on the day of your project: one to two hours. Project time: one to two hours.

People

This project is ideal for families with children between the ages of 3 and 18.

This event involves quite a bit of setup, cleanup, and work running the games, so it will be important to recruit at least six volunteers from your organization to help. Volunteers will set up and run the various "net" type carnival booths, sell game tickets, and take donations from those who want to contribute tax-deductible funds to the cause.

Materials

- 1 or 2 basketball nets and basketballs (for older teens and adults)
- 1 or 2 child-size basketball nets and basketballs
- 1 small children's swimming pool filled with water and rubber ducks
- 1 small fishing net
- 1 permanent marker
- Balls and larger fishing nets (balls should fit in the nets)
- 4 stopwatches or timers
- 500 to 1,000 game tickets
- 4 money collection boxes or envelopes (with change)
- 4 whiteboards, 4 whiteboard markers, and 4 whiteboard erasers
- 1 copy of the handout "Facts About Malaria" (page 54) for each family
- Optional: 4 prizes

Consider asking families to lend game supplies to your event, such as basketballs and basketball nets, or you can purchase most of them at discount stores such as Target, Kmart, or Walmart. Game tickets and rubber ducks are available at www.orientaltrading.com.

Connecting Point

Around the world, 500 million people are infected annually by the life-threatening disease called malaria, which is spread through mosquito bites. Each year, malaria kills 1 million people, and 90 percent of these people are children living in Africa. A simple $10 bed net can protect children from mosquitoes at night, but few families can afford them. The organization Nothing But Nets collects donations to buy and distribute these bed nets.

Doing the Project

1. The day of your event—but well before it begins—set up your "Nets by the Numbers" carnival. Create four game stations: a basketball shoot for teens and adults, a basketball shoot for children, a fishing-for-ducks pond, and a ball toss. You may decide to do other activities in addition to these. Be sure to read all the steps to see how the games work so you'll know how to set them up. Place a whiteboard, whiteboard marker, and whiteboard eraser at each station.

2. Set up a table or booth where a volunteer will sell game tickets (sell each ticket for $1, and have each station cost one ticket to play), and set up another table or booth where a volunteer can collect any additional donations.

3. As families arrive, distribute the "Facts About Malaria" handout and talk about how malaria is one of the world's most deadly diseases.

4. Briefly introduce the four stations to families and show them where to buy game tickets.

5. For the basketball games: Give participants 20 seconds to shoot basketballs into the net, count the number of baskets they make within 20 seconds, and write that number on the whiteboard.

6. For the ball toss: Give participants 20 seconds to throw as many balls as they can into mounted fishing nets. As with the basketball games, keep track of scores on the whiteboard.

7. For the fishing game at the swimming pool, write numbers representing points with a permanent marker on the bottom of each rubber duck. See how many points a player can get in 20 seconds by scooping ducks with a small fishing net. Make the numbers large, such as 100, 200, 300, and so on. Have players stand behind a line or kneel on a chair to keep them from leaning over (or into) the pool. Add up

each player's total score and write it on the whiteboard.

8. Have volunteers at each station track the high score for that station. Continue to do this until the end of the event.

9. Consider having a prize for the winner of each station. Visit www.nothingbutnets.net for possible prizes from the site's store, or ask local businesses to donate items.

10. After debriefing the event, announce the winners and also announce how much money you raised. Divide that total by 10 to calculate how many nets your fundraiser will buy (each net costs $10).

Debriefing the Project

- What did you think of playing games with nets to raise money to buy bed nets?

- What would it be like to know that a mosquito could bite you and give you a disease that kills you?

- How would you feel if someone gave you a gift that could save your life?

- Why is it important to help people who live on the other side of the world?

- How else can we help fight malaria?

Helpful Resources

- For children: *Why Mosquitoes Buzz in People's Ears: A West African Tale* by Verna Aardema (Penguin, 1993), a story about why Africans dislike mosquitoes.

- For teens: *The World Malaria Report,* published annually by the World Health Organization and distributed by the Malaria Foundation International, can be downloaded for free from the foundation's website at www.malaria.org.

Bonus Ideas

- Get further information and activity ideas from Scholastic on this subject at www.scholastic.com. Click on "Teachers," select "Teachers Home," then search for "malaria."

- If someone among your volunteers has lived in Africa or has had malaria, ask that person to give a short presentation about the experience.

Foster Kids Suitcases

Purpose

Give foster children something they need but may not own: a suitcase of their own.

Possible Recipients

- Local options: a local social service agency that works with foster children and foster families
- Other options: Suitcases for Kids (www.suitcasesforkids.org)

Time Requirement

Planning time before the project: one to two hours. Gathering materials: one hour. Setup time on the day of your project: 30 minutes to an hour. Project time: one hour.

People

This project is ideal for families with children between the ages of 5 and 18.

Materials

- New (or gently used) suitcases, large duffle bags, and backpacks
- 1 sheet of notepaper for every participant
- 1 pen or pencil for every participant
- 5 washable markers in various colors for each family
- Other possible decorating materials, such as glitter glue and stickers

Ask families to donate the suitcases. The decorating materials are available at discount stores, such as Target, Kmart, and Walmart.

Connecting Point

The average child in foster care moves to seven different homes during childhood, and many foster kids have nothing more than a large plastic garbage bag to move their belongings. Imagine how a foster child would feel if he or she had a suitcase, a large duffel bag, or even a backpack.

Doing the Project

1. Before your event, ask families for gently used (or new) suitcases, large duffel bags, and backpacks to give to children living in foster care. Make the case about how few foster kids have their own suitcase. Also mention that sometimes we have gently used suitcases, duffel bags, and backpacks that are rarely used, and this is a great way to recycle them—by giving them to kids who really need them.

2. Set up a spot for families to leave their donated suitcases, duffel bags, or backpacks in your project area. Leave it up for two weeks before your event.

3. Write a sample note to include with a suitcase.

4. As families arrive at your event, give each person a sheet of notepaper, a pen or pencil, and markers. Encourage him or her to write a letter to a foster child and decorate the page by drawing pictures. Have extra paper available for individuals who wish to do it over—and for those who would like to make more than one.

5. When people finish, ask for volunteers to read aloud what they wrote, then collect the letters.

6. Gather around all the donated suitcases, duffel bags, and backpacks. Count them and talk about how many foster care children you're helping.

7. Provide the letters in the way the recipient organization requires. Some may want the letters collected all together in one batch. Others may want them placed individually into each suitcase.

Debriefing the Project

- What does a suitcase mean to you? Why?
- What do you think a suitcase means for a foster child?

- How would it feel to move from home to home when you don't know anyone in the family you're going to live with?
- What if you had to do that seven times as a child?
- What other ways could we help foster kids?

Helpful Resources

- For children: *Kids Need to Be Safe: A Book for Children in Foster Care* by Julie Nelson (Free Spirit Publishing, 2006), a book that explains why some kids move to foster homes, what foster parents do, and how kids might feel during foster care. The text makes it clear that the troubles in kids' lives are not their fault, and they deserve to be safe.
- For teens: *Another Place at the Table* by Kathy Harrison (Jeremy P. Tarcher/Putnam, 2003), a true, wrenching story about the author's life as a foster parent to more than 100 children.

Bonus Ideas

- Check with the recipient agency to see if families can also add something to the suitcase, such as a teddy bear or a cosmetic bag (with toothbrush and toothpaste, comb, and shampoo). If so, consider collecting these items as well.
- Read about Aubyn Burnside, a 10-year-old from Hickory, North Carolina, who started Suitcases for Kids and has collected hundreds of suitcases for foster care kids. Read her story at www.suitcasesforkids.org/history. Include her story as part of your event.
- Invite a foster parent in to talk about what it's like to be a foster parent and how he or she helps foster kids feel at home.
- If you know of talented artists (children, teenagers, or adults), ask them to make posters to publicize the event. They could draw outlines of suitcases, make a display of suitcases, or even create a poster that includes a black garbage bag, asking the question, *Would you want to move all your belongings in this?*

18 Home-Starter Kits

Purpose

Create home-starter kits for individuals and families moving from a shelter into their own home.

Possible Recipients

- A homeless shelter, domestic-abuse shelter, or some other type of shelter. Also consider an agency that helps individuals and families move from shelters to their own housing. Check with local homeless shelters or domestic-abuse shelters for suggestions.

Time Requirement

Planning time before the project: one to two hours. Gathering materials: one hour. Setup time on the day of your project: 30 minutes to an hour. Project time: 30 minutes.

People

This project is ideal for families with children between the ages of 3 and 18. Expect each family to put together one home-starter kit during the 30-minute event.

Materials

- Enough new, unopened items to make at least 1 home-starter kit per participating family. Items include trash bags, cleaning supplies, brooms, dustpans, paper towels, cleaning gloves, dish towels, bath towels, buckets, and so on.
- 1 cardboard box (preferably with slots for carrying) for each home-starter kit

- 2 sheets of notepaper for each family you expect (in case anyone wants to make more than one, or if someone makes a mistake and wants to start over)
- 5 washable markers in various colors for each family

Ask families to donate trash bags, cleaning supplies, and other new items for the home-starter kits. Grocery stores often are willing to donate the cardboard boxes with slots for carrying if you ask.

Connecting Point

Ask participants if they have ever experienced moving to a new home. Talk about how what a big, wonderful step it is for people to move from a shelter into a home of their own. When people live in a shelter, they don't have any privacy. There are people everywhere. They may have a bed to sleep in each night, but some can't even count on that. Imagine having to sleep in a room with 10 to 20 strangers. Think about what it would be like if you could move from a shelter into your very own home. How would that feel?

Doing the Project

1. A few weeks before your event, decide how you will gather materials and who will be in charge of this step. You will get the most enthusiastic participation if you ask families to bring items to your event, such as trash bags, cleaning supplies, and other new items necessary when moving into a new home. Alternatively, you could ask for donations from local businesses, or you could buy the items yourself and ask families to donate a fee to participate in the event. Try to collect a minimum of four to six items for the kits.

2. Make a sample home-starter kit to show as an example.

3. As families arrive on the day of your event, separate the home-starter supplies into piles and stations. For example, place all the cleaning supplies together in one area, the trash bags in another, and so on.

4. Ask for volunteers to count up the number of supplies at each station. Then determine how many home-starter kits you can make. Count out the number of boxes you'll need to hold the home-starter kits.

5. Divide your families into as many groups as you have kits—each group will work on one kit. Keep families together instead of splitting them up. Give each group a box. Have families use markers to decorate the home-starter kit. Encourage them to write "Your home-starter kit" on the box and then decorate it with drawings.

6. Have groups collect a certain number of each item to place in their decorated box.

7. Have each family or group write a personal note with congratulatory comments and sign their first names. Children might draw pictures of a house or of household scenes. When they finish, they can place the notes in the box.

Debriefing the Project

- What do you think it would be like to be moving into your first home?
- In most areas, affordable housing is in short supply. Why do you think that is?
- Why do you think so many people live in shelters?
- What else could we do to support people moving from shelters into their own homes?

Helpful Resources

- For children: *Lakas and the Makibaka Hotel/ Si Lakas at ang Makibaka Hotel* by Anthony D. Robles (Children's Book Press, 2006), a bilingual picture book in English and Tagalog that tells the story of Lakas and his Fillipino-American community's struggle to stop the demolition of their home.
- For teens: *White Lilacs* by Carolyn Meyer (Harcourt, 2007). When the white residents of Dillon, Texas, decide to raze the city's black enclave and build a park in its place, young Rose Lee Jefferson and her neighbors must fight for their homes and their lives.

Bonus Ideas

- Consider creating "Home Sweet Home" signs that residents can display in their new homes. Visit your local craft stores to find easy, professional-looking supplies for making these signs.

- Consider creating a picture book in which each family writes one page. On the top of each page, start with "What Home Means to Me." Families can then write a short note about what it means to them and young people can draw a picture. Then collect all the pages, photocopy them, and assemble them into books to include in the home-starter kits.

19 Donate Food in a Creative Way

Purpose

Help combat hunger by filling empty shelves at your local food bank while being creative and having fun in the process.

Possible Recipients

- Local options: a local food bank, community kitchen, or some other local agency that collects food to distribute
- Other options: Feeding America at www.feedingamerica.org

Time Requirement

Planning time before the project: one to two hours. Gathering materials: one hour. Setup time on the day of your project: 30 minutes to an hour. Project time: one hour.

People

This project is ideal for families with children between the ages of 3 and 18. Find a volunteer who has a camera and other volunteers who can help with building food designs and writing a press release.

Materials

- Enough copies of the "Donate Food: Help Those Who Are Hungry" handout (page 55) to publicize your event to families
- A large space to create designs out of the donated food

- A camera
- Photos of dry (canned or boxed) food items arranged into designs by architectural and engineering experts (available at www .canstruction.org)
- Various food items
- Optional: collection box

Ask families to donate food or ask for donations from a grocery store.

Connecting Point

Many food shelves cannot keep up with the demand for food from hungry families. Whenever the economy gets bad, their requests multiply— even when donations do not. A food shelf always welcomes donations of food and money to help those in need.

Doing the Project

1. Consider setting up a donation box about two weeks before your event and asking people to donate food. Some people like to donate and may be unable to attend your event.

2. As families arrive at the event, have them separate the donations into groups of similar types: soup cans, peanut butter, noodles, and so on.

3. Have your creative volunteers spread out among the families. They should show families the pictures of food displays and work with them to come up with designs for their own displays.

4. Explain that families are not to compete with the displays that these experts have made, but that these displays may inspire them to create something unique. Have families work together to build some type of design with the donated food. You may have a number of designs happening simultaneously—or you may end up with only one or two designs.

5. Photograph the end results.

6. Dismantle the display and find volunteers to deliver all the food to your local food bank.

Debriefing the Project

- When you open your kitchen cupboards and refrigerator, what do you see? Have you ever seen an empty cupboard?

- What would you do if your family couldn't afford food? Why?

- Why is it important to continue to give donations to a food bank—and not just do it one time?

- How else can we help hungry people in our community?

Helpful Resources

- For children: *The Can-Do Thanksgiving* by Marion Hess Pomeranc (Albert Whitman, 1998), a story about Dee, who brings a can of peas to school for the canned food drive and keeps asking, "Where do my peas go?" Her questioning results in a class project to prepare and serve food for people in need at Thanksgiving.

- For teens: *What the World Eats* by Faith D'Aluisio and Peter Menzel (Tricycle Press, 2008), which takes readers to 21 countries to see local shopping lists and what's on tables. Readers are also shown the connection between nutrition and politics and circumstance.

Bonus Ideas

- Consider having a monthlong food drive with suggestions of what people can donate each week. For example: Week 1: Donate soup. Week 2: Donate canned fruits and vegetables. Week 3: Donate breakfast cereal. Week 4: Donate crackers.

- Consider creating a food costume (or two) for a volunteer to wear, such as a can of soup or a stalk of celery.

- Decorate boxes for families to take home and collect food they wish to donate. You can often find storage file boxes at local office-supply stores—or you can ask a grocery store to donate boxes.

- Have a focused food bank drive, such as a "Breakfast of Champions" food drive, during which everyone brings healthy cereals and nonperishable breakfast items.

20 Baby Kits

Purpose

Provide baby necessities for a baby in need.

Possible Recipients

- Local options: any local cause that serves families with young children, such as a crisis nursery, family homeless shelter, or domestic-abuse shelter for families

- Other options: Church World Service at www.churchworldservice.org. Click on "Kits," then "Baby Care Kit."

Time Requirement

Planning time before the project: one to two hours. Gathering materials: one hour. Setup time on the day of your project: 30 minutes to an hour. Project time: 30 minutes.

People

This project is ideal for families with children between the ages of 3 and 18. Expect five or six families to collaborate on each baby kit.

Materials

- Enough copies of the "Help Create a Baby Kit" handout (page 56) to publicize your event with families (about 3 times as many as the number of families you wish to attract)
- 1 cardboard box for each baby kit
- Enough baby kit items (see handout) to make all the baby kits you plan to donate

Ask families to donate kit items. You can find cardboard boxes at grocery stores.

Connecting Point

Keeping a baby warm, dry, and clothed is expensive, and many families cannot afford to do this. Baby kits help families get a good start in raising their babies well.

Doing the Project

1. About three weeks before your event, distribute the handout "Help Create a Baby Kit" to families. Fill in the blanks with checkmarks or numbers so families know which items you're asking them to bring. Some organizations print six handouts and place a checkmark by one of the six items—so that across the six handouts all six items are checked—before making more copies. That way they ensure that all the items for the baby kits will be supplied. (You can still give families a choice of which item they want to shop for or of shopping for additional items.) Also provide the opportunity for families to give a monetary donation instead of shopping.

2. Make a sample baby kit to show as an example.

3. At the event, figure out how many families will collaborate on each kit based on how many families are present and how many items were donated. Have each group create a complete baby kit from the list of items and wrap all the items inside one of the receiving blankets, securing it with both diaper pins. Pack each complete kit in its own box.

Debriefing the Project

- Why do babies need so many clothes and diapers?
- Why is poverty particularly hard on families with young children?
- When your family had young children, did your family get help from anyone, like a grandparent or friend? How important was this help?
- How else could we help poor families with babies?

Helpful Resources

- For children: *What Baby Needs* by William Sears (Little Brown, 2001), a heartwarming story about all the things (and people) babies need to grow up well.
- For teens: *The First Part Last* by Angela Johnson (Simon & Schuster Children's Publishing, 2003), a Coretta Scott King Award–winner that tells the story of a 16-year-old boy who is trying to figure out how to be a good father to his newborn daughter while also balancing school, friends, and family.

Bonus Ideas

- Visit the Presbyterian Disaster Assistance website (www.pcusa.org) and search for "Gift of the Heart Kits." Use the graphic in promotion and print resources.
- If you have a crisis nursery in your area, consider asking a representative to speak to your group—or to arrange a tour for your group.

Birthday Bag Bash

Create a birthday bag for a child in need

Every kid deserves to celebrate his or her birthday. Brighten a child's day by helping make special birthday bags at our Birthday Bag Bash.

Date: _____

Time: _____

Place: _____

Please bring:

Nine inexpensive, small toys, plus one more significant toy, such as a stuffed animal or picture book that will fit into a gift bag. You can find inexpensive toys at dollar stores, educational stores that have prizes, toy stores, and other places. You also can bring in unopened new toys from fast-food kids meals.

Toy ideas include: small stuffed toys, whistles, puzzles, books, coloring books, washable markers, crayons, small notepads, and so on.

If you wish to donate larger or more expensive toys, such as Legos or picture books, feel free to do so.

Please RSVP by _____

(date)

to _____.

(project coordinator)

Facts About Malaria

Malaria is one of the world's most deadly diseases, and medical experts say it is one of the leading causes of sickness in the world. Yet, it is also a disease that can easily be prevented with insecticide-treated nets and medication. Other facts about malaria:

- In 2008, 109 countries around the world reported cases of malaria.

- The disease is spread by getting bit by a malaria-carrying mosquito.

- Of the 1 million people who die from malaria, most are children younger than five years old.

- More than half of the world's population (3.3 billion) is at risk of getting malaria.

- The disease is becoming more prevalent because more mosquitoes have developed a resistance to pesticides and some treatment drugs.

- On average, 1,500 malaria cases are reported in the United States every year, even though the disease was eradicated there in the early 1950s.

- Most of those who die from malaria are children who live in sub-Saharan Africa.

- Only one out of three African homes owns an insecticide-treated net.

- Only 23 percent of children and 27 percent of pregnant women in Africa sleep under an insecticide-treated net.

- In Africa, about two people die every minute from malaria.

Sources

WGBH Educational Foundation, *Rx for Survival—A Global Health Challenge, Deadly Diseases: Malaria* (Boston: WGBH Educational Foundation, 2005).

Centers for Disease Control, *Malaria Facts* (Atlanta: Centers for Disease Control, April 11, 2007).

World Health Organization, *World Malaria Report 2008* (Geneva, Switzerland: World Health Organization, 2008), vii.

Donate Food: Help Those Who Are Hungry

You can make a difference by helping those who experience hunger in our community. The next time you go grocery shopping, pick up some extra items to bring to our event.

Date: _____

Time: _____

Place: _____

Before you buy food, carefully check the expiration date. We need food that will stay good for a long time.

Suggested items:

- Canned soup
- Canned tuna or meat
- Peanut butter
- Nuts
- Canned fruits
- Canned vegetables
- Juice (not from the fresh or frozen sections)
- Tomato sauce
- Breakfast cereal
- Brown rice
- Boxed macaroni and cheese
- Whole-wheat pasta
- Crackers
- Granola bars
- Dried beans
- Canned beans

Thank you! Everything you donate will help a family in need.

Help Create a Baby Kit

You're invited to help families care for their babies by creating baby kits.

Come to our event:

Date: _____

Time: _____

Place: _____

Please bring the following NEW items:

_____ 6 diapers

_____ 2 baby T-shirts or undershirts (no onesies)

_____ 2 baby washcloths and 2 diaper pins

_____ 2 baby gowns or baby sleepers

_____ 1 baby sweater or sweatshirt

_____ 2 receiving blankets (one can
be a hand-knitted or crocheted
baby blanket)

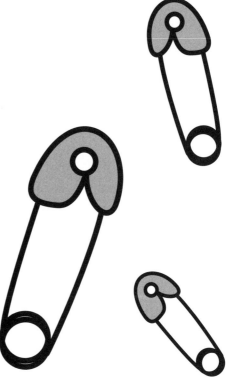

Chapter 3
Projects to Help Those Who Are Sick, Aging, and Disabled

Many people who are sick, disabled, or growing old feel forgotten, isolated, or overlooked in a society that values health and youth. Reach out to those people with the following creative, caring family service projects.

(21) Caring Cards

Purpose

Send cards to cheer up children or adults who are living with a long-term illness.

Possible Recipients

- Local options: a pediatric cancer ward, hospital, nursing home, or social service agency that specializes in home care
- Other options: Make a Child Smile at www.makeachildsmile.org, or Hugs and Hope at www.hugsandhope.org.

Time Requirement

Planning time before the project: one to two hours. Gathering materials: one hour. Setup time on the day of your project: 30 minutes to an hour. Project time: 30 minutes.

People

This project is ideal for families with children between the ages of 5 and 18. Expect each family to make one to two cards during the 30-minute event.

Materials

- 1 piece of 11" x 17" white paper for each family (plus extras for those who want to do more), or inexpensive blank cards and envelopes
- 1 9" x 12" manila envelope for each family (plus extras for those who want to do more)
- 5 washable markers in various colors for each family
- Optional: Stickers
- Optional: Postage stamps

Inexpensive blank cards and envelopes can be found at craft stores such as Michael's.

Connecting Point

Ask participants to imagine what it would be like to be sick for a long time in the hospital without any hope of getting well. Explain that there are children, teenagers, and adults who are struggling with long-term illnesses, and there are also many people who are disabled or are old and sick. A handmade card, made with loving care, boosts a person's spirits.

Doing the Project

1. Before your event, make a sample card to show as an example.
2. Set up the area where you will have the family service project.
3. As families arrive to your event, give each one a piece of paper and manila envelope (or a blank card and envelope). Have families fold the paper in half so that it looks like a large greeting card.
4. Talk about appropriate messages to write on the card. For example, families could write "Hi" on the outside of the card and "Thinking of you" on the inside of the card. Or they could you write "Thinking" on the outside of the card and "of you" on the inside of the card. Brainstorm other messages so families have many from which to choose. Encourage families not to write "get well" messages, since many of the recipients won't be getting well.
5. Create the greeting cards using markers. Encourage families to make them colorful, cheerful, and bright. Encourage them to decorate the envelopes as well, leaving space for the sending and return addresses and stamp.
6. When families finish, have them sign their first names on the inside of the card.
7. If you have time and supplies, families may make additional cards.
8. If you're mailing the cards, ask families each to consider donating $1 per card created to cover postage costs.

Debriefing the Project

- How would you feel if you received a hand-made card of this size? Why?
- Why is it important to send notes to people who are sick, lonely, or disabled?
- When has someone mailed a card to you? How did you feel about that?
- What else can we do to raise the spirits of those who are sick, isolated, or disabled?

Helpful Resources

- For children: *The Hospital* by Debbie Bailey (Annick Press, 2000), a book that uses photos to depict different aspects of what kids can expect if they go to a hospital.
- For teens: *I Still Dream Big: Stories of Teens Living with Chronic Illness* by Penny Wolf (AuthorHouse, 2009), stories by 17 young adults about living with chronic illness.

Bonus Ideas

- Consider other creative ways to make cards, such as taping together a bunch of 8½" x 11" paper in an accordion fan and writing a long note.
- If you have a tight budget, consider doing the same project with 8½" x 11" paper folded in half with 6" x 9" manila envelopes.
- Make a mailbox (or get one from a home-improvement store) so families can "mail" the cards when they finish.
- If choosing nonlocal recipients, show photos and read short biographies of the children to whom the families are writing. These photos can be found on the Make a Child Smile Foundation website, www.makeachildsmile.org, or the Hugs and Hope website at www.hugsandhope.org. Or put the photos and short stories of the kids in plastic frames on the tables to make a display.
- Consider making bookmarks to include with the cards.
- Stamps and stamp pads are also great for decorating the cards.

(22) Breakfast Bags

Purpose

Make quick, easy-to-grab breakfasts for families staying at a Ronald McDonald House while their children receive medical treatment at a nearby hospital.

Possible Recipients

A local Ronald McDonald House (visit www.rmhc.org to find one near you. Click on "Chapter Search" under "Who We Are")

Time Requirement

Planning time before the project: one to two hours. Gathering materials: one hour. Setup time on the day of your project: 30 minutes to an hour. Project time: one hour.

People

This project is ideal for families with children between the ages of 3 and 18. Expect each family to make one or two breakfast bags during the one-hour event.

Materials

- Various single-serving individually wrapped breakfast items such as fruit, fruit cups, granola bars, juice boxes, yogurt, breakfast bars, muffins, breads, and so on. (Each breakfast bag needs about 4 different items. Ask your local Ronald McDonald House which items they would like included; they may require nonperishable items only.)
- 1 paper lunch bag for each family
- 5 washable markers in various colors for each family

Ask families to donate the breakfast items.

Connecting Point

Explain how hard it would be to have a very ill child and the stress not only of the illness but of the medical expense. In many areas, there are Ronald McDonald Houses where families can stay for a small fee (such as $15 a night) while the sick child receives medical treatment at a nearby hospital. Since these families spend most of their time at the hospital, the Ronald McDonald House provides easy-to-make and easy-to-grab breakfasts, which volunteers often donate.

Doing the Project

1. About three weeks before your event, email or distribute a list of acceptable breakfast foods that families can donate. Encourage families to bring at least three items. You might also ask a corporation or local grocery store to donate items.

2. When families arrive at your event, tell them what breakfast is like at a Ronald McDonald House. You can read excerpts from the "A Day in the Life at a House" section at the Ronald McDonald House website.

3. Have families sort the breakfast items they brought. Place all the fruit cups together, all the granola bars together, all the breads together, and so on.

4. Figure out how many breakfast bags your group can make with about four items per paper lunch bag.

5. Have families use markers to decorate the paper lunch bags.

6. Once families finish, form an assembly line. Have each family place three to four different items into their breakfast lunch bags.

7. Collect all the breakfast bags in one area and count them. Talk about how that many families (such as 20, 50, or 100) will now have breakfast, thanks to your group's efforts.

Debriefing the Project

- What did you experience when you went shopping for the breakfast items?
- What did you think about as you decorated the bag?
- How do you think the family who receives your breakfast bag will feel when they see it? Why?
- What would it be like to have a family member in the hospital?
- What else can we do to help families staying at a Ronald McDonald House?

Helpful Resources

- For children: Read aloud a story about a real family staying at a Ronald McDonald House. The website has a number of short stories that capture what it's like. Visit www.rmhc.org and click on "News and events."
- For teens: *Tuesdays with Morrie: An Old Man, a Young Man, and Life's Greatest Lesson* by Mitch Albom (Broadway, 2002), a true story about a former college student visiting his dying college professor, who teaches important lessons about living and dying through the last 14 weeks of his life.

Bonus Ideas

- Ask your local Ronald McDonald House what other needs it has that your group could create and donate.
- Create thinking-of-you cards for individual families to read while they're waiting at the hospital for medical procedures.
- Consider asking your local Ronald McDonald House if anyone could speak to your group about the important work they do.

(23) Smile Drawings

Purpose

Give people living in nursing homes (or those who are homebound) something to smile about when they receive colorful drawings from children.

Possible Recipients

- Local options: a nursing home, local Meals on Wheels chapter, congregation that has a number of homebound members, or some other senior agency
- Other options: Color A Smile, at www .colorasmile.org, an organization that collects and distributes hand-colored drawings for people who live in nursing homes or who live alone and receive Meals on Wheels

Time Requirement

Planning time before the project: one to two hours. Gathering materials: one hour. Setup time on the day of your project: 30 minutes to an hour. Project time: 30 minutes.

People

This project is ideal for families with children between the ages of 3 and 12. Expect each person to create one to two smile drawings during the 30-minute event.

Materials

- 1 copy of the coloring template from the Color A Smile website for each person attending (go to www.colorasmile.org and click on "Coloring book"), plus extras for those who want more
- Lots of 8½" x 11" white paper (about 4 to 5 pieces per person)
- 5 to 10 crayons of various colors for each person
- 1 9" x 12" manila envelope (if you plan to mail the drawings to Color A Smile)
- Postage (if you plan to mail the drawings to Color A Smile)

Connecting Point

Ask kids about times they've been sick. Were they happy or sad? Could they play with their friends when they were sick? Why or why not? Talk about how sad and lonely older people can get when they are either sick or disabled. Explain how sending them a colorful picture can lift their spirits and make their day brighter.

Doing the Project

1. Before your event, print out color examples of pictures children have drawn and donated. You can find these at www.colorasmile.org/masterpieces.html.

2. When families arrive for the event, show them the color examples and have a group discussion about why they're important pictures. Explain how people display handmade art in their homes and how touched they are when someone creates something just for them.

3. Give each person paper and crayons. Encourage individuals to draw and color their own masterpieces. Or you can use the templates Color A Smile has online.

4. As families create their drawings, read aloud some of the thank-you notes from past recipients. You can find these at the Color A Smile website.

5. If some people finish early, encourage them to make another drawing to donate.

6. When families finish, ask participants to take turns showing their illustrations to the group. After everyone has done this, applaud.

7. Place all the finished drawings in one area for delivery or mailing.

Debriefing the Project

- How did seeing other children's masterpieces first help you with your drawing?
- Why is it so important to give colorful drawings to elderly and disabled people?

- If you received one of these drawings, where would you display it in your home?
- How do you think the person receiving your picture will feel? Why?
- What else can we do to help elderly and disabled people?

Helpful Resources

- For children: *Wilfrid Gordon McDonald Partridge* by Mem Fox (Kane/Miller Book Publishers, 1989), a story about a boy with four names who lives next door to a nursing home and has made friends with the residents.
- For teens: *The Cay* by Theodore Taylor (Laurel Leaf, 2003), a story of a friendship that evolves between a young boy and an older man stranded on a raft together.

Bonus Ideas

- Make color photocopies of some of the drawings and use them the next time you do a similar project. (Or display the color photocopies along with information about your service project.)
- If some families would be interested in doing this type of project on a regular basis, see if a local agency would be interested in connecting families with a specific elderly or disabled person. Then they could send pictures and notes once a month.
- If you use Color A Smile as your recipient agency, consider providing families with the Color A Smile website information so they can continue to send their children's drawings. A lot of families are happy to share their children's artwork when so much is generated.

(24) Sweet Somethings

Purpose

Brighten the day of people who feel isolated or lonely by decorating cookies to donate to them.

Possible Recipients

- A local nursing home, Meals on Wheels chapter, congregation that has a number of homebound members, group home for disabled adults, or some other senior agency

Time Requirement

Planning time before the project: one to three hours. Gathering materials: one to two hours. Setup time on the day of your project: one to two hours. Project time: one to two hours.

People

This project is ideal for families with children between the ages of 5 and 18. Expect each family to decorate 10 to 25 cookies during the one- to two-hour event.

Materials

- 10–25 store-bought, plain sugar cookies per family
- 2 tubs of frosting for each cookie-decorating station
- A variety of cake and cookie decorations, such as edible pearls, sugar sanding, and sprinkles so that each cookie-decorating station has 2 to 4 different ones
- 1 plastic knife for each person
- 3 to 4 sheets of foot-long wax paper for each cookie-decorating station
- Shallow boxes or cookie tins for delivering the finished cookies
- 3 to 4 bottles of hand sanitizers

You can find shallow boxes or cookie tins in the baking department of a craft store.

Connecting Point

Ask participants how it feels to get a tasty, hand-decorated treat as a gift. Explain that decorated cookies are often associated with the holidays and with families making them for people they love. People who are sick or homebound often don't receive these types of treats. When they do, they feel excited and cared for.

Doing the Project

1. If you've never frosted or decorated cookies before, try it before you lead this project so you know how it works.

2. The day of your event, set up for your family service project by creating cookie-decorating stations. Place ready-to-decorate cookies, frosting, cookie decorations, wax paper, and plastic knives at each station.

3. As families arrive, have them sanitize their hands. Then ask them to cluster around a station and begin to decorate the cookies. If you have many younger children, give instructions on how to decorate cookies, such as using a thin layer of frosting and not overdecorating the cookies.

4. After everyone finishes, place all the cookies in shallow boxes or cookie tins for delivery. Encourage families to help with cleanup of materials.

Debriefing the Project

- What was your experience in decorating these cookies? Why?

- Why are decorated cookies something that boosts people's spirits?

- Why is it important to make things for people you don't know who feel lonely?

- How else can we help people who feel isolated or lonely?

Helpful Resources

- For children: *Sitti's Secrets* by Naomi Shihab Nye (Aladdin, 1997), a heartwarming story about a young girl visiting her grandmother in a Palestinian village and how their love transcends differences in language and culture.

- For teens: *If I Live to Be 100: Lessons from the Centenarians* by Neenah Ellis (Three Rivers Press, 2004), a book that includes stories of more than a dozen people who have lived a century or more.

Bonus Ideas

- If you have access to a large kitchen, consider baking the cookies rather than buying them. You can either make them from scratch (which requires more time and effort) or you can buy ready-to-bake dough in the refrigerator section of your local supermarket.

- Consider inviting families who enjoy baking and decorating sugar cookies to make them around certain holidays, such as Valentine's Day (heart-shaped cookies), Halloween (pumpkin-shaped), Christmas (tree- or ornament-shaped), or Hanukkah (star-of-David- or dreidel-shaped).

25 Toy Treasures

Purpose

Provide new toys for children who are sick or disabled.

Possible Recipients

- Local options: a hospital pediatric ward, Ronald McDonald House, or some other long-term clinic for kids

- Other options: Spencer's Treasures at www.spencerstreasures.org

Time Requirement

Planning time before the project: one to two hours. Gathering materials: one hour. Setup time on the day of your project: 30 minutes to an hour. Project time: one hour.

People

This project is ideal for families with children between the ages of 3 and 18.

Materials

- Enough copies of the "Help Brighten a Sick Child's Day" handout (page 74) to publicize your event with families

- 1 large cardboard box for every 2 to 3 families to decorate together (if you're giving the donation to a local organization)

- Enough decorating materials for each group of families to decorate a box, including washable markers, stickers, and other supplies (if you're giving the donation to a local organization)

- Optional: A laptop computer, projector, and wireless Internet access to show the video from the Spencer's Treasures website at www.spencerstreasures.org. Click on "Recipients."

- Optional: Shipping boxes, tape, and labels (if you're shipping the toys to Spencer's Treasures)

- Postage (if you're shipping the boxes to Spencer's Treasures)

Connecting Point

Ask participants if anyone has ever seen a treasure chest of toys at the dentist, doctor, or restaurant where they got to choose a toy. Explain that an organization called Spencer's Treasures sets up treasure chests in hospitals for pediatric patients to choose a new toy after a procedure. This makes their hospital stay less stressful.

Doing the Project

1. Distribute the handout "Help Brighten a Sick Child's Day" about two to three weeks before your event. Consider designating a place for families to donate toys in case some families want to donate and are unable to attend your event.

2. As families arrive for the event, have them sort the toys by type. Remove all the price tags and stickers.

3. If you're shipping the toys to Spencer's Treasures, talk about the organization using the information at www.spencerstreasures.org. Click on "About Us." If you have a laptop computer, projector, and wireless access, show the video which you can find by clicking on "Recipients." (It is only a few minutes long.)

4. If you're donating the toys locally, have families work together to decorate the boxes. Then fill the boxes with a variety of new toys. If you're shipping the toys to Spencer's Treasures, pack the toys for shipping.

Debriefing the Project

- What did you think of as you bought or found the new toys to donate?

- Why are toys so important for kids?

- How often do you think kids who are disabled or sick get to play? Why?

- Why is it important to help kids who are sick or disabled?

- How else can we help children who are sick or who have special needs?

Helpful Resources

- For children: *Mama Zooms* by Jane Cowen-Fletcher (Scholastic, 1996), a story about a boy who uses his imagination as he expresses the pleasure he finds with his mom in her wheelchair.

- For teens: *Petey* by Ben Mikaelsen (Hyperion, 2010), a story about Petey, who has cerebral palsy and is raised in a psychiatric hospital because of his misdiagnosis.

Bonus Ideas

- Consider finding someone who can make or purchase a toy chest. Then find a local hospital, pediatric ward, or some other facility that would be willing to receive a toy chest. (You will need to fill it on a regular basis.)

- Consider setting up a collection box for people to donate unopened toys from fast-food meals. Many adults enjoy buying children's meals for themselves and then donating the toys to a worthy cause.

(26) Healthcare Kits

Purpose

Provide healthcare kits for people who don't have these everyday necessities, such as those who live in a homeless shelter or domestic-abuse shelter.

Possible Recipients

- Local options: a homeless shelter, domestic-abuse shelter, food shelf, public school district, or some other type of social service agency that would collect these types of donations

- Other options: UMCOR (United Methodist Committee on Relief) at new.gbgm-umc.org (search for "relief supply kits"), or Church World Service at www.churchworldservice.org (click on "Kits" then "Hygiene Kit")

Time Requirement

Planning time before the project: one to two hours. Gathering materials: one hour. Setup time on the day of your project: 30 minutes to an hour. Project time: 30 minutes.

People

This project is ideal for families with children between the ages of 3 and 18. Three families will usually collaborate on one health kit.

Materials

- Enough copies of the handout "Be a Healthcare Helper" (page 75) to publicize your event with families

- Enough healthcare items (see "Be a Healthcare Helper" handout) to complete all the kits

- 1 gallon-size sealable plastic bag for each kit (if you're donating the materials to a local charity)

- Small boxes and other items for shipping the materials (if you're sending them to UMCOR or Church World Service; for up-to-date shipping specifics, visit their websites)

Ask families to donate the items for the healthcare kits and shipping materials.

Connecting Point

Around the world, natural disasters and wars force people to leave their homes. Some people are homeless because of other circumstances. People without homes often lack the basic essentials of hygiene and health. When people have their own healthcare kits and the knowledge of why hygiene is important, they tend to live healthier, longer lives.

Doing the Project

1. About two to three weeks in advance of your project, distribute copies of the "Be a Healthcare Helper" handout. If you want to ensure that you'll get a variety of materials to make complete kits (the list on the handout is what is needed for two kits), have families sign up to bring different items. You can put a number or checkmark in front of items you want families to donate. If families want to bring more, encourage them to do so, since the items on this list are often inexpensive compared with items in other types of kits. Fill in the amount of cash you want families to donate—$2 or $4. (If you're shipping kits to UMCOR, you'll need $4, $2 for the kits and $2 to help cover shipping costs.)

2. Consider establishing a drop-off spot for families to leave donations for the healthcare kits. Some families may wish to donate items but are unable to attend your family service project.

3. Before your event, make one healthcare kit to show as an example.

4. As families arrive for the project, have them place their donations by type into separate piles. (For example, place all the hand towels in one place and all the combs in another place.)

5. Give each family (or two or three families working together) a plastic bag (or a small box if you're shipping them to UMCOR). Have them walk through the stations and pick up items at each station: one hand towel, one washcloth, one comb, one nail file or finger-nail clippers, one bar of soap, one toothbrush, six plastic strip sterile bandages.

6. Once families finish, have them dump out their bags (or boxes) and double-check the kit to make sure it's complete. Read aloud each item from the list and have families place that item back into their empty bag as you read.

7. Ask each family to place one of the dollars they brought into the bag, which will purchase toothpaste. (In the past, people donated toothpaste, but it expires. The dollar ensures that people can get fresh toothpaste.)

8. If you're donating the kits to UMCOR, ask one family to collect the other dollar from families. That dollar is to help cover the cost of shipping these items.

9. Talk about the connection between daily hygiene habits (brushing your teeth, washing your face and body, clipping your nails, and so on) and health.

10. Count the number of healthcare kits your group put together.

Debriefing the Project

- Why is each of these items in these healthcare kits important?
- When do you use the items in this healthcare kit? Why?
- How would you feel if you became homeless because of a natural disaster, war, or some other means?
- Why is it important to make healthcare kits?
- How else can we help people with their medical needs?

Helpful Resources

- For children: *Happy Healthy Monsters: All Squeaky Clean (All About Hygiene)* by Kara McMahon (Random House, 2006), a story about the monsters of *Sesame Street* (Elmo, Grover, Cookie Monster, and so on) learning the importance of hygiene and health.
- *Mountains Beyond Mountains: The Quest of Dr. Paul Farmer, a Man Who Would Cure the World* by Tracy Kidder (Random House Trade Paperbacks, 2009), the powerful story of doctor and human rights activist Paul Farmer's dedication to public health work in Haiti.

Bonus Ideas

- Healthcare kits aren't the only type of medical kits needed. You can also create medicine boxes or "Healthy Homes, Healthy Families" kits. For more information, visit the UMCOR website and click on "Get Connected," then on "Send Relief Supplies."

- Some shelters and agencies create a regular collection spot for people wanting to donate toothbrushes, small tubes of toothpaste, and sample sizes of dental floss (after a dental

visit) or the small shampoos and lotions acquired when they visit hotels. All these small, unopened items are often heartily accepted by local shelters.

27 Ponytail Power

Purpose

Boost the confidence of children who suffer from long-term medical hair loss by donating hair to create high-quality hairpieces.

Possible Recipients

- Locks of Love at www.locksoflove.org

Time Requirement

Planning time before the project: one to two hours. Gathering materials: one hour. Setup time on the day of your project: 30 minutes to an hour. Project time: one hour. Allow 20 months for people to grow hair before the event.

People

This project is ideal for families with children between the ages of 5 and 18.

Materials

- Enough copies of the handout "Grow Out Your Hair for a Good Cause" (page 76) to publicize your project with families
- 1 gallon-size zip-top plastic bag for each ponytail or braid
- 1 padded envelope for each ponytail or braid
- 1 yardstick
- 1 large shipping box, permanent marker, strapping tape
- Postage
- Optional: laptop computer, projector, and wireless Internet connection

Connecting Point

When children get cancer and lose their hair because of chemotherapy, or get some other type of disease that causes them to lose their hair, they often suffer emotionally because they don't like the way they look. Getting a realistic-looking hairpiece is expensive (they can cost up to $6,000 each). Locks of Love has been accepting hair donations since 1997, and they have provided more than 2,000 hairpieces in all 50 states and Canada.

Doing the Project

1. Visit the Locks of Love website at www .locksoflove.org to learn about the specifics of creating a family service project where individuals donate hair.

2. Set an approximate date for your family service project about 20 months in the future.

3. Publicize your need for kids (and adults) to grow out their hair. Use the "Grow Your Hair for a Good Cause" handout. Note that it takes about one month to grow a half-inch of hair, so you need about 20 months for people to grow 10 inches of hair, which is the minimum length required for a donation. (Some people with long hair may be willing to donate sooner.)

4. Send out monthly reminders to keep families inspired as they grow out their hair. (Request to be added to the Locks of Love e-newsletter subscription so you can receive additional information from the organization.)

5. A week or so before your event, email families instructions on how to cut off their hair, using the specifications listed on the Locks of Love website, so they can bring their hair to your event. Anyone can cut the hair, but it must be in a ponytail or braid to donate. Go to www .locksoflove.org/donate.

6. As families arrive on the day of your event, have donors place their ponytails or braids of hair on a donation table.

7. Give families the opportunity to make a financial donation to Locks of Love if they didn't participate in the hair donation.

8. Line up all the donated hair in a long line. Have families measure to see how much was donated. Total up the financial donations as well.

9. If possible, show photos of the recipients, which you can find on the Locks of Love website. Click on "LOL Kids" and then "Recipient photos."

10. Place each individual donation in a plastic bag and then in a padded envelope for mailing.

Debriefing the Project

- If you grew out your hair to donate, why did you decide to do this?

- Was it hard to grow out your hair? Why or why not? (It's easier for some people than for others.)

- How would you feel if you lost all your hair for good?

- What other ways could we help kids who have lost all their hair?

Helpful Resources

- For children: *The Girl with No Hair: A Story About Alopecia Areata* by Elizabeth Murphy-Melas (Health Press NA Inc., 2003), a story about a girl who loses all her hair because of an autoimmune disease.

- For teens: *Bald as a Bean* by Nancy Parsons (Nancy Parsons Pub, 2006), a true story about a woman who suddenly goes bald because of alopecia areata universalis.

Bonus Ideas

- Consider having hair stylists donate their time. Instead of having families get their hair cut before the family service project, have a number of hair stylists available to cut the hair for free at the event (to the specifications required by Locks of Love).

- Encourage local hair salons to become a Locks of Love Participating Salon. Whenever a client asks a hair stylist to cut off 10 inches of hair or more, the stylist can request to keep the hair and donate it to Locks of Love. You also could have many hair salons participating at the same time as your family service event so you have more hair to donate.

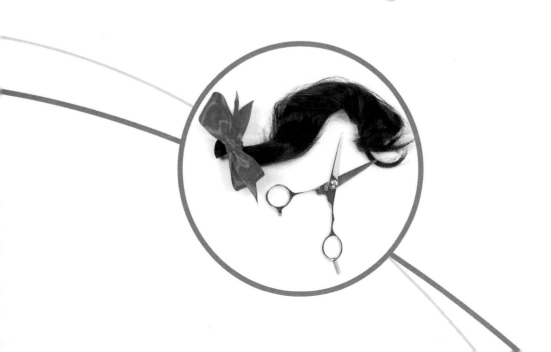

(28) New Eyes to See

Purpose

Collect used prescription eyeglasses and prescription or nonprescription sunglasses to donate to someone in need who lives in a developing country or low-income area of your country.

Possible Recipients

- Local options: eyeglass stores and service clubs (such as the Rotary or Lions Club) that collect glasses and sunglasses
- Other option: New Eyes for the Needy at www.neweyesfortheneedy.org

Time Requirement

Planning time before the project: one to two hours. Gathering materials: one hour. Setup time on the day of your project: 30 minutes to an hour. Project time: one hour.

People

This project is ideal for families with children between the ages of 3 and 18.

Materials

- Used prescription eyeglasses that individuals no longer use
- New and used sunglasses (either prescription or nonprescription)
- New and used reading glasses
- Old eyeglasses that may be in too bad of shape to donate
- Petroleum jelly
- Optional: Shipping materials (see specifics at www.neweyesfortheneedy.org)

Families will donate the new and used glasses.

Connecting Point

Ask participants if they have ever experienced not being able to see clearly. (This is often the case for individuals who need prescription eyeglasses for the first time—or for people who wear a prescription that changes.) Have them tell what it was like to try to see. Explain that in some developing countries, prescription eyeglasses are too expensive for many people who need them. In some areas, it costs three months' salary for a pair of eyeglasses—they must buy food, clothing, and shelter instead and therefore go without glasses. In addition, many people need sunglasses, but don't have the means to buy any. Donating prescription eyeglasses and sunglasses can help many people in need.

Doing the Project

1. About two to three weeks before your event, get the word out for families to bring prescription eyeglasses they no longer use and sunglasses (either prescription or nonprescription) to your family service project. (Encourage them to call extended family members and connect with others who may be interested in donating used eyeglasses and sunglasses to this worthy cause.)

2. Consider creating a drop-off spot to collect donations and leaving it up for the weeks leading up to your event. Sometimes you can collect more items this way from families who would like to donate but can't make it to the event.

3. As families arrive on the day of the event, separate their donations into four groupings: prescription eyeglasses, prescription sunglasses, reading glasses, and nonprescription sunglasses.

4. Rub petroleum jelly on the lenses of some of the eyeglasses you brought in (that cannot be donated). Give children turns putting on these eyeglasses and ask them to talk about what it's like to try to see through them. (It will be blurry and hard to see.) If families can spot children carefully, let the children try to take a few steps.

5. Talk about how important it is to see well, and how good eyesight makes life better.

6. Count up the number of eyeglass donations.

7. If you're shipping your donations to New Eyes for the Needy, follow the shipping instructions at the organization's website. Click on "Impact: How You Can Help" and then on "Shipping Instructions."

Debriefing the Project

- Were you surprised how many old eyeglasses or sunglasses you had at home? Why or why not?

- Why do you think it is easy for us to take our eyesight for granted?

- What would you choose to buy if you didn't have enough money to buy glasses, food, shelter, *and* clothing? Why?

- What else could we do to support people who have trouble seeing and can't afford prescription eyeglasses?

Helpful Resources

- For children: *Luna and the Big Blur: A Story for Children Who Wear Glasses* by Shirley Day (American Psychological Association, 2008), the story of a girl who learns to feel proud of her glasses and her name.

- For teens: *Eye Care in Developing Nations* by Larry Schwab (Manson Publishing, 2007), a book that gives an overview of what's needed to help people with eye problems in countries that don't have enough resources.

Bonus Ideas

- Consider inviting someone who is blind (or has poor sight) and uses Braille items (such as Braille books, dice, and other things) to talk about what it's like and how these Braille items help them.

- Find prescription eyeglass drop-off facilities near you (such as some LensCrafters or Pearle Vision stores and Lions Clubs) so people can continue to donate glasses after your service project ends.

 **Penny Power**

Purpose

Collect pennies to donate to the Leukemia & Lymphoma Society's annual Pennies for Patients program to help children diagnosed with cancer.

Possible Recipients

- The Leukemia & Lymphoma Society School & Youth programs at www.schoolandyouth.org

Time Requirement

Planning time before the project: one to two hours. Gathering materials: one hour. Setup time on the day of your project: 30 minutes to an hour. Project time: one hour.

People

This project is ideal for families with children between the ages of 3 and 18.

Materials

- Lots of pennies

- 1 copy of the forms from the School & Youth website (see step one under Doing the Project)

Invite families to collect pennies and any other type of spare change over a certain period of time and bring them to your family service project. Also consider asking families to donate money in other ways, since some may not have spare change to bring.

Connecting Point

Each year, more than 14,000 kids are diagnosed with cancer. Of those, more than 5,000 get a blood cancer, which is called leukemia or lymphoma. The Leukemia & Lymphoma Society started Pennies for Patients to raise money to improve the lives of children with the diseases and for research to find a cure. In 2007, schools and youth organizations raised $18 million dollars through programs such as Pennies for Patients.

Doing the Project

1. Before your event, consider downloading the helpful forms from School & Youth at www.schoolandyouth.org, such as the coordinator guide and creative campaign ideas. Click on "Program Coordinators."

2. When families arrive at your event, have them place their pennies and other spare change into piles according to the coin: one for pennies, one for nickels, one for dimes, and one for quarters. If appropriate, you may also make one pile for other donations (such as bills and checks).

3. Seat families at tables and give each table about 50 coins. Explain that you're going to play a game. Place all the coins in the middle of the table.

4. Play a game called "Give and Take." First play the game where the point is to try to get as many coins as possible. The trick, however, is that the coins cannot leave the table, you cannot get out of your chair, and you cannot hurt anyone. You can try to get as many free coins as possible and also try to get coins from others at your table. This will seem like a free-for-all in grabbing coins. Give families time to play, but monitor the games to make sure no one gets too aggressive.

5. After a few minutes, stop the game. Have everyone return all the coins to the middle of the table. Play the game again, except this time have individuals try to give away as much money as they can—and keep coins from getting to them. Again, monitor the game to make sure no one gets too aggressive.

6. End the game. Ask questions such as these: Which was more fun: trying to take coins or give them away? Why? Which game made

you angrier or more frustrated? Why? What is the point of this game?

7. Return all the coins to the original donation piles. Have families count the coins and add up the total donations.

8. Package the coins for delivery. See the School & Youth website for more information.

Debriefing the Project

- How did you save coins? Did you have a certain container?

- Were you surprised by how many coins you could—or couldn't—save? Why?

- Why do you think this organization emphasizes giving pennies and coins (instead of other types of donations)?

- How else can we help people with blood cancers?

Helpful Resources

- For children: *The Amazing Hannah: Look at Everything I Can Do!* by Amy and Dave Klett (Candlelighters Childhood Cancer Foundation, 2002), a story created for a preschooler with leukemia to explain what the disease and medical procedures are all about. Get a free copy from the American Childhood Cancer Organization at www.candlelighters .org or email staff@acco.org.

- For teens: *Here and Now: Inspiring Stories of Cancer Survivors* by Elena Dorfman and Heidi Schultz Adams (De Capo Press, 2001), a collection of true stories of people who survived cancer, including famous actors, musicians, and authors.

Bonus Ideas

- The Leukemia & Lymphoma Society School & Youth Programs website also has a video you can show if you have a laptop computer, a projector, and access to wireless Internet. Click on "Participating Educators" and then "Video."

- The Leukemia & Lymphoma Society offers many different ways to raise money for cancer patients and research. Visit www.leukemia-lymphoma.org for more ideas. Click on "How to Help" on the left-hand tool bar. Then click on "Participate in Events."

(30) Forever Flowers

Purpose

Make a lonely person's day with colorful, hand-made flowers that last forever.

Possible Recipients

- A nursing home, local Meals on Wheels chapter, congregation that has a number of home-bound members, group home for disabled adults, or some other senior agency

Time Requirement

Planning time before the project: one to two hours. Gathering materials: one hour. Setup time on the day of your project: 30 minutes to an hour. Project time: one hour.

People

This project is ideal for families with children between the ages of 5 and 18. Expect each family to make one bouquet of about five flowers during the one-hour event.

Materials

- 1 used vase for each family
- A variety of tissue-paper squares in many colors (one 25-sheet tissue-paper pack will make about 300 tissue flowers)
- 5 green pipe cleaners for each family (plus extras for those who want to make more flowers)
- 1 ruler, yardstick, or measuring tape for each table
- 1 pair of scissors for each family
- 1 roll of clear tape for each family

Ask families to donate vases. Tissue paper can be found in the wrapping paper section of a discount or craft store. Tissue paper usually comes in packages of 25 sheets that measure 18" x 24". Other materials are available at craft stores such as Michael's or Jo-Ann Fabrics & Crafts.

Connecting Point

People who are homebound, sick, or disabled often do not receive many visitors or gifts and may feel very lonely. These handmade flowers will brighten rooms and show people they're cared for.

Doing the Project

1. Before your event, make a flower bouquet so you know how it's put together and to show as an example.

2. Set up tables for your event. At each table, have a variety of tissue paper, pipe cleaners, and scissors.

3. As families arrive, have them find a table. Talk about what kinds of gifts we tend to bring people who are sick, homebound, or disabled. (Listen for someone to say flowers and then talk about why flowers cheer up people. Flowers represent new life, they're colorful, and some have a wonderful aroma.)

4. Explain that each family is going to create a tissue-flower bouquet of about five flowers. Each flower requires three squares of tissue paper. They can all be the same color or different colors.

5. Explain that the squares must be 6" x 6". Have families measure and cut out the squares.

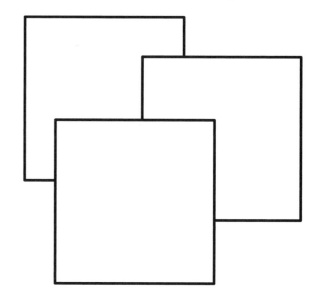

6. To make a flower, place all three tissue squares on top of each other, then fold the paper back and forth like an accordion-style paper fan. Make the folds about ½" to ¾" wide.

7. Fold the fan in half. Wrap one end of a pipe cleaner around the fold to secure it. Explain that the pipe cleaner is going to be the stem.

8. To add interest to the petals, before unfolding the fan, encourage families to trim each side of the tissue paper. Families could trim the ends into a point, round out the ends like a half circle, create a jagged cut, or cut into the sides close together like a fringe to add interest.

9. Pull open the tissue paper gently on one side, layer by layer. Be careful not to do this too quickly, since tissue paper rips easily. Then do the other side. Grab the point where the flower is connected to the stem and fluff it up toward the middle of the flower until it looks like a blooming flower. (Help children who struggle with this step. Children who want to do it themselves can tape the top ends together with a small piece of tape.)

10. Place the completed flower into a vase and make at least four more flowers to form a bouquet. Encourage families to make flowers of different colors so the bouquet is colorful.

11. If the vase has a wide mouth, encourage families to wrap the stems of the five flowers together so that the flowers make a tighter bouquet.

Debriefing the Project

- Why do you think people enjoy receiving handmade gifts?
- Why do people sometimes give real flowers? Why did we give handmade flowers?
- What did you talk about as you made your flowers?
- What do you think the recipient will say when he or she sees your bouquet?
- How else could we help people who are sick, homebound, or disabled?

Helpful Resources

- For children: *Sunshine Home* by Eve Bunting (Sandpiper, 2003), a touching story of a boy visiting his grandmother in a nursing home.
- For teens: *The Short Bus: A Journey Beyond Normal* by Jonathan Mooney (Holt Paperbacks, 2008), the memoir of a man with dyslexia who challenges people's preconceptions of people with disabilities and what it means to be "normal."

Bonus Ideas

- Consider making handmade, personal cards to accompany the flower bouquet.
- Make fuller flowers by using more tissue paper. Try using six pieces—or 12—and see what happens. Or make larger flowers by using 9" x 9" squares.
- Sometimes you have someone in your community who is struggling with a major disease and the community is rallying to help that person. Consider making many bouquets and giving them all to this one person to show your support and care.

Help Brighten a Sick Child's Day

Children love to play, and children who are sick get excited when they receive new toys. The next time you go shopping, pick up some small toys to bring to our family service project. Feel free to visit dollar stores and other discount stores to find toys.

Date: _____

Time: _____

Place: _____

Note: All toys need to be small and new, in an unopened container.

Suggested items:

- Unopened toys from fast-food kids meals
- New miniature cars
- Small stuffed animals
- Small books
- Playing cards
- Small bath toys
- Small crayon sets
- Pez-head dispensers
- Small dolls
- Small action figures
- Small jewelry sets
- Collectible cards: football, baseball, basketball, Pokémon, Yu-Gi-Oh!, Magic, and so on
- Novelty pencils or pens
- Bubbles to blow
- Gift certificates to movie houses or stores (if you're donating locally)
- Any new toy small enough to fit in a child's hand

Thank you! Everything you donate will help a child in need.

Be a Healthcare Helper

You're invited to help homeless individuals and families by creating healthcare kits. Come to our family service project.

Date: _____

Time: _____

Place: _____

Please bring $_____ and the following NEW items:

_____ 2 hand towels (each can be 15" x 25" up to 17" x 27"—not kitchen towels)

_____ 2 washcloths

_____ 2 combs (large and sturdy, not pocket-size, no hair brushes)

_____ 2 nail files or fingernail clippers (no emery boards or toenail clippers)

_____ 2 bath-size bars of soap (3 ounces and larger)

_____ 2 toothbrushes (single brushes only, in the original wrapper; no child-size brushes)

_____ 12 adhesive plastic strip sterile bandages

Grow Out Your Hair for a Good Cause

When children lose their hair due to disease or chemotherapy, they often suffer emotionally because they don't like the way they look. Since realistic-looking hairpieces can cost up to $6,000 apiece, this service project is critical for many children in need.

Locks of Love is one organization that collects hair donations to make hairpieces for kids. It has been doing this since 1997, and since then the organization has helped more than 2,000 children under the age of 18. If you'd like to see how important this work is, please visit www.locksoflove.org.

We encourage you and your family members to participate in a long-term family service project by growing out your hair to donate to Locks of Love. It takes about 20 months to grow 10 inches of hair (which is the minimum length required for a donation).

We'll meet on _____ to collect your donations.
(date)

If you're interested in helping a child, start growing out your hair and let us know so we can keep in touch along the way.

Remember: Every inch of hair matters!

Chapter 4
Projects to Help Promote Education and Literacy

One out of five people in the world is illiterate, reports the United Nations Educational, Scientific and Cultural Organization.* Literacy—the ability to read and write—is critical for an individual to succeed at school, at work, at home, and in the community. Help promote education and literacy with these family service projects.

*UNESCO Institute for Statistics, *International Literacy Statistics: A Review of Concepts, Methodology and Current Data* (Montreal, Quebec: UNESCO Institute for Statistics, 2008), 9.

(31) Whisper Phones

Purpose

Help English language learners (ELL) or young readers learn to read quicker by building and donating whisper phones.

Possible Recipients

- An elementary school (public or private) or ELL classrooms for children through a local school district or community education

Time Requirement

Planning time before the project: one to two hours. Gathering materials: one hour. Setup time on the day of your project: 30 minutes to an hour. Project time: one hour.

People

This project is ideal for families with children between the ages of 5 and 18. Expect each family to make one whisper phone during the one-hour event.

If possible, recruit several volunteers to cut PVC pipe at your event in addition to the volunteers who normally help with planning, organizing, and running the event. Shoot for four volunteers for every 20 families or so.

Materials

- 1 piece of ¾" diameter PVC pipe (5" long) for each family
- 2 PVC elbows that match the PVC pipe for each family
- 4 hacksaws
- 4 rulers or tape measures
- 1 gallon-size sealable plastic bag for each family
- 1 index card for each family
- 1 pen for each family
- 2 to 3 fine- and medium-point permanent markers in a variety of colors for each family

PVC pipe, elbows, and hacksaws are available at home-improvement stores such as The Home Depot and Menards. PVC pipe generally comes in foot-long (or longer) pieces. A 5-foot piece can be cut into a dozen 5-inch pieces. Check with your home-improvement center to see if they'll cut the PVC pipe to your specifications for free. (Some may do so, and that would save you a number of steps in this project.)

Connecting Point

Ask participants to say the alphabet slowly. Then ask how many different ways you can say a certain letter, such as the letter A (short A and long A). Explain that when children are learning to read, it's important for them to hear these subtle differences.

Doing the Project

1. Before your event, find enough volunteer adults or older teenagers to saw the PVC pipe.

2. Make a sample whisper phone so you know how it's put together and to show as an example. Have the parts to show how to assemble one at your event.

3. Once families arrive to your event, ask for a volunteer. Have that person assemble one whisper phone with your guidance by placing one PVC elbow on one end of the 5-inch straight PVC pipe and another elbow on the other end of the straight PVC pipe. Have the volunteer show how it looks like a phone.

4. Ask the volunteer to whisper into the phone. What does he or she hear? (It should amplify what is said so that he or she can hear better.) Talk about how this amplification helps young children and children who are learning English as a second language to discern differences in the sounds of language. In a class, children can read along by whispering and be able to hear what they're saying through the whisper phone.

5. Have volunteers measure and mark 5-inch pieces on the long PVC pipe and saw the pieces while the families continue with the next step.

6. Distribute an index card and pen to each family. Ask them to choose a family member who has very neat printing to write the following on the card: *To sanitize your whisper phone, soak it in a tub with one tablespoon of bleach per one gallon of water. Or you can have children wipe it off with a wet wipe when they're finished using it. Or you can wash the phone in the top rack of a dishwasher.*

7. By now the volunteers who have been sawing should be finished. Distribute pieces of the whisper phone (one straight piece and two elbows) so families can put the phones together.

8. Have families decorate the whisper phones with permanent markers.

9. When they finish, have them try the whisper phone to see why it's helpful. Then have them place one whisper phone with the instruction card in a sealable plastic bag for delivery to recipients.

Debriefing the Project

- Do you remember learning how to read—or teaching someone how to read? How long did it take?

- Why is it important to learn how to read well?

- How does using a whisper phone make learning how to read more fun?

- What else can we do to help people learn how to read?

Helpful Resources

- For children: *Eating the Alphabet: Fruits & Vegetables from A to Z* by Lois Ehlert (Harcourt, 1994). Learn the alphabet through colorful pictures of fruits and vegetables.

- For teens: *You Can't Read This: Forbidden Books, Lost Writing, Mistranslations, and Codes* by Val Ross (Tundra Books, 2006). These eighteen stories describe the persistent struggles of individuals, scholars, believers, and transgressors to engage in writing and reading in civilizations across the globe throughout history.

Bonus Ideas

- If you find a teacher who uses the whisper phones often, see if your group can make a new batch each year for his or her classroom. That way, each child can receive a personal whisper phone and continue using it at home after the school year is done.

- Consider making a bookmark to add to the zip-top bag and whisper phone. Or have a book drive and also enclose an easy-to-read book.

(32) Storybook Magic

Purpose

Create books for children in northern Uganda, where a long civil war has caused a lot of tragedy, so children can find momentary peace of mind through a story.

Possible Recipients

- Books of Hope (www.booksofhope.org)

Time Requirement

Planning time before the project: two to six hours. Gathering materials: one to two hours. Setup time on the day of your project: one to two hours. Project time: 90 minutes.

People

This project is ideal for families with children between the ages of 5 and 18. Expect two to four families to collaborate on each book, so if you'd like to donate five books, you'll need about 10 to 20 families.

In addition to the usual volunteers who help with setup, cleanup, publicity, and running the event, you may also want to recruit volunteers to photograph your event (or ask families to do this).

Materials

- 1 facilitator packet from www.booksofhope .org (click on "Facilitator Resources," then "Facilitator Packet")
- $125 to $475, depending on your participation level (see the payment instructions page of the facilitator packet)
- Mailing supplies: ReadyPost mailing cartons and plastic bags to wrap books in (see step 2 to determine how many you'll need)
- 1 computer for each book you plan to make
- 1 printer for each book you plan to make
- 27 pieces of 8½" x 11" white paper for each book you plan to make
- 10 washable markers in various colors for each family

- 1 report cover for each book you plan to make
- 1 three-hole punch
- 3 to 4 digital cameras
- 1 pen for each family
- writing paper or stationery

Connecting Point

Because of the war in northern Uganda, about 1.7 million people were living in camps to keep safe until just a few years ago. Many of the children were upset because they were separated from their families. In 2006, a tentative truce was made that allowed children to go back to their families. But many are still traumatized, and they're very behind in their schooling. Books of Hope encourages schools and organizations to create books for these children.

Doing the Project

1. Read the facilitator packet from the Books of Hope website. Note the deadline for the project: Books of Hope collects books between mid-May and mid-June each year.

2. Decide on your participation level. It costs $125 to $475 for various participation levels. For $125 you can ship one box, a ReadyPost® 15" x 12" x 10" mailing carton from the U.S. Postal Service®, which you can fill with as many books as will fit.

3. Purchase the ReadyPost mailing carton from your local post office so you can determine how many books (each wrapped in a plastic bag to weatherproof it) can fit.

4. Register through Books of Hope at www.booksofhope.org.

5. Once you have registered, choose a school and decide which type of books your families will be making. **Note:** Your group can choose books for three different age groups: elementary (ages 3 to 8), intermediate (ages 9 to 13), and advanced (ages 14 and 18) in eight different subject areas.

6. Become familiar with the instructions for constructing the books from the "Instructions for Making Books" in the facilitator packet. Use the list of book topics that the school you have selected has requested when deciding which books to make during your service project.

7. Make a sample blank book so you know how it's put together and to show as an example. Be sure you know how to assemble the book with the type of report cover you're using.

8. Find out which of your participants enjoy writing and which enjoy drawing pictures. Depending on the type of books your group is making, create small groups with one or two people writing a book (at a computer) and one or two people drawing the pictures for the book. (Some families might stick together to create a book—or they might mix with other families, depending on their interest.)

9. Have groups create the books using the guidelines that fit the recipient school's needs.

10. Have a volunteer photograph the writing, illustrating, and assembly process of the books to include with your donation.

11. When a book is finished, assemble it into your report cover.

12. Have each book group write a letter (and have a book-group photo taken by the photographer). Make the letter a message of hope and friendship to the children in Uganda who will be reading this book.

13. Schedule a follow-up gathering at a later date. Books of Hope will send photographs, a written update about your sponsored school, and letters the children may have written.

Debriefing the Project

- How would you feel if your school didn't have any books?
- What do you think it is like to live in a country where war is going on?

- Why is it important to make books for children who don't have any?
- What else can we do to help children who don't have any books?

Helpful Resources

- For children: *Beatrice's Goat* by Page McBrier (Atheneum Books for Young Children, 2001). When a goat is donated to Beatrice's family in northern Uganda, Beatrice's parents could finally afford to send Beatrice and her siblings to school. This true story helps readers see the long-term effects of a single act of kindness.

- For teens: *Girl Soldier: A Story of Hope for Northern Uganda's Children* by Faith J. H. McDonnell and Grace Akallo (Chosen Books, 2007). This is the true account of 15-year-old Grace Akallo's abduction from her family in northern Uganda. Faith J. H. McDonnell provides historical background of this horrific war and the more than 30,000 children who, like Grace, have been forced to fight their captors' war.

Bonus Ideas

- The Books of Hope website has a video you can show during the event. Click on "For Prospective Participants."

- The story *Beatrice's Goat* is true, and it was developed as a story for *60 Minutes* on June 12, 2005. Consider viewing it at your event. (Many libraries have it for you to borrow, or you can purchase it from Amazon.com.)

- Create books using other types of illustration, such as painting, stencils, ink stamps, or crayon rubbings. See the "Suggestions for Illustrating Your Books" in the Books of Hope facilitator's guide.

- Consider expanding this service project to your local school classrooms. Since there are eight major subject areas (with a list of topics for each one), educators may find this is a worthwhile classroom service project as well.

(33) Secondhand-Book Sale

Purpose

Sell used books in order to raise funds and promote the love of reading with young children or English language learners.

Possible Recipients

- A local literacy or educational organization, library, classroom, or childcare center. You may decide to serve two organizations: a school to promote literacy and a childcare center to donate the leftover children's books from your book sale.

Time Requirement

Planning time before the project: about four hours. Gathering materials: one to two hours. Setup time on the day of your project: two hours. Project time: six hours. Take-down time after your project: two hours. Have families sign up for different time slots so no one is required to volunteer more than one to two hours.

People

This project is ideal for families with children between the ages of 3 and 18. Expect each family to volunteer for one hour during the 6-hour event.

If possible, recruit four volunteers from your organization to sort books, handle donations, and set up the book sale.

Materials

- Lots of used books
- Enough tables to display the books
- Enough copies of the "It's a Book Sale—And You Can Help!" handout (page 92) to solicit books and publicize your event
- 25 pieces of heavyweight paper (65-pound paper)
- 25 markers
- 10 pieces of poster paper

- Something to collect money (with lots of coins and one-dollar bills to make change)
- Optional: boxes for collecting and moving books

Ask families to donate the used books.

Connecting Point

One out of five graduating high school students cannot read his or her diploma, reports Readfaster .com. Too many Americans struggle with reading and haven't been given the opportunity to find books that get them excited about reading. Book sales help promote reading by getting books into the hands of individuals. When people find books they're excited about, they're more likely to read. In addition to getting more books into people's hands, this sale will raise money you can donate (along with the books you don't sell) to a local literary or educational organization, library, classroom, or childcare center.

Doing the Project

1. About two to three weeks before your book sale, begin asking families and individuals to donate gently used hardcover and paperback books for your secondhand-book sale. Use email, newsletters, the "It's a Book Sale—And You Can Help!" handout, and other methods of communication. Explain where the money raised will be donated.

2. Designate a clear drop-off spot for donated books and have a volunteer be in charge of these donations. This volunteer will periodically check the book drop-off and move books as it fills up. Ask this person to keep you posted about the number of book donations coming in.

3. Ask for at least one volunteer (or family) who knows books well to develop categories and a system for displaying books for the sale. Ideally, you'll want three broad categories: books for children, books for teens, and books for adults.

Then you'll want topical categories within those larger categories. Separate nonfiction books from fiction.

4. Ask for volunteers to create posters for the book sale and post them around your community. Be clear about times and when special events will happen. For example, if you have a book sale from 11 a.m. to 5 p.m. on a Saturday, you might say that all books will go on sale for $1 from 3 p.m. to 4 p.m., and that there will be a book-bag sale (where people can use a grocery-size bag and fill it with books for $5 per bag) from 4 p.m. to 5 p.m. (You'll want to have some specials close to the end of your sale to encourage people to move out as many books as possible.)

5. Have families sign up for various shifts during the book sale. Find families to sort the books before the book sale, price them, and set up the tables. Make labels to clearly mark which types of books are on which tables.

6. Enjoy the sale.

7. After the sale, have volunteers collect all the unsold books and donate them to a second-hand bookstore or an interested place (such as a childcare center). Donate the money raised to the organization you're serving.

8. Set up another 30-minute time for all your family volunteers to gather to debrief the project.

Debriefing the Project

- What was it like to go through your books at home and look for ones to donate?
- Why is reading important?
- Why is it important to have a used-book fundraising sale?

- What would happen to the books in your home if you didn't periodically go through them? Why?
- What else can we do to get people excited about reading?

Helpful Resources

- For children: *Tomás and the Library Lady* by Pat Mora (Dragonfly Books, 2000). Based on a true story, Tomás Rivera takes refuge from the heat in a nearby library and is surprised to find a new friend in the librarian who teaches him the many joys of reading.
- For teens: *The Book Thief* by Markus Zusak (Knopf, 2007). Nine-year-old Liesel Meminger likes to steal books. She steals from libraries, from cemeteries, and from Nazi book burnings. Liesel's love for books help her write her own story of survival in World War II Germany.

Bonus Ideas

- Have other events going on during your book sale: Ask someone to dress as a character from a children's book and read aloud that book, or consider having children's activities, such as creating bookmarks.
- Promote a love of reading by helping people find lists of high-quality books that will appeal to them. A helpful resource is the National Education Association's many book lists that are posted on www.nea.org. Search for "Read Across America" and go to "For Parents."
- Because people learn in so many different ways, you may want to expand this service project to include more than books. Consider adding music on CDs, movies and TV shows on VHS or DVD, educational computer games, or even children's video games.

(34) Book Walk

Purpose

Raise funds, promote the love of reading, and have fun at a book walk.

Possible Recipients

- A local library, classroom, childcare center, or other organization

Time Requirement

Planning time before the project: one to two hours. Gathering materials: one hour. Setup time on the day of your project: 30 minutes to an hour. Project time: one hour.

People

This project is ideal for families with children between the ages of 3 and 18. Expect each family to buy game tickets for a total of $3 to $5 in the one-hour event, so if you'd like to donate about $50, you'll need about 10 to 20 families.

In addition to the volunteers you find to help with setup, cleanup, and publicity, you will need several volunteers to help run the project on the day of your event. These volunteers will sell tickets to the book walks and play the music. You'll also need a volunteer to help collect and organize book donations in the weeks leading up to your event.

Materials

- Lots of used books
- Tables to display the books
- 50 sheets of 8½" x 11" paper
- markers
- 1 roll of masking tape if you have a noncarpeted floor
- Large, open space for the book walks
- Music CDs and a system to play them on
- Game tickets to sell
- A money-collection box (with lots of change)
- A small box or bowl
- 15 small pieces of paper

Ask families to donate used books. You may also ask families to lend a music system for your event.

Connecting Point

Ask participants what gets them excited about reading books. Is it the genre (such as science fiction or mystery)? Is it the characters (such as Arthur and D.W. in the Marc Brown books)? Is it the clever story (such as the Horrible Harry books by Suzy Kline)? Talk about how important it is to discover new books constantly and how a book walk can introduce you to new books.

Doing the Project

1. About two to three weeks before your book-walk event, begin asking families and individuals to donate gently used hardcover and paperback books for your book walk. Explain where the money raised will be donated.

2. Designate a clear drop-off spot for donated books and have a volunteer be in charge of these donations. This volunteer will periodically check the book drop-off and move books as it fills up. Ask this person to keep you posted about how many book donations are coming in.

3. Ask for at least one volunteer (or family) who knows books well to develop categories and a system for displaying the books. Ideally, you'll want three broad categories: books for children, books for teens, and books for adults. Then you'll want topical categories within those larger categories. Separate nonfiction books from fiction.

4. On the 8½" x 11" sheets of paper, draw or print out one large number on each sheet to make three sets of 15 numbers (each set numbered from one to 15). Consider making each set a different color of paper or ink. These will be the 15 steps for three separate book-walk areas.

5. Make another set of numbers from one to 15 on the small pieces of paper (they could all be written or printed out on one sheet of paper and cut up). Place them into the small box or bowl.

6. The day of your event, set up the area where you will have the family service project by placing the large numbers in a large circle (as you would for a cake walk) so that when you stand outside the circle the numbers face you. Create three areas with numbers. (With three sets of book walks going on simultaneously, you can have 45 people participating at once.)

7. Greet families as they arrive and show them where to buy tickets for the book walks. Consider selling tickets for 25 cents each so families can play many times.

8. To do a book walk, have people who have bought tickets stand on a large number in one of the circles. Play the music and have people walk around the circle. After about 30 seconds, stop the music. When the music stops, each person should stand on the closest number. Make sure that everyone is standing on one number and that no one is sharing a number.

9. Draw a number from the box or bowl and announce it. The person at each circle who is standing on that number gets to go to the book table and choose one book as a prize.

10. Repeat the book walk until the books are all gone.

11. Count the money raised and announce the total. Send the money to the recipient organization.

Debriefing the Project

- Have you ever done a book walk before? If so, where?
- What do you think of a book walk— compared with a cake or cupcake walk?
- Why is it exciting to win?
- How hard was it to choose a book when you won?
- Why is it important to find more books to read?
- How else can we help promote the love of reading?

Helpful Resources

- For children: *Richard Wright and the Library Card* by William Miller (Lee & Low Books, 1997), a story of how an African American got access to the magic of books and libraries during a time when libraries didn't admit African Americans.
- For teens: *Reading Magic: Why Reading Aloud to Our Children Will Change Their Lives Forever* by Mem Fox (Harcourt, 2001), a book that makes the case for reading aloud.

Bonus Ideas

- Consider having other literacy or book activities going on at the same time. For example, if you have a local author in your community, ask the author to sign books. Consider having a well-known adult wear a Cat-in-the-Hat costume or hat and let kids have their picture taken with that person.
- Have a time during your event when families with similar-age children get together and talk about the books that get them excited. This helps families discover new books to read.

35 Family Read-a-Thon

Purpose

Raise money to promote literacy while encouraging families to read.

Possible Recipients

- A local library, classroom, or childcare center, or other organization that's important to your group

Time Requirement

Planning time before the project: one to two hours. Gathering materials: one hour. Setup time for the kickoff gathering of your project: 30 minutes to an hour. Kickoff gathering time: up to one hour. Reading at home: two weeks. Setup time for the final gathering of your project: 30 minutes to an hour. Final gathering time: up to one hour.

People

This project is ideal for families with children between the ages of 3 and 18.

Materials

- Enough copies of the handouts "Reading for a Good Cause" (page 93) and "How Many Books Did Your Family Read?" (page 94) for all families involved (you may want additional copies of the handout "How Many Books Did Your Family Read?" for families who want extras)
- A picture book to read aloud (see Helpful Resources on page 87)

Connecting Point

Ask: How often does your family read? Why? Explain how it's easy not to spend much time reading because of so many other activities and possibilities. Yet reading is not only fun, it helps people succeed in school and in the workplace. A read-a-thon will raise money for a good cause and help promote reading within your family.

Doing the Project

1. Set two event dates (one for your kickoff event and one about two weeks later for the final gathering).
2. For your kickoff event, consider doing another reading-related family service project from this book, such as 32: Storybook Magic, 33: Secondhand-Book Sale, or 34: Book Walk. Follow all the steps for that project during your event.
3. At your kickoff event, distribute the two handouts so all families get one of each. Talk about how you want families to read books and raise money for the organization you're serving, and tell a bit about the organization. Together, fill in the blanks on the "Reading for a Good Cause" handout with the organization, cause, and number of books.
4. Encourage families to collect donations from family and friends during the one to two weeks before your second meeting. Use the "Reading for a Good Cause" handout.
5. If your organization has nonprofit status, consider having people make checks out to your organization—or the nonprofit organization you're donating the money to—so that all the donations can be tax deductible.
6. Send encouraging reminders during the two- to three-week family reading time to keep families reading and excited about reading.
7. Have families bring their completed handouts and donations to your final event.
8. While you read a picture book aloud (or do some other type of reading activity from the Bonus Ideas), have volunteers add up the total donations and also the total books read.
9. Announce the total amount of money raised and the total number of books read.

Debriefing the Project

- How many books did you think you would read before you started this service project?

- How did that compare with what you actually read?
- Did the time go slowly or quickly as you read books for this service project? Why?
- Why is it important to raise money for good causes?
- How else can we help promote reading?

Helpful Resources

- For children: *Little Witch Learns to Read* by Deborah Hautzig (Random House, 2003), a story about a child witch who learns how to read when her family doesn't want her to.
- For teens: *You Can't Read This! Why Books Get Banned* by Pamela Jain Dell (Compass Point Books, 2010). Learn about book censorship throughout history. Could your favorite book be banned?

Bonus Ideas

- Consider having one of your volunteers dress up like a character in a book, such as Alice in Wonderland, Curious George, Cinderella, or the tin man from the Wizard of Oz and read the book (or part of the book) at your event.

Find adult-size costumes at www.costumesupercenter.com.

- This is a popular service project that has many benefits besides raising money, and some organizations do this type of project once a year. They keep track of the number of books read and the collective amount raised and challenge families to raise those numbers again the following year.
- If you have a number of families that are transient and you worry about having attendance drop off between the kickoff event and the final celebratory event, consider having a one-time read-a-thon event at your organization for a designated amount of time (about two hours) and see how many books people can read within that time frame.
- Some families enjoy the competition of reading between family members. (Since not all families do, be sensitive to this idea, especially since some kids have learning differences or may have different abilities and interest in reading books.) Some families may want to have separate reading sheets for each family member so each can track his or her own reading.

(36) School-Supply Kits

Purpose

Provide school supplies for kids who do not have the resources to buy them.

Possible Recipients

- A local public school district or some other type of social agency that would collect these types of donations

Time Requirement

Planning time before the project: one to two hours. Gathering materials: one hour. Setup time on the day of your project: 30 minutes to an hour. Project time: one hour.

People

This project is ideal for families with children between the ages of 3 and 18. Expect about three families to collaborate on each school-supply kit during the one-hour event, so if you'd like to donate 10 school-supply kits, you'll need about 30 families.

Materials

- 1 copy of the "Help Create a School-Supply Kit" handout (page 95) for each family
- Kit items listed on the handout

- 1 gallon-size, zip-top plastic bag for each school-supply kit
- 1 pen for each family

If you want to ensure that you'll get a variety of materials to make complete kits (the list on the handout is what is needed in one kit), assign families to bring different items from the list. If families want to bring more, encourage them to do so. Note that the backpack is the most expensive item on the list, so one family could donate just the backpack, and other families can donate several of the less-expensive items on the list.

Connecting Point

Around the world, many children do not have school supplies. Many live in underdeveloped countries, such as Afghanistan, Mexico, Uganda, and Nicaragua. Others reside in poor areas of the United States. By giving them a school-supply kit, we're making it possible for them to get a better education than they otherwise would receive.

Doing the Project

1. A few weeks before your event, distribute the "Help Create a School-Supply Kit" handout to families. Checkmark different items on families' forms to ensure that you get a variety of supplies. For example, on one-third of the handouts, checkmark the first five items. On another third, checkmark the next five items. On another third, checkmark the backpack.

2. Before your event, make a school-supply kit to show as an example.

3. As families arrive to your event, have them sort their donations by type into separate piles. (For example, place all the scissors in one place and all the rulers in another.)

4. Give each family a backpack (or zip-top bag if there aren't enough backpacks). Have them walk through the stations and pick up one item at each station.

5. Once families finish, have them dump out their backpacks (or bags) and double-check the kit to make sure it's complete. Read aloud each item slowly and have families place that item back into the empty backpack (or bag).

6. At the end of the event, count the number of school-supply kits your group put together.

Debriefing the Project

- Why is each of these items in these school-supply kits important?
- How would you feel if you could go to school, but you couldn't afford school supplies?
- Why is it important to create school-supply kits for kids who need them?
- How else can we help students with their school-supply needs?

Helpful Resources

- For children: *Amazing Grace* by Mary Hoffman (Frances Lincoln Childrens Books, 2007), a story about Grace, who loves to act out stories. When she decides to try out for the role of Peter Pan in her school's production, some of her classmates tell her she can't be Peter because she is black and a girl. Grace's story shows kids how to be self-confident and courageous in the classroom.
- For teens: *The View from Saturday* by E. L. Konigsburg (Atheneum, 1996) about a group of students who develop a special bond with each other and their paraplegic teachers during an Academic Bowl.

Bonus Ideas

- Help fulfill classroom wish lists. Find specific wish lists organized by state at www.donorschoose.org.
- Instead of collecting backpacks, consider raising funds to purchase school backpacks. You can send donations to Give a Kid a Backpack at www.giveakidabackpack.org.
- Some sites create a regular collection spot for people wanting to donate school supplies or gently used backpacks. Many of these sites do this during early August, when stores often have school-supply sales.
- If the recipient organization is open to personalization, consider making cards to include with each kit.

37 Seek-and-Find Instruments

Purpose

Provide children with opportunities to participate in band or orchestra by collecting and donating used musical instruments.

Possible Recipients

- Any local school districts with band and orchestra music departments, or a community band or orchestra seeking donations

Time Requirement

Planning time before the project: one to two hours. Gathering materials: one hour. Set-up time on the day of your project: 30 minutes to an hour. Project time: 15 minutes.

People

This project is ideal for families with children between the ages of 5 and 18. Expect each family either to donate one instrument or bring a $5 donation for the 15-minute event.

Materials

- Enough copies of the "Donate a Used Musical Instrument (or Money to Buy One)" handout (page 96) to publicize your event with families
- A music teacher who can accept the donations and talk about why they're so important
- Musical instruments to donate

Ask families to donate used instruments for your event or consider making a financial donation.

Connecting Point

School budgets are regularly being cut. Because of these cutbacks, fewer and fewer children get the opportunity to learn to play a musical instrument. Yet many used instruments are sitting unplayed in the closets, attics, and basements of people in our community. When we donate musical instruments that are no longer being used, we give interested children the chance to learn to make music.

Doing the Project

1. About two to three weeks before your event, begin asking families and individuals to look for gently used musical instruments that they would be interested in donating. Explain who will receive the donated instruments. Ask families to bring the instruments to your event.

2. As families arrive at your event, have them sort the instruments they've donated by type—all the flutes together, all the violins together, and so on.

3. If possible, have a music teacher accept the donations and make the case for why it's important to donate instruments to a school.

Debriefing the Project

- If you donated a musical instrument, why did you decide to do this?
- How hard was it to let go of the instrument? Why?
- How would you feel if you were a child and really wanted to learn a musical instrument but couldn't afford to rent or buy one?
- What other ways could we help kids who want to play musical instruments and don't have access to them?

Helpful Resources

- For children: *Music, Music for Everyone* by Vera B. Williams (Greenwillow, 1988), a story about Rosa and her friends who play in a band to raise money to help pay the healthcare expenses of an ailing grandmother.
- For teens: *Song Shoots Out of My Mouth: A Celebration of Music* by Jaime Adoff (Dutton Children's Books, 2002), rhythmic poems that celebrate all types of music, from jazz to Mozart, and from hip-hop to air guitar. Musicians will also appreciate the theory-based wordplay.

Bonus Ideas

- Find another 15- to 30-minute project from this book and combine it with this one to make it a longer event.
- Consider having an ongoing collection spot for donated musical instruments. People's lives and interests continue to change, and schools are always in need of donated instruments. Some families who enjoy going to garage and estate sales may want to keep an eye out for used instruments.
- Check with your local school district to see if there are other items your group could collect and donate, such as art supplies, physical-education supplies, books for the library, and so on.
- Give families the opportunity to try out the instruments.

38 Dr. Seuss Day

Purpose

Collect books to donate to facilities that encourage child development and reading.

Possible Recipients

- A local childcare center, preschool, or elementary school

Time Requirement

Planning time before the project: one to two hours. Gathering materials: one hour. Setup time on the day of your project: 30 minutes to an hour. Project time: one hour.

People

This project is ideal for families with children between the ages of 3 and 18. Expect each family to donate one Dr. Seuss book or give $5 during the one-hour event.

Materials

- Lots of new or gently used Dr. Seuss books
- Optional: A hat like the one in the book *The Cat in the Hat* for a leader to wear

Ask families to donate gently used and new Dr. Seuss books for your event. A Cat-in-the-Hat hat is available from places such as Target and Toys R Us, or online at Amazon.com.

Connecting Point

Building a classroom library at a childcare center, preschool, or elementary school is often costly. Yet books are a critical part of childcare. By donating books, you're making it easier for teachers and students to incorporate reading into their daily routines.

Doing the Project

1. About two to three weeks before your event, begin asking families and individuals to donate new and gently used Dr. Seuss books for your project. Explain where the books will be donated.
2. Consider setting up a book drop-off spot in case families want to contribute but are unable to attend your event.
3. As families arrive to your event, separate the Dr. Seuss book donations that families brought into groupings by title, such as putting all the *The Cat in the Hat* books together and all the *Green Eggs and Ham* books together. Encourage others to give a monetary donation.
4. Read aloud some of the Dr. Seuss books.
5. Reorganize the books into groupings so that each grouping has only one of each title. That way you can give one group of books to one classroom and have other groups available for other classrooms.

6. Count up the number of book donations. How many schools or organizations will you be able to donate Dr. Seuss books to?

Debriefing the Project

- Why are Dr. Seuss books so popular?
- How do you feel when you hear a Dr. Seuss book read aloud? Why?
- Why is it important for classrooms to have books for kids to read?
- What else could we do to supply books to schools?

Helpful Resources

- For children: *The Cat in the Hat* by Dr. Seuss (Random House, 1957) or *One Fish, Two Fish, Red Fish, Blue Fish* by Dr. Seuss (Random House, 1960).
- For teens: *Oh, the Places You'll Go!* by Dr. Seuss (Random House, 1990) or *The Secret Art of Dr. Seuss* by Theodor Geisel and Maurice Sendak (Random House, 1995).

Bonus Ideas

- If you have several laptops or one computer with which you can project images onto a screen, introduce families to the activities, games, and information about Dr. Seuss and his books at www.seussville.com. Talk about—and play—the games in the "Playground" portion of the website, including "The Grinch Grow Your Heart Game" and "One Fish Two Fish Concentration Game."
- March 2 is the anniversary of Dr. Seuss's birth. Consider having your family service project around that date.
- Many Dr. Seuss books have been translated into other languages, including Spanish and Chinese. If you have a diverse group, consider having some of the books read in another language.
- Read Across America Day is also celebrated on March 2. (For more information, visit www.nea.org and search for "Read Across America.") Instead of having a Dr. Seuss family service project, have an around-the-world family service project for which families donate children's picture books about various cultures around the world.

It's a Book Sale—And You Can Help!

_____ is holding a used book sale on _____.
(our organization)   (date and time)

All the money we raise will go directly to support _____.
                                                                    (organization we're supporting)

You can help in three ways.

1. Donate used books. Look through your bookshelves, closets, attics, basements, and other places for books you can donate to our sale. Clear out the clutter! Donate one or two books . . . or 20. Every book helps. Please bring book donations to _____ by _____.
(drop-off spot)   (date)

We're looking for:

- Children's picture books
- Adults novels
- Teen fiction
- Children's chapter books
- Cookbooks
- Adult nonfiction
- Teen graphic novels
- Comic books
- Teen nonfiction
- Books on tape or CD
- Best sellers
- Classics
- Travel books
- Any type of book!

2. Sign up to help staff the sale. Can you take a one-hour shift? See _____ for times needed.
(event organizer)

3. Come to the sale and buy books. You're bound to find something you'll love. Remember, all sale money goes to a good cause.

Reading for a Good Cause

Our family is working with _____
(organization)

to raise money for _____.
(cause)

It's a good cause. Please consider giving a one-time donation or making a pledge according to the number of books we plan to read. Our family's goal is to read _____ books.

(Because we're all so busy, we'd prefer that you donate now so we don't have to bother you later to collect.)

Donor's Name	Donor's Address	Donor's Phone	Amount Donated
Total Amount Donated			$

Thank you! We appreciate your donation!

How Many Books Did Your Family Read?

Family Members: _____

_____

Our Goal (How Many Books We Thought We Would Read): _____

How Many Books We Actually Read: _____

Depending on your reading ability, you can count each book as one book read or each chapter within a chapter book as one book read.

	Family Member Reading	Book (or Chapter) Read	Date Finished
1			
2			
3			
4			
5			
6			
7			
8			
9			
10			
11			
12			
13			
14			
15			
16			

Use the back if you need more space.

Help Create a School-Supply Kit

You're invited to help children in poverty by creating school-supply kits. Come to our event:

Date: _____

Time: _____

Place: _____

Please bring the following NEW items that are checked:

_____ 1 pair of blunt scissors

_____ 1 12-inch ruler

_____ 12 new #2 pencils with erasers

_____ Small pencil sharpener

_____ 1 large eraser

_____ 1 box of colored pencils

_____ 12 new pens

_____ 2 folders with inside pockets

_____ 1 zippered pencil bag

_____ 1 gently used or new backpack

Donate a Used Musical Instrument (or Money to Buy One)

Many students in our community wish to play a musical instrument but cannot afford to rent or buy one. Do you have a musical instrument that's no longer being used? Check your closets. Check your attic. Check your basement.

Or if you prefer, donate money to help buy an instrument for a child.

We're collecting instruments for a family service project that will be held:

Date: _____

Time: _____

Place: _____

Thank you for helping students who want to make music!

Chapter 5
Projects to Raise Funds

The service projects in this chapter not only provide creative ways to raise funds for the good causes of your choice, but also bring families together in fun new ways. Many people get tired of more typical fundraisers, but these projects will breathe new life into family service—and into raising money.

If possible, match the recipient organization with the type of fundraiser you've chosen. For example, an organization focused on health issues, such as the American Lung Association, would be an ideal one to receive funds from the Family Moving-Along-a-Thon (39). Donations from your Guess-a-Thon (46) might go to a group that helps children, such as a family shelter or crisis nursery.

(39) Family Moving-Along-a-Thon

Purpose

Raise money by getting families physically active.

Possible Recipients

- Any worthy cause that promotes health, such as the American Heart Association (www.americanheart.org) or the American Diabetes Association (www.diabetes.org)

Time Requirement

Planning time before the project: one to three hours. Gathering materials: one to two hours. Setup time on the day of your project: one to two hours. Project time: 90 minutes.

People

This project is ideal for families with children between the ages of 3 and 12.

This event involves families participating in seven exercise stations; you will need to recruit volunteers to help set up and run these stations (you could have a parent-child team in charge of a station). Match the volunteers' interests and skills to the exercise station they will be staffing. You'll also need someone to collect and add up donations.

Materials

- Enough copies of the "Exercising for a Great Cause" handout (page 116) to publicize your event with families
- A large gymnasium or open area
- A music system and upbeat music
- 1 whistle
- 1 timer with minutes
- About 10 jump ropes
- 20 easy-to-inflate round balloons
- 2 beach balls
- About 10 towels, exercise mats, or yoga mats
- 7 pieces of 8½" x 11" white paper

- 3 black markers
- 1 roll of masking tape

Consider asking families to lend a music system for your event.

Connecting Point

Talk about the recipient organization you've chosen and how the organization uses its donations. Then talk about the importance of exercise and physical fitness. According to the Centers for Disease Control and Prevention, two out of five adults say they never engage in any exercise, sport, or physical activity, and children are increasingly sedentary as well. People who are sedentary are more likely to develop heart disease, colon cancer, and diabetes. The obesity rate is rising in the United States. With this fundraiser, you can raise money for a good cause (perhaps a health-related one) while having fun and getting exercise at the same time.

Doing the Project

1. Well before your event, choose an organization you wish to raise funds for. Learn more about this organization so you can make the case about why it's important to support it.

2. Decide how you will use the service project to raise funds. You can have families collect donations using the "Exercising for a Great Cause" handout or simply charge an entrance fee for the project.

3. Just before the service project, set up your event space for the exercise activities. Plan exercise activities that will be fun and appropriate for your community. The materials listed on this page fit these seven activities: (1) a jump-rope station; (2) a beach-ball roll, where family members sit on the ground with their legs in front of them in a V and roll the beach ball to each other; (3) walking or jogging around the perimeter of your area; (4) a yoga or stretching station; (5) a workout-routine station with toe touches, jumping jacks, sit-ups,

push-ups, and more; (6) a balloon-batting station, where players try to keep a balloon in the air by bumping it with their hands (and without anyone hitting the balloon more than once in a row) for as many bumps as they can before it hits the ground; (7) a dance station.

4. Make seven signs with the paper and markers to clearly mark the seven stations. On each piece of paper, write one number from one to seven in large print. Display these signs by hanging them up with masking tape.

5. When families arrive, collect their donations. Have a volunteer add up the donations while everyone is doing the activities.

6. Divide the families into seven groups and have each group go to a specific station. Each group will stay at a station for five minutes, when a whistle will signal to stop. Then the group goes to the station with the next number (such as moving from station three to station four). If you're at station seven, then you move to station one. Explain that each station has a volunteer who will lead the group in the exercise activity.

7. Set the timer for five minutes and begin. Play upbeat music to make it fun (people at the dance station will dance to this music). After five minutes, blow the whistle to signal people to stop and change stations. Do this six more times so that everyone goes through all seven stations.

8. After everyone has gone through all the stations, gather together as a group. Announce how much money was raised. Talk about the cause you're giving the money to (and why).

Debriefing the Project

- How do you feel about exercising? Why?
- What makes exercise a chore for you? What makes exercise enjoyable for you?
- Why do you think there are so many fundraisers that involve walking or running?
- How else can we raise money in ways that are interesting?

Helpful Resources

- For children: *Get Up and Go!* by Nancy Carlson (Puffin, 2008), a picture book about animals that exercise to relax and make friends while learning about their hearts and bodies.
- For teens: *Be Fit, Be Strong, Be You* by Rebecca Kajander and Timothy Culbert (Free Spirit Publishing, 2010), a book full of specific tips on eating, exercise, and building self-confidence to give kids and teens a positive, holistic approach to health and wellness.

Bonus Ideas

- Consider getting stickers or buttons that say, "I did it!" to distribute to each person who participated.
- Consider finding a physical education expert who could recommend fun, easy ways for families to play and exercise together, and create a service project with those activities. Or check out resources such as *The Ultimate Playground and Recess Game Book* by Guy Bailey (Educators Press, 2001) or *Great Big Book of Children's Games* by Debra Wise (McGraw-Hill, 2003).

40 Quarter Rally

Purpose

Raise money by empowering family members to choose the aspects of charitable causes they feel most strongly about.

Possible Recipients

- Any worthy cause in your area

Time Requirement

Planning time before the project: one to two hours. Gathering materials: one hour. Setup time on the day of your project: 30 minutes to an hour. Project time: one hour.

People

This project is ideal for families with children between the ages of 3 and 18.

Materials

- Lots of quarters
- 2 to 3 rolls of ¾" wide (or 1" wide) double-sided masking tape (or regular masking tape if you can't find double-sided)
- Handmade signs (made on 8½" x 11" paper) designating various aspects of a worthy cause that you're raising money for (see step 3)
- Optional: A music system and music that fits with the theme of your cause; for example, if you're raising money for a crisis nursery, you might play nursery music; if you're raising money for an animal shelter, you might play music with animal nature sounds

Ask families to bring their own quarters; you'll want to get some extra rolls, too, in case families forget. You can get rolls of quarters at any bank or credit union, but call ahead if you're requesting more than two rolls, because the bank may not have many in stock.

Connecting Point

Talk about the organization you're raising money for and why. Then talk about this unique way of giving. Families who regularly donate money are aware of which causes they want to support. With this service project, while your organization has chosen a cause that it's raising money for, family members get the chance to show which aspects of the cause they're most excited about by voting with their quarters. Helping kids learn about making charitable gifts is an important way to teach them about family service.

Doing the Project

1. Well before the family service event, choose a worthy cause to raise money for, such a crisis nursery. Learn more about this organization so you can make the case about why it's important to support it.

2. Publicize your event through your organization, encouraging families to bring as many quarters as they wish to donate to your cause.

3. Make signs designating different aspects of your cause that people might choose to direct their donations toward. Find pictures in magazines or catalogs or on the Internet, or create your own. For example, if your cause is a crisis nursery, you could have pictures of a crib, baby bottle, diapers, baby food, rocking chair, baby toys, baby clothes, a rattle, and so on. (If you choose an animal shelter, you could have pictures of different types of animals served.) Try to avoid, however, using photos or pictures of people—you don't want participants voting for people based on their looks.

4. The day of your event, hang the signs around the room at about eye level for someone who is 5 feet tall. Then place a line of double-sided tape below the signs with the line connecting all the pictures. If you are using single-sided tape, put the sticky side out and secure it to the wall using vertical strips of tape between

the signs and on the ends. (Otherwise the tape could sag and break once families start placing quarters on it.)

5. When families arrive, explain how the fundraiser works. Families walk around the room with their quarters, looking at the signs and voting for the aspect of the fundraiser they're most excited about, such as the crib or the rattle, by sticking a quarter onto the tape below the picture of that aspect. Encourage them to press hard so that quarters stick well. Tell them they can give as much as they want. They can also vote for everything not only once, but many times.

6. If you have music, play it.

7. Once all the families have finished voting (placing their quarters on the masking tape), have them look at the line of quarters surrounding you. (It's impressive.) Consider having volunteers count the coins (while leaving them displayed) to find out how much you raised.

8. Make your donation after the event. Depending on the recipient organization, use the quarters to buy the items to donate, or donate the money and let the organization know how families voted for the money to be used.

Debriefing the Project

- What was different about this fundraiser? Why?
- Most of the time when we give money, we hand over a check or cash and then we're done. How did it feel to give it in quarters? Why?

- Why does it matter that we are excited about the causes we raise money for?
- How else could we help this organization?
- How else could we raise money in creative ways?

Helpful Resources

- For children: *The Giving Tree* by Shel Silverstein (HarperCollins, 1987), a classic story about a tree that will keep giving to make a boy happy.
- For teens: *The Power of Serving Others* by Gary Morsch (Berrett-Koehler, 2006), a book that makes the case for serving others and starting where you are.

Bonus Ideas

- Consider using any kind of coin instead of quarters (although you'll likely raise less money).
- Some groups have put the line of tape along the floor, which makes it less likely quarters will fall off. (However, it makes it harder to visualize the end result, and some adults find it hard to bend down to place money on the floor.)
- If you have a lot of people, make two rows of tape.
- Consider taking photos of this fundraiser. The recipient organization may like a few photos for their newsletter or other public-relation pieces to encourage others to hold a similar type of fundraiser—and also to celebrate your donation.

(41) Supporters Wall

Purpose

Raise money for a worthy cause by selling paper cutout stars and displaying them on a wall.

Possible Recipients

- Any worthy cause in your area

Time Requirement

Planning time before the project: one to two hours. Gathering materials: one hour. Setup time on the day of your project: 30 minutes to an hour. Project time: 15 minutes.

People

This project is ideal for families with children between the ages of 3 and 18.

Materials

- Lots of paper cutout stars
- A large empty wall to display all the cutout stars
- 10 to 15 fine-point permanent black markers
- 2 to 3 rolls of masking tape
- Something to hold the money collected, such as an envelope or a change box
- A lot of one-dollar bills (about 40)

You can find cutout stars at teacher-supply and education stores or online, or have a group of families gather beforehand to cut out stars.

Connecting Point

When we give money to a good cause, we make a difference. In this fundraiser, participants will create a "wall of support" that highlights the contributions every person makes. By the end, there will be a wall of star supporters. Talk about the organization you're raising money for and why.

Doing the Project

1. Well before your event, choose an organization you wish to raise funds for. Learn more about this organization so you can make the case about why it's important to support it.

2. Make a sample star with your name on it so you can show it as a sample.

3. When families arrive on the day of your event, sell individual cutout stars for an amount that fits your community's economy, such as 50¢ or $1 each. Have a volunteer collect the money. When people buy stars, have them write their first names on them (and decorate them if they wish), then use masking tape (by making a loop and placing it on the back of the star) to secure it to the wall of support. The goal is to fill the wall with stars. Encourage people to buy as many stars as they wish. They also can buy a star in honor or memory of someone and write that person's name on the star.

4. When your wall is filled, keep it displayed for a period of time (such as a week) so others can see it. It's a great visual to show how each person makes a difference—and also how together, our contributions really add up.

Debriefing the Project

- How did it feel to see your name on a star on the wall? Why?
- What did you think as you saw the wall fill up with stars?
- What other shapes could we have used instead of stars? Why?
- What else can we do to raise money for worthy causes?

Helpful Resources

- For children: *Twinkle* illustrated by Scott M. Fischer (Simon & Schuster Children's Publishing, 2007), a creative, colorful book based on the nursery rhyme *Twinkle, Twinkle, Little Star.*
- For teens: *Making the Most of Today: Daily Readings on Self-Awareness, Creativity, and Self-Esteem* by Pamela Espeland and Rosemary

Wallner (Free Spirit Publishing, 1998), daily readings of inspiring quotations, essays, and affirmations encouraging readers to think deeply and make good choices.

Bonus Ideas

- Consider having cutout stars of different sizes. Then sell the small stars for $1, the medium stars for $5, and the large stars for $10.
- Consider using a variety of shapes, such as red hearts (to show that each person cares). Then sell the different shapes for different amounts,

such as 50¢ for hearts, $1 for stars, and $2 for balloon shapes.

- Consider having three charities for people to choose from. Have three different envelopes (or money boxes) to keep the donated money separate. Then make three different areas on the wall (or use three different walls) for people to place stars on. Label each area (or wall) with the name of your recipient organization. Some families get competitive and buy multiple stars for one charity—and some families buy stars to support all three!

(42) Super Silent Auction

Purpose

Raise money for a worthy cause by having a silent auction with artistic, unusual, and family-oriented items.

Possible Recipients

- Any worthy cause in your area

Time Requirement

Planning time before the project: three to five hours. Gathering materials: six to 10 hours. Planning and gathering materials can be longer if you're planning a large event. Setup time on the day of your project: one to two hours. Project time: 90 minutes.

People

This project is ideal for families with children between the ages of 5 and 18.

A silent auction can involve a lot of work soliciting donations and setting up displays on the day of your event, so it is important that you recruit several volunteers to help.

Materials

- A variety of items donated to the silent auction, such as artwork that students and professionals have done, services (such as cooking a meal, planting flowers, babysitting), gift certificates, books or other purchased gifts, and other valuables that people donate
- Tables to display the items
- 1 copy of the "What's Your Bid?" handout (page 117) for each item you'll have up for bid
- 1 to 2 pens for each item at the auction

Ask families and other individuals to donate items to the silent auction. Suggest they consider items or services that appeal to families, such as a spaghetti dinner cooked by another family, tickets to a sporting event or amusement park, or tickets to the zoo. Ask families to solicit donations from organizations, such as gift certificates to restaurants. See if any individuals wish to donate money so you can purchase tickets and items that would appeal to families.

Connecting Point

A super silent auction can raise a lot of money while also highlighting the talents, interests, and expertise of family members. Talk about the organization you're raising money for and why.

Doing the Project

1. Well before your event, choose an organization you wish to raise funds for and publicize it with your group. Learn more about this organization so you can make the case about why it's important to support it.

2. About a month before your event, begin asking families to submit donations. Encourage family members (and members of your organization) to donate an art project, a service, or something else to raise funds for your worthy cause. Suggest they donate something that they enjoy doing or are passionate about. Maybe a musician will perform for someone, a family will bake a cake, or an artist will give a piece of art. Consider supplementing these items by asking businesses for donations, as well.

3. Set a deadline a few days before your auction for all donations to be in hand.

4. Advertise widely for your super silent auction so you get lots of potential bidders to attend. Be sure to describe the organization the event is supporting.

5. On the day of your super silent auction, creatively display each donation. Have a copy of the "What's Your Bid?" handout and a pen next to each donation. Make sure you fill out the pertinent information at the top of the handout. Have extra pens available in case the ink runs out.

6. During the auction, bidders write their bids on the bid sheet for each item, with each subsequent bid going higher by a set amount (indicated on each bid sheet). If someone is really interested in a particular item, they may need to keep bidding as other bids come in. The winner of each item will be the last person on the sheet (with the highest bid).

7. About 30 minutes before the end of your event, announce that the bidding will close in 10 minutes. After the 10 minutes are up, collect the sheets. Announce the winners of each item, collect the money bid from each winner, and distribute the items.

8. Total up the amount of money raised and announce it.

Debriefing the Project

- If you donated something, how hard or easy was it to think of something to donate? Why?

- What did you think of all the items and services that were in the super silent auction? Why?

- How would this auction be different if it was a traditional auction with an auctioneer and live bidding? Why?

- How could we have an even better auction next time?

- What else can we do to raise money for a good cause?

Helpful Resources

- For children: *Auction!* by Tres Seymour (Candlewick Press, 2005), about people coming to an auction and bidding on everything from a stuffed groundhog to a potbellied stove.

- For teens: *Fundraising for Dummies* by John Mutz and Katherine Murray (For Dummies, 2010), a helpful book full of strategies on how to raise money for good causes.

Bonus Ideas

- Consider teaming up with a school art teacher or music teacher and seeing if they would be interested in working with students to create donations for your super silent auction.

- If you have a lot of creative donations, consider taking photographs and writing a press release featuring some of the donors (particularly if they are kids or families with kids), and then sending them to a local newspaper before the event. Sometimes you can generate a lot of publicity for this type of fundraiser (and get more potential bidders to attend).

- If you have a lot of young kids, consider making it a literal "super silent" auction where the loudest noise allowed is a whisper.

- Make it a real party by having music and refreshments. Have a slightly longer event, so people have a chance to socialize—and bid—more.

(43) Creative Cookbooks

Purpose

Raise funds for a worthy cause by creating and selling a cookbook with recipes from a wide variety of families.

Possible Recipients

- Any worthy cause in your area

Time Requirement

Planning time before the project: one to two hours. Gathering materials: one hour. Setup time on the day of your project: 30 minutes to an hour. Project time: one hour. Cookbook assembly after the event: two to four hours.

People

This project is ideal for families with children between the ages of 3 and 18. Expect each family to bring two to three recipes for the one-hour event to help create the cookbook.

You will need volunteers, either from your organization or from families, to assemble the cookbooks after the event. You will need at least one person who has access to a computer, scanner, and printer—and knows how to use them.

Materials

- 2 or 3 favorite family recipes from each family
- 1 fine-point black marker for each person (plus extras)
- 4 pieces of 8½" x 11" white paper for each person
- 1 pencil for each child or teenager
- After the event: A computer, scanner, printer, and spiral-binding machine

If your organization doesn't have the equipment needed for cookbook assembly, ask families if they do, and if they would be willing to lend it (or volunteer to do the assembly). You may need to go to a copy store to use a spiral-binding machine.

Connecting Point

Families are often looking for new recipes and easy, creative ways to make healthy meals. During the event, families can share favorite recipes and get new recipes to try, all while raising money for the good cause you've chosen. Discuss the cause and why you're supporting it.

Doing the Project

1. Well before the event, choose an organization you wish to raise funds for. Learn more about this organization so you can make the case about why it's important to support it.

2. Encourage families to bring two or three of their favorite family recipes to your event. Encourage them to find a variety of recipes, such as one main course, one side dish, and one bread to ensure you get a good mix for your book. These recipes need to be copyright free and cannot come from published, copyrighted cookbooks.

3. Consider creating a cookbook that's laid out landscape style: 11 inches wide by 8½ inches high. Make a template of a finished recipe page (either hand-sketched or laid out on a computer) so you can show families as a model.

4. When families arrive to your event, distribute the paper and markers. Have someone in each family clearly print their family's recipe on a piece of paper. Have children and teenagers draw a picture to illustrate each recipe on a separate piece of paper. If you're planning on publishing a cookbook that's landscape, make sure everyone writes and draws on the paper in this fashion.

5. When families finish, have them write their name on the recipe (so everyone will know who submitted it). Have the kids turn the illustrations over and write (in pencil) the name of the recipe that the picture is illustrating. Then have families turn in the recipes and illustrations.

6. Explain that once the cookbooks are assembled after the event, they'll be available for sale.

7. Host a subsequent event for families and volunteers who have agreed to help assemble the books. Using the template you created as a model and a word-processing or design program, have them put each recipe on a single page with its illustration. Have some volunteers type up the recipes, others scan illustrations, and others put each recipe together into the template. Another volunteer or group of volunteers can work on an attractive cover.

8. To assemble the cookbook, place all the recipes of each category together (such as appetizers, main courses, side dishes, breads, desserts, beverages, etc.). Consider using a published cookbook for a guide. Print the pages and bind them together using a spiral-binding machine, which you can find at a copy store or perhaps at your organization.

9. Once the cookbooks are finished, publicize their availability. Consider having families come together again to purchase them.

10. Encourage families not only to buy one for themselves but also to buy extra copies to give to extended family members, friends, and neighbors. Set the price for the cookbook at a reasonable cost (such as $5 or $10, depending on the economy of your area and the finished result of your cookbook). Sell the cookbooks and see how much money you can raise for your cause.

Debriefing the Project

- How hard was it to find favorite family recipes? Why?
- What do you like best about cooking? Least? Why?
- Why do you think we drew illustrations in addition to writing up the recipes?
- Where else could we try to sell our cookbook?
- What else can we do to raise money for this good cause?

Helpful Resources

- For children: *Cook-a-Doodle-Do* by Janet Stevens and Susan Stevens Crummel (Harcourt Children's Books, 1999), a creative spin on *The Little Red Hen,* in which Rooster, tired of chicken feed, tries to bake a cake with the questionable help of his friends, Turtle, Iguana, and Pig.
- For teens: *How to Cook Everything: 2,000 Simple Recipes for Great Food (Completely Revised Tenth Anniversary Edition)* by Mark Bittman (Wiley, 2008), a helpful book that teaches individuals how to cook.

Bonus Ideas

- If your group loves desserts, consider creating a cookbook containing only desserts.
- There might be someone in your organization who is a graphic designer or publications specialist. Tap the expertise of this individual to create a first-class cookbook.
- To celebrate your cookbook, have families bring in food for a potluck using the recipes they included in the cookbook.
- If you have access to a kitchen, consider making a simple recipe during your service project so everyone can experience cooking—and have a snack.

Banana Bread Recipe

3 bananas
2 cups flour
1/2 cup brown sugar
1/2 cup applesauce
1/4 cup olive oil
2 eggs
1/2 tsp baking soda
1 pinch salt
1/2 cup walnuts

Mix all ingredients.
Bake at 375 degrees for 30–40 minutes.
It's done when the knife comes out clean!

44 Rubber-Duck Race

Purpose

Raise funds for a worthy cause and make a splash with a rubber-duck race.

Possible Recipients

- Any worthy cause in your area

Time Requirement

Planning time before the project: one to two hours. Gathering materials: one hour. Setup time on the day of your project: 30 minutes to an hour. Project time: one hour.

People

This project is ideal for families with children between the ages of 3 and 18.

You will need volunteers to help write numbers on the rubber ducks, collect donations, and conduct the race.

Materials

- An outdoor stream or shallow river that has moving water
- 1 rubber duck for each person you expect to attend
- 5 fine-point permanent black markers
- Game tickets that are numbered from 1 and up
- 1 whistle
- Large boxes or containers to hold the ducks
- Something to hold the donated money, such as an envelope or money box
- Prizes for the individuals with winning ducks

Game tickets and rubber ducks are available through Oriental Trading at www.orientaltrading.com.

Connecting Point

Ask participants what gets them excited about sport competitions. Usually, people love to see the action that occurs and what eventually leads to a winner. With the rubber-duck race, you're cheering on rubber ducks, which makes it a fun-filled fundraiser. Talk about the organization you're supporting and why.

Doing the Project

1. Before you do the project, find a place to do the race, such as a small stream or a shallow river. One option is to inquire at a nearby water park about using a moving water feature (such as a "lazy river").

2. Choose an organization you wish to raise funds for. Learn more about this organization so you can make the case about why it's important to support it.

3. Before your event, have volunteers mark numbers on the bottoms of the rubber ducks with the permanent markers (starting with 1 and matching the numbers on your game tickets).

4. When families arrive for the event, sell each duck for 50¢, $1, $2, or whatever price is suitable for your community. (Encourage people to buy more than one.) Give the buyer a game ticket that has the matching number to the duck, and set the duck aside. The buyer will need to hold on to the game ticket to prove that he or she is the winner. (Note: If you want to keep the ducks for other fundraisers, be clear that no one will actually get a duck to keep.)

5. When families have finished buying ducks, put all the purchased ducks into boxes or containers. Have everyone gather at the water source where you will have the race. Have a clear starting and ending point for your race.

6. Ask for volunteers to dump the containers of ducks. Make sure you have a volunteer for each container so that when the whistle blows, all the ducks will be dropped at the same time.

7. Have a couple volunteers positioned at the ending point of the race to grab ducks as they cross the finish line to declare the top five winners.

8. Let families position themselves along the water racetrack. (Anyone who touches a floating duck will be disqualified.)

9. When the volunteers at the starting line are ready, blow the whistle and dump all the ducks into the water at the same time.

10. Watch the ducks float down your watercourse and award a prize to the winner (or prizes for first, second, and third place).

11. Have a volunteer count up the donations and announce the total to the families before they leave.

Debriefing the Project

- What did you think of this fundraiser? Why?
- Why is it fun to cheer on rubber ducks?
- Why is it exciting to win?
- Why is it important for fundraisers to be fun?
- Why is the cause we're raising funds for important?
- How else can we raise funds for the worthy cause that we chose?

Helpful Resources

- For children: *10 Little Rubber Ducks* by Eric Carle (HarperCollins, 2005), a story of 10 adventuresome rubber ducks who are tossed overboard when a storm strikes a cargo ship.
- For teens: *Fundraising for Dummies* by John Mutz and Katherine Murray (For Dummies, 2010), a resource book with lots of tips and strategies for raising money.

Bonus Ideas

- This type of fundraiser often can get press coverage (since it's so visual and fun). Consider typing up a press release before your event and sending it to local media.
- To add more levity to the event, consider renting a duck costume for someone to wear. Costume stores, theater stores, and local theater costume closets often rent this type of costume.
- If you received permission to hold the event at a water park, ask the owners if families can stay afterward to swim. This would be a great way to celebrate the event.

(45) Giving Boxes

Purpose

Make "giving boxes" so families can collect money at home to donate to a worthy charity.

Possible Recipients

- Any worthy cause in your area

Time Requirement

Planning time before the project: one to three hours. Gathering materials: one to two hours. Setup time on the day of your project: one to two hours. Project time: 90 minutes.

People

This project is ideal for families with children between the ages of 3 and 18.

Materials

- Coffee cans with lids, shoe boxes with lids, or other containers with lids
- 2 sheets of colored 8½" x 11" colored paper (such as colored photocopy paper or construction paper) for each family
- 1 pair of scissors for each family
- Adhesives (such as glue, glue guns, double-sided tape, or tape)
- 5 washable markers in various colors for each family

Ask families to bring their own containers with lids, plus an extra or two, if they can, for people who may forget.

Connecting Point

Giving isn't a one-time, check-it-off-your-list activity. Giving is something we can incorporate into our day-to-day living. When we make a giving box and place it in a prominent place in our homes, we can add money to the box each time a positive event occurs (or through part of a weekly allowance) as a way of sharing our good fortune. A giving box is a great way to show our kids how we can keep giving every day. Talk about the organization you're raising money for and why.

Doing the Project

1. Well before your event, choose an organization you wish to contribute to through this family service project. Learn about this organization so you can make the case for why it's important to support it.

2. In your publicity for this event, ask families to bring a coffee can with the lid, a shoe box with the lid, a plastic soup container from a deli with the lid, or some other container with a lid to your event. Encourage them to bring extras in case other families forget.

3. Create two or three giving boxes as samples. Try to make each one unique to encourage families to be creative.

4. As families arrive to your event, set them up at tables where they'll do their project. Have the art materials—such as colored paper, scissors, glue, and washable markers—at the tables.

5. To start, have families each create a slot (using scissors) in the top of their giving container so it looks like a bank.

6. Decorate the container with the art supplies. Encourage families to be creative and to make something they would want to display permanently in their homes.

7. When families finish, or as they're working, talk about how families use these giving boxes. Some families have them sitting on their dining room tables to remind them to give daily. Others have a special place in the living room where the giving box sits. Each time something positive happens in the family (such as a child getting a high grade on a test or a parent

finishing the tax forms before April 15), the family gathers and places money in the box. Some families require a percentage of each child's allowance (and each parent's paycheck) to go into the giving box on a weekly or bi-weekly basis. Some organizations have each family member give up something each week (such as lattes for adults and sodas for kids) and put the money they don't use for those items into their giving box.

8. Give families time to talk about where they want to keep their giving boxes and how they want to use them.

9. Then discuss when to contribute the accumulated funds to your cause. Some families donate their money only when the giving box is full. Others empty the box when good causes come along, even if the box is only half full. Consider setting a date (about two to four weeks later) for families to bring in their giving boxes to donate funds to your worthy cause.

10. Develop a plan for promoting your cause (or other worthy causes) throughout the year for families to contribute from their giving boxes. Some organizations designate a different worthy cause each month, encouraging families to bring in their money from their giving boxes. Some create a large, secured giving box where families can deposit their money whenever they wish to donate.

11. Keep in touch about the giving boxes and encourage families to continue using them.

Debriefing the Project

- Have you ever seen a giving box before? If so, where? What did you think of it?
- Why is it important to take time to decorate the giving box well?
- Why is it important to place the giving box in a prominent place in your home?
- Which charitable causes would you like your family to support? Why?
- How else can we promote giving?

Helpful Resources

- For children: *The Giving Book: Open the Door to a Lifetime of Giving* by Ellen Sabin (Watering Can, 2004), an interactive book that inspires kids to give and keep giving.

- For teens: *Classified: How to Stop Hiding Your Privilege and Use It for Social Change* by Karen Pittleman and Resource Generation (Soft Skull Press, 2006), a book cowritten by the Resource Generation—a group of wealthy young people working for social justice—that uses role-playing games, comics, and quizzes to help readers understand the importance of being honest about their own wealth and giving back.

Bonus Ideas

- Allow families to decide for themselves where to donate the money they accumulate in their boxes. This encourages family members to have conversations among themselves about the charities that are important to them.

- A great, out-of-print resource that you may be able to find at your local library or at a used bookstore is *The Giving Box: Create a Tradition of Giving with Your Children* by Fred Rogers (Running Press, 2000), a kit that has folktales, fables, and an already-made giving box.

- Have older children and teenagers learn how to search for information about specific charities on the Internet. Helpful, informative websites include Charity Navigator (www .charitynavigator.org), the Better Business Bureau Wise Giving Alliance (www.give.org), Guide Star (www.guidestar.org), and Global Giving (www.globalgiving.com).

- A number of religious traditions also promote the use of giving boxes. For example, many of those in the Jewish faith have *tzedakah* boxes, which is a form of a giving box. Introduce this information or have families learn more about these traditions if that fits your organization's mission.

46 Guess-a-Thon

Purpose

To get people talking and guessing while raising money for a good cause.

Possible Recipients

- Any worthy cause in your area

Time Requirement

Planning time before the project: one to two hours. Gathering materials: one hour. Setup time on the day of your project: 30 minutes to an hour. Project time: 30 minutes.

People

This project is ideal for families with children between the ages of 3 and 18.

You will need one volunteer to collect the completed handouts and calculate the total length of the stuffed animals, one or more volunteers to sell bear shapes, and another volunteer (or family) to lend a collection of stuffed animals for display during the event.

Materials

- Enough copies of the "Guess for a Good Cause" handout (page 118) to publicize your event with families

- At least 1 teddy-bear cutout for each person who attends

- 2 to 3 rolls of masking tape

- 5 markers that will work on the teddy-bear cutouts (experiment first)

- Paper, pen, and calculator
- A large, empty wall to display the teddy-bear cutouts
- Something to hold the donations, such as an envelope or money box
- A bunch of stuffed animals for display
- Optional: A small gift or prize for the winner who guesses the closest total length of stuffed animals, such as a gift certificate to a local ice-cream shop or fast-food restaurant

Teddy-bear cutouts can be found at teacher-supply or educational stores such as Lakeshore Learning Materials. Ask one family (or volunteer) who has a lot of stuffed animals to bring in their collection (this is for display only).

Connecting Point

Talk about the organization you're raising money for and why. Then talk about how most of us take for granted how much we have. If we look only at the stuffed animals we own, we may be surprised how many there are. Some people aren't as fortunate. With this project, we can gain an appreciation for how much we have and help others at the same time.

Doing the Project

1. Well before your event, choose an organization you wish to raise funds for. Learn about this organization so you can make the case about why it's important to support it.

2. Assemble a stuffed-animal display in a prominent place for your event.

3. As you publicize your event with families, distribute the "Guess for a Good Cause" handout and ask families to bring it to the event completed. Explain that family members are going to guess how many total feet in length all the stuffed animals are when they're lined up side by side.

4. On the day of the event, have families turn in their "Guess for a Good Cause" handouts with the total number of stuffed animals each family member owns. If they forgot to complete the sheet, have each family member estimate the number of stuffed animals he or she owns.

5. After families have turned in their handouts, have them buy one or more teddy-bear cutouts. (Have a set price that's appropriate for your community, or ask for any donation.)

6. On each teddy bear they buy, have families write their guesses for total number of feet all the stuffed animals would be if laid out side by side. (This figure will come from adding up the total number of all stuffed animals on all forms and multiplying that total by five, which is assuming each animal is about 5 inches wide, and then dividing that total by 12 to get a total in feet.) Encourage family members to buy a teddy-bear cutout for each family member. Write the guesser's first and last name along with the guess on the teddy bear. Then use masking tape to attach the guesses to the blank wall. Try to group the guesses roughly by number (so it will be easy to find the winner).

7. Meanwhile, have one volunteer separate from the group and calculate the total length in feet that all the families' stuffed animals would be if they were lined up side by side.

8. At the end, announce the total feet of everyone's stuffed animals. Then ask someone to figure out how many miles (or part of a mile) that would be. One mile equals 5,280 feet.

9. Find the teddy-bear cutout that has the number closest to the final number. Recognize the person who had the best guess. Consider giving a small gift or prize to the winner, such as a gift certificate.

10. Announce the amount of money raised for your cause and donate it.

Debriefing the Project

- When you counted your stuffed animals at home, what did you find? Were you surprised by how many you have?
- Why is it important to pay attention to what we have?
- Once you discovered how many stuffed animals you have, were you motivated to donate more or less to our cause today? Why?
- How else can we help those in need?

Helpful Resources

- For children: *The Berenstain Bears Think of Those in Need* by Stan and Jan Berenstain (Random House Books for Young Readers, 1999), a delightful story about a family who starts donating to charity when they realize they have way too much stuff!

- For teens: *The Compassionate Instinct: The Science of Human Goodness* edited by Dacher Keltner, et. al. (W. W. Norton & Co., 2010), a thought-provoking book on the new science of human goodness.

Bonus Ideas

- If your group is small, consider asking families to bring in their stuffed animals. Seeing the actual long line of stuffed animals is a great visual of how much we all have collectively.

- The Council on Foundations is a helpful organization for raising money. It has a resource available called the *Giving Family: Raising Our Children to Help Others* by Susan Crites Price (Council on Foundations, 2001) that has good ideas for families becoming more giving.

47 Clip and Collect

Purpose

Raise money for a worthy cause by collecting labels and box tops from certain household items that otherwise would get tossed.

Possible Recipients

- Any local school in your area

Time Requirement

Planning time before the project: one to two hours. Gathering materials: one hour. Setup time on the day of your project: 30 minutes to an hour. Project time: 15 minutes.

People

This project is ideal for families with children between the ages of 3 and 18.

Materials

- A container to hold the label and box-top donations

Connecting Point

Many schools struggle with finances, meaning programs may be cut and fewer teachers hired, resulting in an overall less rich education for kids. Collecting labels and designated box tops can help raise essential funds for schools. By becoming aware of what can be collected, we can raise a lot of money together. Talk about the organization you're raising money for and why.

Doing the Project

1. Before the project, choose which label and box-top programs you will participate in. See the "Collecting Made Easy" box on page 113 for ideas. Some organizations do several programs simultaneously.

2. Decide whether you will have an ongoing collection without an event, an ongoing collection with an event, or just an event where everyone brings in what they collected.

3. Publicize your event with families, letting them know which specific items you plan to collect (such as Campbell's Labels for Education, Tyson Project A+, or Kemps Nickels for Schools). You might use email, make flyers to send home or post on a bulletin board, or mention the collection program in any regular communication.

Collecting Made Easy

Many companies and organizations offer ways to raise money for education. Consider exploring these possibilities:

- Campbell's Labels for Education (www.labelsforeducation.com)
- Kemps Nickels for Schools (www.kemps.com); click on "Promotion" and then "Nickels for Schools"
- General Mills Box Tops for Education (www.boxtops4education.com)
- Land O Lakes Save Five for Schools (www.savefiveforschools.com)
- Target Take Charge of Education Program (www.target.com); scroll down to "Company Information" and click on "Take Charge of Education"
- Tyson Project A+ (www.tyson.com/projectaplus)

4. If you plan to do this as an ongoing project, set up a permanent drop-off place for donations. To keep families motivated to continue to collect labels and box tops, provide monthly updates so families are aware of progress being made.

5. If you have a single event, give families one to two months to collect before your event. (Consider combining this event with another, such as project 46: Guess-a-Thon, to make it a longer and more substantive event.) Have families separate the labels into piles when they arrive, so all the Campbells' Labels for Education are together, the Tyson labels are together, the Kemps caps are together, and so on. Ask families to count the number of items in each pile and donate them to the school you have chosen.

Debriefing the Project

- What was it like to start collecting labels and box tops? Why?
- Where did your family keep these labels until you turned them in?
- Why is it important to collect labels and box tops for schools?
- What other ways could we help support our schools?

Helpful Resources

- For children: *How Much, How Many, How Far, How Heavy, How Long, How Tall Is 1000?* by Helen Nolan (Kids Can Press, 2001), a book with lots of fun facts about numbers.
- For teens: *Honey, Baby, Sweetheart* by Deb Caletti (Simon Pulse, 2008), a fictional story about a high school junior trying to make sense of her life, school, relationships, and the book club she's in, called the Casserole Queens.

Bonus Ideas

- Visit the websites featured in the "Collecting Made Easy" box on this page to find more activities and ideas you can do during your family service project.
- Network with other schools in your area to find out about other potential label and box-top collecting programs that you may not know about.

(48) Community Babysitting

Purpose

Raise funds for a worthy cause by providing an important service for families with young children: babysitting.

Possible Recipients

- Any worthy cause in your area, such as a child-care center or a preschool

Time Requirement

Planning time before the project: one to three hours. Gathering materials: one to two hours. Setup time on the day of your project: one to two hours. Project time: three hours, or adjust as appropriate for your group.

People

This project is ideal for families with children between the ages of 12 and 18.

You will need volunteers to do the babysitting, which you can recruit from your organization or from families. You will also need volunteers with expertise in childcare or education who know about laws and guidelines that you will be required to meet for your babysitting activity, and at least one volunteer who has been trained in CPR and first aid.

Materials

- A childcare center or school that can provide space for your babysitting activity
- Flyers to advertise the event
- Items to entertain children (games, toys, movies, books, crafts, and so on)

Connecting Point

Many families with young children do not have a regular babysitter or for other reasons don't often get out without their kids. Your group can provide a valuable service to these families—a babysitting night or afternoon—while also raising funds for the organization you've chosen to support. Talk about the organization you're raising money for and why.

Doing the Project

1. Well before your event, choose an organization you wish to raise funds for. Learn more about this organization so you can make the case for why it's important to support it. For example, many high schools will do this type of a fundraiser to help raise money to send students on an international or out-of-state school trip.

2. Before you do this project, make sure you have secured a space to have the babysitting night or afternoon (usually for about three hours). Check with local childcare centers and schools for possibilities. Then connect with experts in this area who will know what laws and guidelines you need to meet to ensure the safety of the children you're caring for (and also for those volunteering to staff this event). These experts will also know about staff-to-child ratios and how many kids can be cared for at one time. Or visit the National Child Care Information and Technical Assistance Center at nccic.acf.hhs.gov for each state's guidelines. Search for "State Requirements for Child-Staff Ratios."

3. Set the date and begin recruiting volunteers to babysit.

4. Publicize your event with families who may need babysitting services. Make flyers that include information about the organization you're raising funds for, the date and time of your babysitting event, the qualifications of the babysitters, a minimum suggested donation, and an email address and phone number for families to RSVP (since you most likely will be able to care for only a certain number of children). Set a deadline for the RSVP. Encourage families to get the word out to their friends.

5. Plan a variety of activities for the children so kids will not be bored and restless during the babysitting time. Consider craft activities, games, books to read aloud, puppet plays, a short (age-appropriate) movie, and physical activities.

6. On the day (or evening) of the event, encourage your babysitters to welcome families by smiling at them, introducing themselves, asking for the name of their child, and squatting down to look the child in the eye and say hello. Help kids feel safe and welcome.

7. Get a contact phone number (home and cell phone) for parents while they are away in case of an emergency.

8. joy playing with the kids while the parents away. Have fun.

9. Collect donations from parents when they return. Thank them for bringing their kids and for donating to your worthy cause. Be warm and friendly.

Debriefing the Project

- Why is it helpful to have a community babysitting fundraiser?

- What was it like to care for the young children? What would make it better next time?

- What surprised you about this type of fundraiser?

- What else could we do to raise funds and provide a service to families at the same time?

Helpful Resources

- For children: *The Berenstain Bears and the Sitter* by Stan and Jan Berenstain (Random House Books for Young Readers, 1981), a story about Brother and Sister Bear who aren't happy that Mrs. Grizzle comes to babysit them—until Mrs. Grizzle surprises them.

- For teens: *It's Our World, Too! Young People Who Are Making a Difference* by Phillip M. Hoose (Farrar, Straus and Giroux, 2002), stories of young people who have made a difference, along with tips on what you can do to contribute.

Bonus Ideas

- Consider creating a list of certified teen babysitters to give to families with young children in your organization. (Make sure you get written permission first from the parents of the teenagers.) Although this doesn't raise funds, it does provide a valuable service to families with young children and an opportunity for teens to earn money.

- Some organizations have found that this type of fundraiser is especially popular in early December, so families can shop for the holidays. Others have discovered that having it once a month on a Saturday evening, so parents can go out for dinner or to a movie, also generates a lot of interest.

Exercising for a Great Cause

Our family will be joining many others to exercise, play, and socialize at a Family Moving-Along-a-Thon in order to raise money for _____.

(name of organization)

It's a great cause. Please consider sponsoring our family with a donation.

Family Moving-Along-a-Thon: _____

(date)

Donor's Name	Donor's Address	Donor's Phone	Amount Donated
Total Amount Donated			$

Thank you! We appreciate your donation!

What's Your Bid?

Item: _____

Description: _____

Minimum bid: _____   Minimum raise: _____

First and Last Name (Print clearly)	Your Bid

Guess for a Good Cause

You're invited to help raise money for _____.
Come to our event: (name of organization)

Date: _____

Time: _____

Place: _____

At this event, we will be guessing the total length (when placed side by side) of all the stuffed animals owned by participating families. (We'll estimate that each stuffed animal is about 5 inches wide.)

Count the number of stuffed animals each family member has and write those totals on this sheet. Bring this sheet with you to the event.

Family Member's Name	Total Number of Stuffed Animals

Be ready to guess the total length of stuffed animals when you get here!
(And bring some money to donate to our worthy cause.)

From *Doing Good Together: 101 Easy, Meaningful Service Projects for Families, Schools, and Communities* by Jenny Friedman, Ph.D., and Jolene Roehlkepartain, copyright © 2010. Free Spirit Publishing Inc., Minneapolis, MN; 800-735-7323; www.freespirit.com. This page may be reproduced for individual and small group work only. For other uses, contact www.freespirit.com/company/permissions.cfm.

Chapter 6
Projects to Promote Peace, Justice, and Social Action

We live in a world full of conflict and injustice where many countries are at war and people are discriminated against for their race, age, gender, ethnicity, sexual orientation, religion, economic class, disability, and beliefs. Families can do service projects that make the world a bit better by promoting peace and advocating for justice. These projects are a call to social action with the hope of slowly reversing injustices.

(49) Adopt a Well

Purpose

Give people in developing countries access to clean water by adopting a well.

Possible Recipients

- The Water Project at www.thewaterproject.org

Time Requirement

Planning time before the project: one to two hours. Gathering materials: one hour. Setup time on the day of your project: 30 minutes to an hour. Introductory session project time: 30 minutes. Concluding project time (two weeks after the introductory session): 30 minutes.

People

This project is ideal for families with children between the ages of 3 and 18.

Materials

- A paper cup for each family
- 1 copy of the "Water Challenge Savings Scorecard" from the free Water Challenge Fundraiser Kit for each family (see the Water Project website)
- Optional: Free water wristbands
- Optional: Laptop computer, screen, and speakers to show the Water Project videos

Find the "Water Challenge Savings Scorecard," the free wristbands, and the Water Project videos by searching at the Water Project website (www.thewaterproject.org).

Connecting Point

Have you ever been thirsty? What did you do? Most likely, you drank something. But there are some people in the world who do not have access to clean water. They're thirsty a lot. Some even die because they drink polluted, untreated water that makes them sick. We can help people in countries like Kenya, where water is dirty and scarce, by raising money to drill wells that will give them access to clean water.

Doing the Project

1. Before you do the project, download the free Water Challenge Fundraiser Kit from the Water Project at www.thewaterproject.org. Decide whether your group will raise funds for school wells in Kenya and the Sudan or for general wells in India, the Sudan, Sierra Leone, or Haiti.

2. Set the date for your introductory session and concluding project two weeks afterward.

3. As families arrive at your introductory event, give each family a paper cup (and the wristband, if you've opted to get them). Talk about the need for wells in areas of the world that do not have access to clean water. If possible, show the Week One video from the Water Project website.

4. Explain that each family will keep its paper cup in a prominent place at home and add money to the cup every time family members get something to drink. (If you distribute the wristbands, have people wear them for the entire two weeks as reminders of those who don't have access to clean water.)

5. Distribute a copy of the "Water Challenge Savings Scorecard" to each family. Challenge family members to drink only water in the next two weeks. Whenever they drink water (instead of something else), have them mark their scorecard. For example, if they drink water at a restaurant instead of milk, they would mark the second item: Milk Restaurant at $1.50 a serving. They would then add $1.50 to the paper cup you gave them. Every time they drink water, they are to decide what they might have otherwise chosen and mark their scorecard before adding the designated amount of money to the cup.

6. Ask families to bring their cups filled with money and their scorecards to your second event.

7. At the second event, show the Week Two video from the Water Project website if possible.

8. Count up the funds raised and divide the total by $10. (Ten dollars provides clean water for one person through the Water Project.) For example, if you raised $250 dollars, that means your group will provide fresh, clean water for 25 people through a new well or new water system.

9. If possible, show some of the ongoing and completed projects posted on the Water Project website. Pictures tell a moving story.

Debriefing the Project

- Was it hard or easy to drink only water for two weeks? Why?
- Why do you think it is easy to take drinking water for granted?
- Why do you think some people live in parts of the world where there isn't access to clean drinking water?
- How else can we help people dig wells and get access to clean drinking water?

Helpful Resources

- For children: *A Cool Drink of Water* by Barbara Kerley (National Geographic Children's Books, 2006), a book of full-page color photos that show people drinking water from around the world.
- For teens: *The Unheard: A Memoir of Deafness and Africa* by Josh Swiller (Holt, 2007), a true story about a man who joined the Peace Corps to dig wells in Zambia.

Bonus Ideas

- Consider getting the "I gave water" stickers from the Water Project website to distribute to families at the second meeting.
- Learn about Ryan Hreljac, who became inspired in first grade (at the age of 6) to help provide clean water to people in developing countries. Read about his story at his website at www.ryanswell.ca or in the book *Ryan and Jimmy: And the Well in Africa that Brought Them Together* by Herb Shoveller (Kids Can Press, 2006).

(50) Worldwide Humanity

Purpose

Advocate for human rights with Amnesty International through a letter-writing campaign.

Possible Recipients

- Amnesty International's Freedom Writers Network (go to www.amnestyusa.org and search for "Freedom Writers")

Time Requirement

Planning time before the project: one to two hours. Gathering materials: one hour. Setup time on the day of your project: 30 minutes to an hour. Project time: one hour.

People

This project is ideal for families with children between the ages of 10 and 18. Expect each person to write one letter during the one-hour event.

Materials

- 1 copy of the Freedom Writers handouts "Basic Letter Writing Tips" and "Sample Messages" for each family
- 1 copy of the current Freedom Writers case sheet for everyone who is attending your event
- 2 to 3 pieces of 8½" x 11" paper for each person
- 1 pen for each teenager and adult
- 1 pencil for each child ages 10 to 12

- 1 business-size envelope for each person
- 1 98¢ international stamp for each person

The "Basic Letter Writing Tips" and "Sample Messages" handouts can be downloaded from the Amnesty International website by searching for "Freedom Writers," then searching in the "Resources" section from the left-hand menu. The current case sheet can be found by clicking on "Sample letter and more case details" at the bottom of the Freedom Writers page.

Connecting Point

Amnesty International is the world's largest volunteer human-rights organization, with more than 1 million members in 90 countries. Members take action to protect people from human-rights violations—trying to free political prisoners, for example, and working to ensure that everyone receives a fair trial. The Freedom Writers program includes a case sheet that gives information about a group or individual who needs help. Families can read the report together and write letters, asking officials to take notice of the human-rights violations and stop them.

Doing the Project

1. Well before your event, learn more about this project by going to the Amnesty International website and searching for Freedom Writers. Read about some of the organization's success stories by clicking on "Updates on Previous Freedom Writers Cases" from the left-hand menu that appears.

2. Read the case sheet to familiarize yourself with the current Freedom Writers cause so you'll be comfortable discussing it at your event. (The causes periodically change.)

3. As families arrive on the day of your event, hand out copies of the "Basic Letter Writing Tips" and "Sample Messages" handouts, the Freedom Writers case sheet, paper, pen or pencil, an envelope, and an international stamp to each person. Go over letter writing handouts as a group; they have helpful tips on how to write an effective appeal.

4. Even though many families can read the case sheet together, it may be helpful to read parts of it aloud because of the different literacy skills of families. For families who have never done this type of service project before, it's often helpful to walk through the case sheet with them so they understand how it works.

5. Give individuals time to write their letters. The "Recommended Action" portion of the case sheet gives explicit instructions of what to write. For example, in a case sheet about a journalist who has received death threats in Honduras, it was suggested that people ask for a public condemnation of killings and threats against journalists and for protection for all journalists. Since many families no longer write letters often, it's often helpful to brainstorm ideas of what to write and give pointers for how to be courteous.

6. When families finish, have them fold their letters into thirds, place them into envelopes, address the envelopes, and place an international stamp on each one.

7. Collect all the letters for mailing.

Debriefing the Project

- How was the Freedom Writers case sheet helpful?
- After you read the case sheet, did you become more concerned about this issue? Why or why not?
- Why is it important to write letters to protect people from human-rights violations?
- How else could we help Amnesty International?
- How else could we help people who live in unjust situations?

Helpful Resources

- For children: *We Are All Born Free: The Universal Declaration of Human Rights in Pictures* by Amnesty International (Frances Lincoln, 2008), a book for children about human rights.
- For teens: *Speak Truth to Power: Human Rights Defenders Who Are Changing Our World* by Kerry Kennedy Cuomo (Crown Publishers, 2000), a book that includes portraits of and interviews with human-rights advocates from around the world.

Bonus Ideas

- Get even more letter-writing tips by searching for "Mr. Rights' Letter Writing Guide" at the Amnesty International website.

- Consider using some of the other activities and topics from the AIKids' Urgent Action program that are listed at the website, such as the games and activities, writing guidelines, photo gallery, and the global write-a-thon. Search for "AI Kids" at the website.

- Visit the United Nations Convention on the Rights of the Child at www.unicef.org. Click on "The State of the World's Children." Also search for "Convention on the Rights of the Child" and click on "About the Convention." This website has helpful information about what's happening with children around the world, which you can incorporate into your Connecting Point.

- Consider organizing an email campaign. Today, many people advocate for change by sending emails to the legislators at the state and federal level.

- Encourage families to join the Urgent Action Network so they can write letters on their own each month. It's a powerful way for families to contribute and make a difference.

51 100 Steps to Peace

Purpose

Raise awareness about the need for peace in our world by creating a wall display of 100 footprints.

Possible Recipients

- Any worthy peace cause, such as the Institute for Peace and Justice (www.ipj-ppj.org), the Alliance for Global Justice (www.clrlabor.org), or the Carter Center (www.cartercenter.org)

Time Requirement

Planning time before the project: one to three hours. Gathering materials: one to two hours. Setup time on the day of your project: one to two hours. Project time: 90 minutes.

People

This project is ideal for families with children between the ages of 5 and 18.

Materials

- A large, empty wall to display all the ideas for peace

- 100 foot cutouts, which you can find at teacher-supply and education stores

- 1 fine-point permanent black marker for each family

- 2 pieces of 8½" x 11" paper for each family

- 1 pen for each person

- 2 to 3 rolls of masking tape

- Something to hold the money collected, such as a cash box or manila envelope

- A lot of one-dollar bills (about 40)

- 1 timer

- Enough copies of the "100 Steps to Peace— Add *Your* Steps" handout (page 133) to publicize your event with families

Foot cutouts are available through teacher-supply or educational stores, such as Lakeshore Learning Materials.

Connecting Point

Peace is precarious for many. Many countries are at war, and we often hear about violence in the news. Terrorism and other threats can make us afraid and cause us to wonder if peace is even possible. When we identify easy ways to take a step toward peace right now, right here, we can begin to have hope that we can change our world step by step toward a more peaceful one. For this project, we will name 100 creative ways to live in peace.

Doing the Project

1. Well before your event, choose a worthy peace cause to raise funds for. Learn more about the cause or organization so you can make the case for why it's important to support it.

2. Distribute the handout "100 Steps to Peace—Add *Your* Steps" to families you hope will attend your event. They can prepare for the event by thinking of easy ways to promote peace.

3. As families arrive to your event, have each one find one or two other families to work with. Give each group paper and each person a pen.

4. Explain that each group is to brainstorm a list of ways friends are kind to each other. Examples could include listening to each other, eating together, laughing at each other's jokes, and so on. Have each group designate a recorder (someone who will write down all the brainstorm ideas). Give the groups 10 minutes to come up with as many ideas as they can think of.

5. When 10 minutes are up, explain that these simple, kind actions we do between friends are actually peace actions. Whenever we're kind to each other, we're promoting peace. We want to live lives of peace.

6. Divide the 100 foot cutouts evenly among your groups. For example, if you have 10 groups, give each group 10. Give the recorder in each group the cutouts and a permanent marker.

7. Ask the groups to choose their best ideas and write one on each of the feet.

8. After groups finish, call them up one at a time and have them announce their ideas to everyone, and then attach the feet to the wall with a rolled piece of masking tape. Create a display that shows 100 steps to peace.

9. After all the groups have given their ideas and you have 100 feet on the wall, make the case for families to give money to your peaceful cause. See how much money you can raise. For example, ask each family to give 10¢ per foot on the wall (which would equal $10 per family).

10. Keep your wall display for a period of time, such as one week, so others can see it. It's a great visual to show how each step can create a lifestyle of peace for everyone.

Debriefing the Project

- Was it hard or easy to come up with kindness ideas in your group? Why?

- Was it harder or easier to choose your best ideas to write on the foot cutouts? Why?

- What did you think when you saw the 100 feet displayed on the wall?

- How can you promote peace at home? At school? At work? In our community?

- What else can we do to promote peace?

Helpful Resources

- For children: *The Peace Book* by Todd Parr (Little Brown, 2009), a colorful book that gives many different definitions of the word *peace*.

- For teens: *Peace Tales: World Folktales to Talk About* by Margaret Read MacDonald (August House, 2006), a collection of tales from around the world that get teens thinking about how war starts and what leads to peace.

Bonus Ideas

- Consider expanding the fundraiser beyond your family service project. Promote the cause as 100 Steps to Peace and 100 Donors to Peace, and ask families to help you recruit enough donors to reach that number.

- Consider distributing an outline of a foot on paper and having kids write their three favorite ideas (from the 100 on the wall) for them to take home and start doing right away.

- Learn about other ways to promote peace through Six Billion Paths to Peace at www.sixbillionpaths.org.

52 Fill a Boat with Animals

Purpose

Raise funds for needy families and help the families in your group become more aware of the power of a goat, a chicken, or even a duck for people in a developing country.

Possible Recipients

- The Heifer Project at www.heifer.org

Time Requirement

Planning time before the project: one to three hours. Gathering materials: one to two hours. Setup time on the day of your project: one to two hours. Project time: 90 minutes.

People

This project is ideal for families with children between the ages of 3 and 18.

Materials

- 200 printouts of small photos of animals from the Heifer website at www.heifer.org (at least 10 of each animal). Click on "Give" then "Online Gift Catalog."
- 200 craft sticks
- 2 to 3 rolls of transparent tape
- 2 to 3 rolls of masking tape
- 3 to 4 pairs of scissors
- 1 washable marker for each person
- About 5 animal crackers for each person
- A large boat cut out of brown posterboard
- Something to hold the donations, such as an envelope or a money box
- Optional: Laptop computer with Internet access, speakers, and projector

You can get craft sticks at craft-supply stores such as Michael's.

Connecting Point

Many people in the world do not have enough to eat. They live in areas where farming is hard (or nearly impossible), or they don't have the resources to buy or create their own food. Heifer International helps families become independent by raising food on their own. They donate chickens, ducks, rabbits, pigs, goats, heifers, water buffalo, and other animals to families who use the animals for much-needed food and income.

Doing the Project

1. Before your event, learn more about the Heifer Project so you can make the case for why it's important to support it.

2. Create a large boat out of brown posterboard. All you need to do is make it in the shape of a rowboat so families can clearly see that it's a boat and be able to place their donation pictures on top (as if inside the boat). Display the boat on an empty wall.

3. Cut out the pictures of the animals from the gift catalog page of the Heifer Project website. (These are small pictures that also include information about the price of animals.) Then tape each animal separately onto a craft stick so all 200 sticks have an animal on them. If possible, think of a creative way to display the craft sticks, such as sticking them into a tray of sand or into a Styrofoam block, keeping similar animals together, such as all the pigs in one place and all the ducks in another place.

4. When families arrive at your event, introduce them to the work of Heifer International. Use information from the organization's website. If you have access to a laptop computer, speakers, and projector, consider showing the short video "12 Stones" from the Heifer website. Go to "Inside Heifer," then "Media Center," then "Photos & Video." (The site actually has a number of short videos you can show.)

5. Talk about how one animal can make a difference in the life of a struggling family. An animal can provide eggs for a family to eat and sell. An animal can provide wool for a family to sell and earn money for food. An animal can provide milk.

6. Point out the boat on the wall and the animals on craft sticks. Talk about how you'd like families to fill up (add animals above or on) your boat by donating money to buy an animal. The photos on craft sticks represent the animals they can purchase. (Pull out two examples: a goat and a flock of chicks.) Explain that if a family wanted to do a lot, they could donate $120 to buy one goat. (Show the picture of the goat.) Or a family could buy a share of an animal (goat shares are $10). They could give $20 to buy a flock of chicks. (Show the picture of the chicks.)

7. Give families time to look at all the options. When they decide to purchase an animal (or a share of an animal), have them circle the part of the picture, such as $120 sheep if they gave $120, or $10 share if they gave $10, on one of the craft stick pictures. Have families make checks out to Heifer International and explain that their donations are tax deductible. After they give their donation, they can then take masking tape and tape their craft stick animal to the boat on the wall.

8. Together, watch the boat fill up with animals.

9. Total up the amount of money raised. Serve animal crackers as a snack to celebrate.

Debriefing the Project

- How did you feel when you saw the empty boat at the beginning of our service project? Why?

- How did you feel when you saw the full boat at the end of our service project? Why?

- How can we learn more about the way people live in other countries?

- Why can one animal make such a big difference in the life of one family?

- What else can we do to raise money for Heifer?

Helpful Resources

- For children: *Beatrice's Goat* by Page McBrier (Aladdin, 2004), a heartwarming story about how a goat from the Heifer Project changes the life of a young girl's family in a small African village.

- For teens: *Free? Stories About Human Rights* by Amnesty International (Candlewick, 2010), a book with stories by 14 children's book authors who write about children who have been either human-rights activists or victims of human-rights abuses.

Bonus Ideas

- Consider downloading the free fundraising idea packets that Heifer offers at its website under "Get Involved."

- Heifer also offers many free materials that you can order in advance, such as boat-shaped banks (for coins), fundraising calendars, and more.

- There are several children's books about Heifer and/or the powerful effect that adding an animal can have on a family. Consider these books: *One Hen: How One Small Loan Made a Big Difference* by Katie Smith Milway (Kids Can Press, 2008), *Give a Goat* by Jan West Schrock (Tilbury House Publishers, 2008), or *Faith the Cow* by Susan Barne Hoover (FaithQuest, 1995).

- On June 12, 2005, the TV show *60 Minutes* did a segment on Beatrice and her goat, featured in the book *Beatrice's Goat* (see above). You can purchase a copy of the show through Amazon.com and other vendors. The show is called *60 Minutes: Beatrice's Goat.*

- Some organizations do this type of service project around Mother's Day, advocating that kids "buy a llama for their mama."

(53) Letter-Writing Campaign

Purpose

Raise awareness about an issue you care about by writing letters.

Possible Recipients

- Any worthy peace cause, such as the Institute for Peace and Justice (www.ipj-ppj.org), the Alliance for Global Justice (www.clrlabor.org), or the Carter Center (www.cartercenter.org)
- Have families brainstorm local issues, such as cleaning a waterway or adding a stop sign to a dangerous intersection

Time Requirement

Planning time before the project: one to two hours. Gathering materials: one hour. Setup time on the day of your project: 30 minutes to an hour. Project time: one hour.

People

This project is ideal for families with children between the ages of 10 and 18.

Materials

- 2 to 3 pieces of 8½" by 11" white paper for each person
- 1 pen for each person
- 1 to 2 business-size envelopes for each person
- 1 first-class postage stamp for each person
- Examples of effective, published letters to the editor and letters to legislators that others have written
- Information about the cause you want families to write about

You can usually find information about your cause at the organization's website or by researching the topic on the Internet. Find effective letters to the editor in a local newspaper (in print or on the Web).

Connecting Point

Talk about the cause you're promoting; this is what will get families excited about the event. Talk about the power of the written word. Individuals and families can advocate for social change by writing letters about causes they care about. Some can write letters to the editor, while others write to legislators. When lots of people write letters about the same cause, leaders are likely to take notice.

Doing the Project

1. Before you do the project, research an issue that families are talking about (or feeling strongly about). For example, maybe families wish there was a pedestrian bridge over a busy road so that kids can safely get to a recreational center in your town.

2. Find the addresses for the places you want families to write to. For example, newspapers publish an address for letters to the editor (or their website may provide an email address or online form). You can find the address of your community or state legislature online. Families can write to U.S. senators at (Name of Senator), The United States Senate, Washington, DC 20510, and to their U.S. representative at (Name of Representative), The United States House of Representative, Washington, DC 20515.

3. Find examples of letters to the editor in a local paper or the website of any paper. If possible, find letters that were effective. For example, if the arts project your school district was threatening to cut was kept because many people in the community wrote letters to the school and newspaper, get copies of these letters. If you have samples of letters that people have written to their legislators, get them as well.

4. When families arrive at your event, show the examples of letters to the editor and explain why they're effective.

5. Distribute the paper, pens, envelopes, and stamps so each person has one of each. Give families time to write their letters.

6. When families finish, ask if there are any volunteers who would like to read their letters aloud. (Some families enjoy doing this.) Then have each person address the envelope (provide the address needed), put the letter inside and seal it, and place a first-class stamp on it. Collect all the letters.

7. After the service project, keep an eye on your local paper (if you wrote letters to the editor) and see if any get published. If so, get the word out about publication. If you're following a bill in the legislature, consider giving updates about its progress.

Debriefing the Project

- Why is it important to write letters advocating for change?

- What do you like best about writing letters? The least? Why?

- Who has ever written this kind of letter before? Why did you do that?

- What else can we do to raise awareness about what needs to change?

Helpful Resources

- For children: *Corduroy Writes a Letter* by Alison Inches (Puffin, 2004), a story about a bear named Corduroy who shows that writing letters to express your opinion can make a difference.

- For teens: *Youth! The 26% Youth Solution* by Wendy Schaetzel Lesko and Emanuel Tsourounis (Information USA, 1998), a helpful book for taking action and influencing decision-makers and the press. The Activism 2000 Project is now called the Youth Activism Project and has a website at www.youthactivism.com.

Bonus Ideas

- If your group has done this type of project in the past, display any letters to the editor that have been published. Continue to keep a file of clippings for future use.

- Some organizations print postcards on which families can fill in the recipient's name at the beginning, their own name at the end, and write in the address. Although this type of letter-writing campaign isn't as creative, it does make an impact if 100 families sign postcards about an issue and mail them.

- If your group would prefer to send emails, find out if the organization you're contacting will receive them. Many will, including most government offices. Almost all newspapers will, too.

(54) Steps in the Right Direction

Purpose

Collect and donate gently used shoes to people who otherwise wouldn't have any.

Possible Recipients

- Local options: A homeless shelter or a non-profit that distributes clothing and shoes to those in need
- Other options: Share Your Soles at www.shareyoursoles.org

Time Requirement

Planning time before the project: one to two hours. Gathering materials: one hour. Setup time on the day of your project: 30 minutes to an hour. Project time: one hour.

People

This project is ideal for families with children between the ages of 3 and 18.

Materials

- Enough copies of the "What's in Your Closet?" handout (page 134) to publicize your event with families
- Large boxes to place the shoes in
- Access to sinks and hot water
- 1 bucket for every 2 families (if you don't have many sinks)
- 1 towel for every 3 pairs of shoes
- 1 washcloth for every 5 pairs of shoes
- 1 bottle of bleach and detergent for each sink or bucket
- Shoe laces, enough for each pair of shoes with laces
- 1 can of shoe polish in each of brown, black, and other colors
- Rags for polishing shoes

Connecting Point

When Mona Purdy went to Guatemala to run in a half-marathon, she was shocked to find kids dipping their bare feet in a sticky black substance. When she asked what they were doing, she was told that they put tar on the soles of their feet because they didn't have shoes. They'd been told that tar might protect their feet from cuts and germs. Determined to help, Mona returned to her Illinois home and started the nonprofit organization Share Your Soles. Since its inception, the organization has donated more than 350,000 shoes to people all over the world.

Doing the Project

1. Before your event, distribute the handout "What's in Your Closet?" to get the word out about your project.

2. As families arrive, have them place their donated shoes in one area.

3. Organize families to sort shoes into categories. Start with major categories, such as women's shoes, men's shoes, boys' shoes, and girls' shoes. Then separate them into smaller categories, such as women's running shoes, women's boots, women's dress shoes, and so on.

4. Have families inspect the shoes. If any are in bad shape, throw them away. Wash all running shoes, flip flops, and washable (made of fabric or rubber rather than leather) sandals in hot water with bleach and detergent. (It's best to do this in a sink rather than a washer.) Dip them in the soapy water and scrub them with the washcloths. Then rinse the shoes and lay them out to dry on towels or directly on a non-carpeted floor.

5. Have families determine which shoes need laces and which need to be polished. Then replace laces and polish shoes as needed.

6. When families have finished cleaning and repairing the shoes, and all shoes are dry, place them into boxes according to category.

7. Take or ship the shoes to a collection site. Share Your Soles currently has collection bins in 10 states, and is expanding to other states. Check the website for details.

Debriefing the Project

- How often do you go barefoot? Why?
- What would it be like to have to go barefoot all the time?
- What did you think of collecting shoes to donate? Why?
- How many pairs of shoes did you expect us to collect—compared with what we actually did?
- How else can we help people who don't have shoes?

Helpful Resources

- For children: *Four Feet, Two Sandals* by Karen Lynn Williams (Eerdmans Books for Young Readers, 2007), a story of two girls in a refugee camp who decide to share a pair of sandals they receive from relief workers.
- For teens: *The Kid's Guide to Social Action* by Barbara A. Lewis, (Free Spirit Publishing, 1998), a book full of stories of kids who've made a difference, along with practical tips on how to change the world bit by bit.

Bonus Ideas

- Consider taking photos of all your families with all the collected shoes displayed in one area. Then write a press release about your service project and include photos to send to a local newspaper and other media outlets to publicize what you did. Getting recognition from the media often gets families talking about the service projects that you do and gets them interested in attending future projects.
- Some organizations also encourage families to give a small amount of money to help pay for bleach, detergent, laces, polish, and any other costs.

(55) Paper Peace Quilt

Purpose

Create a giant paper peace quilt to display while raising money for peace efforts.

Possible Recipients

- Any worthy peace cause, such as the Institute for Peace and Justice (www.ipj-ppj.org), the Alliance for Global Justice (www.clrlabor.org), or the Carter Center (www.cartercenter.org)

Time Requirement

Planning time before the project: one to three hours. Gathering materials: one to two hours. Setup time on the day of your project: one to two hours. Project time: 90 minutes.

People

This project is ideal for families with children between the ages of 3 and 18. Expect each person to make one quilt square during the one-hour event. More families means a bigger quilt.

You may need volunteers to help cut paper squares before your event.

Materials

- 1 3" x 3" paper square (in white and other colors) for each person (plus extras)
- 5 washable markers in various colors for each family
- 5 crayons in various colors for each family
- 2 to 3 rolls of transparent tape
- An empty wall to display the peace quilt
- 2 to 3 rolls of masking tape
- Something to hold the monetary donations, such as an envelope or money box

Connecting Point

Children and teenagers have a lot to say about peace. When they're given the opportunity to express their thoughts through words and illustrations, they often come up with thoughtful, thought-provoking ideas. Promote peace by raising money for a worthy organization *and* raising awareness by creating a paper peace quilt that can be displayed. Talk about the organization you are raising money for today.

Doing the Project

1. Before your event, choose an organization you wish to raise funds for. Learn more about this organization so you can make the case for why it's important to support it.

2. Cut lots of 3" x 3" paper squares from photocopy paper (in white and other colors), so each person can have one. If you have a large group (and therefore will need a lot of squares), have a volunteer help with this. Gather all the necessary supplies and locate a wall to display the finished peace quilt.

3. Make four quilt squares and tape them together into a miniature quilt to show as an example.

4. When families arrive to your event, charge them $1 (or another fee appropriate to your community) for each paper square. Explain what the money will be going toward and how you'd love it if every family member could buy at least one to participate in the peace quilt.

5. Have families decorate their squares with a message or illustration showing what peace means to them. Encourage them to be creative and colorful.

6. As people finish, begin assembling the peace quilt by taping together the squares (from the back). Consider making one large peace quilt or a number of smaller ones to display.

7. Hang up the finished peace quilt with masking tape and keep it on display. Ask for volunteers to tell about their squares.

8. Add up the amount of money raised and mail or deliver the funds raised.

Debriefing the Project

- How did you decide what to put on your square? How hard was it to come up with something? Why?

- What was your reaction when you saw the finished peace quilt?

- Which squares of the peace quilt were you drawn to? Why?

- What does peace mean to you?

- How else can we promote peace?

Helpful Resources

- For children: *Martin's Big Words: The Life of Dr. Martin Luther King Jr.* by Doreen Rappaport (Hyperion Books for Children, 2007), a book that introduces children to the life and peace work of Dr. Martin Luther King Jr.

- For teens: *The Butter Battle Book* by Dr. Seuss (Random House, 1984), a thought-provoking book on how the animosity of the Zooks and the Yooks leads to a buildup of weaponry, satirizing how differences and intolerance can get out of hand.

Bonus Ideas

- Consider making the paper peace quilt without the fundraising aspect. Your group can promote and advocate for peace by making the quilt to display.

- If families are interested in making their own peace quilts to display at home, give them the opportunity to make their own as well. Often, 12 squares will make an attractive peace quilt. Some families may want to decorate all 12 squares and then exchange some of them with other families to create collaborative peace quilts.

- Download the free 16-page *Oxfam America Organizing Guide: Tips for Taking Action in Your Community* from Oxfam America at www.oxfamamerica.org. (Use the "advanced search" feature to find it.) You'll learn tips on how to organize a demonstration and how to move forward with your peace and social action efforts.

100 Steps to Peace— Add Your Steps

You're invited to a family service project on peacemaking. Come to our event:

Date: _____

Time: _____

Place: _____

At this event, we will be naming easy ways to promote peace (while also raising money for peace efforts). We'll be taking easy steps in the right direction to promote peace in our families, our schools, our workplaces, and our community.

Find out how to make peace happen—right now.
Come prepared to make a donation of any amount toward peace.
Donations will go toward _____.
(name of organization)

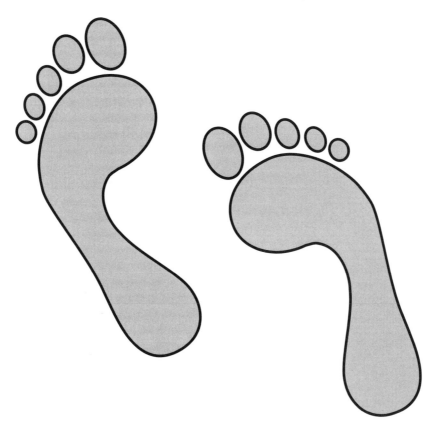

What's in *Your* Closet?

Have you grown out of any shoes lately—or just grown tired of any?
Do you have too many shoes cluttering your closet?

Have you wondered what to do with all those shoes?

Put them to good use! We're collecting gently used shoes at our family service project to donate to needy families all over the world. Please come.

Date: _____

Time: _____

Place: _____

Look through your closets and consider bringing gently used:

- Tennis shoes or running shoes
- Dress shoes
- Boots
- Work shoes
- Infant, toddler, and children's shoes
- Sandals
- Ice skates
- Casual shoes
- Any other kind of shoes (as long as they're still in good shape)

We'll also need:

- Old towels
- Washcloths
- Bleach
- Laundry detergent
- Shoe laces
- Shoe polish
- Buckets

Chapter 7
Projects to Support the Troops

Many American and Canadian soldiers are fighting around the world. They're often deployed for months (if not years), and being separated from their families can take a toll. These family service projects can help our troops feel supported and connected to people who care.

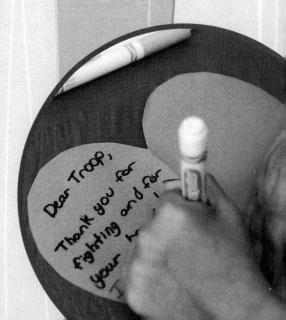

(56) Operation Letters & Cards

Purpose
Let soldiers know they're appreciated by writing and sending them letters and cards.

Possible Recipients
- Local options: a military base in or near your area
- Other options: A Million Thanks at www.amillionthanks.org, or Marine Parents at www.carepackageproject.com. To reach Canadian soldiers, go to www.forces.gc.ca and search for "Any Canadian Forces Member."

Time Requirement
Planning time before the project: one to two hours. Gathering materials: one hour. Setup time on the day of your project: 30 minutes to an hour. Project time: one hour.

People
This project is ideal for families with children between the ages of 5 and 18.

Materials
- 2 pieces of 8½" x 11" white paper for each person
- 1 pen for each person
- 5 washable markers in various colors for each family
- 1 business size envelope for each letter or card
- First-class postage stamps

Connecting Point
Every day, soldiers represent your country around the world. Many are far from home, and they're often deployed for long periods of time. Have you ever been separated from a parent or other loved one for a long time? How did you feel? If you haven't, how do you think you would feel? Help soldiers feel supported and connected by showing your support through cards and letters. Some will enjoy writing back, and you may even develop a friendship in the process.

Doing the Project
1. Before you do the project, read the rules and guidelines posted on the website of the recipient organization you've chosen.
2. When families arrive at your event, have them sit at tables. After introducing the project, give them time to write letters or make cards. Children can draw pictures. Encourage as many family members as possible to make a card or letter of appreciation.
3. Be clear about the writing guidelines. Explain that families should not write about controversial topics: All letters and cards will be screened for security purposes, and letters that rant about politics or criticize military service will be confiscated and not delivered. Encourage letter writers to thank the serviceperson, to tell a little about themselves, and to write about interesting topics (such as a pet and what that pet is doing; activities they're involved in and why; and hobbies).
4. Families that are interested in having contact with a soldier can include their full names and mailing addresses. Not everyone will respond, but some do and enjoy having correspondence during deployment.
5. Place letters together in stacks of 100. (Most likely, you will have fewer than 100, but if you have a large group, you'll need to put them in bundles of 100. This helps with the sorting on the receiving end.)
6. Visit the recipient website to find a drop-off location or mailing address for the letters.

Debriefing the Project
- How often do you receive a personal letter in the mail? How about personal email?
- What do you think of personal letters you receive through the mail? Why?
- What did you discover as your wrote your letter?

- Why is it important to write letters to our servicepeople stationed overseas?
- How else can we support our troops?

Helpful Resources

- For children: *Across the Blue Pacific* by Louise Borden (Houghton Mifflin, 2006), the story of Molly, who writes letters to Ted Walker, a neighborhood man in the Navy, stationed in the Pacific during World War II.
- For teens: *War Is . . . Solders, Survivors, and Storytellers Talk About War* edited by Marc Aronson and Patty Campbell (Candlewick, 2008), a book edited by two writers with opposing viewpoints on war. This book is a collection of essays, letters, and stories written by individuals who have experienced war firsthand.

Bonus Ideas

- Some people feel uncomfortable writing long letters. Consider having postcards available so people can write short supportive messages.
- Consider showing or recommending the video that's posted on A Million Thanks at www .amillionthanks.org. Let everyone know how grateful the soldiers are for mail.
- Some military bases may accept email. Check individual regiments to see if this is an option. (See project 64: Operation Email.)

57 Operation International Children

Purpose

Pack school supplies to send to children living in war zones and create goodwill between the children and the soldiers stationed there.

Possible Recipients

- Operation International Children at www.operationinternationalchildren.org

Time Requirement

Planning time before the project: one to two hours. Gathering materials: one hour. Setup time on the day of your project: 30 minutes to an hour. Project time: one hour.

People

This project is ideal for families with children between the ages of 3 and 18. Expect about three families to collaborate on each school kit.

Materials

- Enough copies of the "Help Create a School Kit for Children Living in War Zones" handout (page 151) to publicize your event with families
- School supply items listed on the "Help Create a School Kit for Children Living in War Zones" handout
- 1 2-gallon-size zip-top plastic bag for each school kit
- 1 sturdy shipping box for every 3 to 4 school kits
- 1 copy of the Operation International Children Donor Information Sheet for each shipping box
- 2 rolls of packing tape
- 3 to 4 permanent markers
- Money to ship the boxes

Donor Information Sheets are found at the Operation International Children website. Click "How You Can Help," then "Build Your Own School-Supply Kits." You can buy shipping boxes at a post office or shipping-supply store, or ask for donations from a grocery store. If you use banana boxes, make sure you tape over the hole in the top and bottom before shipping. Families will donate the school supply items.

Connecting Point

War devastates many countries, and the children who live in these war zones often do not have school supplies. Operation International Children helps organizations donate school-supply kits to children living in war-torn countries such as Afghanistan and Iraq. Not only does this create better educational opportunities for the children, but it also creates goodwill between the children and soldiers, because soldiers give the kits to the children. This type of family service project shows that we care about all children.

Doing the Project

1. Learn more about Operation International Children through the website so you can make the case for why it's important to support it.

2. Before your event, distribute the "Help Create a School Kit for Children Living in War Zones" handout to families. Check three to four school-supply items on each family's sheet, being sure to cover all the items.

3. Make a school-supply kit to show as an example.

4. When families arrive, have them place their donations into separate piles. For example, have one pile for pencils, another for notebook paper, and another for folders.

5. Once all the materials are separated, give each family a 2-gallon zip-top plastic bag (or have two or three families work together, depending on the number of kits you can make). Have them walk through the stations and pick up one of each item and place it in the zip-top bag (except for the folders). Here is the list: one pair of blunt-end scissors, one 12-inch ruler with metric markings, 12 new pencils with erasers, one small pencil sharpener, one large eraser, one box of colored pencils (crayons melt in the summer heat in certain countries, such as Iraq), one package of notebook paper, one composition book, three folders with inside pockets, and one zippered pencil bag.

6. When families are finished, have them dump out their bags and double-check that they have everything included. Read aloud the list slowly and have them put each item back into the bag as you read the items.

7. Count up the number of complete school-supply kits. Make a list of additional items needed to complete additional school-supply kits. (Most likely, you'll have a few extra items left over in certain piles.)

8. Have families pack the shipping boxes and get them ready to ship. (Note: You can include many school-supply kits in one shipping box.) Make sure they fill out and include the Donor Information Sheet. You need one sheet per shipping box.

9. Seal the boxes, address them, and have volunteers ship the kits to Operation International Children.

Debriefing the Project

- Why is it helpful for military personnel to hand out school-supply kits to children in countries that are at war?

- Why would it be hard to go to school if your country was in the middle of a war?

- Why are school supplies so important for learning?

- Why do you think we pack the school-supply kits in see-through plastic bags?

- What else can we do to help children who live in war-torn countries?

Helpful Resources

- For children: *The Librarian of Basra: A True Story from Iraq* by Jeanette Winter (Harcourt Children's Books, 2005), a book that tells the gripping story about an Iraqi librarian who struggles to save her community's collection of books. Based on a true story.

- For teens: *Children of War: Voices of Iraqi Refugees* by Deborah Ellis (Ground wood Books, 2009), interviews with Iraqi child refugees.

Bonus Ideas

- Consider donating other items that Operation International Children is in need of, such as blankets, backpacks, shoes, and tarps. Visit the website for up-to-date information and needs.

- If kids want to include a small stuffed animal or a ball with the school-supply kit, encourage them to do so. However, balls need to be sent deflated, and a small hand pump must be included for reinflating the ball. See the website for more information.

- The website also has other information that you can use for your service project, such as letters from Iraq.

(58) Operation GI Bracelet

Purpose

Donate money to troops and their families by selling GI bracelets that say "for those who serve."

Possible Recipients

- Fisher House (www.fisherhouse.org) or Wounded Warriors Family Support (www.woundedwarriorsfamilysupport.org)

Time Requirement

Planning time before the project: one to two hours. Gathering materials: one hour. Setup time on the day of your project: 30 minutes to an hour. Project time: 30 minutes.

People

This project is ideal for families with children between the ages of 3 and 18.

Materials

- Enough support-our-troop bracelets to sell to your group (about two per family, but try to gauge interest before you order; it's better to have too many than not enough)

- Something to collect the money in, such as a money box or manila envelope

- Change (for larger bills)

You can find inexpensive bracelets at Bumper Sticker Magnets by going to

www.bumperstickermagnet.com and searching for "Support our troops." Or go to Oriental Trading at www.orientaltrading.com and search for "patriotic sayings bracelets." Or personalize your own message by ordering from Wristbands with a Message at www.wristbandswithamessage.com. Note that many military shops also have "support our troops" bracelets, but many are expensive.

Connecting Point

Most people who are in the military do not have high-paying jobs. They joined the military not to make money but to serve their country. Some military families face even more economic hardship when their loved ones who serve are either wounded or killed. We can provide economic support to soldiers and their families by selling GI bracelets.

Doing the Project

1. Decide on a military organization that you'd like to support, such as Wounded Warriors Family Support or Fisher House, and learn about the organization.

2. Before the project, purchase bracelets to sell. Do this well in advance to be sure your order will arrive in time for your event.

3. The day of your event, ask people who have a family member or friend in the military to talk about their loved one. This makes your project

more personal and real for people. It also helps build a sense of community.

4. Sell the bracelets. In determining how much to charge for bracelets, make sure you will recoup the money required for buying and shipping the bracelets *and* raise funds.

5. Encourage families to buy bracelets for themselves and to give to others. This is particularly powerful if your community has a unit that is deployed. Having everyone in the community wearing "Support our troops" bracelets is a great show of support.

Debriefing the Project

- Why does wearing a bracelet show our support for soldiers?
- Why is it important to support soldiers and their families?
- When you wear your bracelet, what does it make you think about? Why?
- How else can we support our troops?

Helpful Resources

- For children: *The Impossible Patriotism Project* by Linda Skeers (Puffin, 2009), a story about Caleb, who is stumped about the true meaning of patriotism until he thinks of his father serving as a soldier.
- For teens: *Sunrise Over Fallujah* by Walter Dean Myers (Scholastic Press, 2008), the story of Robin Perry, a young man who has been deployed to Iraq as part of Operation Iraqi Freedom.

Bonus Ideas

- Consider showing the short video "Remember Me" that's posted on the GI Bracelet website (www.gi-bracelet.org).
- Consider doing this project in conjunction with another short project, such as project 62: Operation Phone Home or 64: Operation Email.

(59) Operation Remember

Purpose

Boost the morale of ill or wounded veterans by sending them uplifting notes on the back of photos.

Possible Recipients

- Veterans at a local veterans hospital

Time Requirement

Planning time before the project: one to two hours. Gathering materials: one hour. Setup time on the day of your project: 30 minutes to an hour. Project time: one hour.

People

This project is ideal for families with children between the ages of 5 and 18.

Ask several volunteers to take photos.

Materials

- 1 pen for each person
- 5 washable markers in various colors for each family
- 1 3" x 3" sticky note for each person
- 1 roll of transparent tape for every 2 families
- 1 digital camera for every 20 families
- A way to print the photos
- 2 pieces of 8½" x 11" white paper for each person
- Optional: 1 brown paper lunch bag for each recipient and items such as candy and toiletries to include in a small care package

Connecting Point

Once soldiers become discharged, people sometimes forget how many sacrifices they made to serve their country. Some veterans become sick and end up in a veterans hospital. You can help ill and wounded veterans and show them how much you appreciate them by sending them uplifting notes and telling them that you're thinking about them.

Doing the Project

1. Contact your local veterans hospital to find out about their policies regarding this type of donation. Ask if you can bring small care packages.

2. Before your event, figure out how you will take photos and get them printed. Many organizations take digital photos and print them on a printer right at the event. Others have them printed at a photo lab, although that makes the project more complex.

3. Take a photo of yourself and attach a message on a sticky note on the back of it (see step 5) to show as an example.

4. As families arrive on the day of your event, take photos of them. If you're expecting a lot of families, have a number of photographing stations so people don't have to wait in line for a long time.

5. Print the photos.

6. Distribute sticky notes to families. Explain that these notes will be attached to their photos. Have them write an uplifting note or draw a picture, and sign their first names. When they've finished, have them attach the sticky notes to the back of the photos and secure them with tape.

7. Some families may be interested in doing more, such as enclosing some candy or toiletries. If so, have these items available. Others may wish to write a longer letter. Encourage those families to do so.

8. Thank families for being sensitive to and remembering our ill and wounded veterans.

9. Ask for family volunteers to take the cards to the veterans hospital to distribute. Some may enjoy passing them out themselves and talking to the patients.

Debriefing the Project

- Do you like having your photo taken? Why or why not?

- How do you feel when you receive a personal photo in the mail or in an email (or see photos online at Facebook or another social networking site)? Why?

- Why is it important to send uplifting notes and photos to ill and wounded veterans?

- How else could we help veterans?

Helpful Resources

- For children: *The Wall* by Eve Bunting (Sandpiper, 1992), a moving story about a young boy and his father visiting the Vietnam War Memorial in Washington, D.C., and finding the name of the boy's grandfather who died in the war. *Susan Laughs* by Jeanne Willis (Henry Holt and Company, 2000), a book that helps readers understand that people with disabilities are people first.

- For teens: *Fallen Angels* by Walter Dean Myers (Scholastic, 2008). This Coretta Scott King Award winner reveals the realities of war when Richie Perry, a teenager from Harlem, enlists in the army and heads to war. *The Disability Rights Movement* by Deborah Kent (Children's Press, 1996), a book about the struggle of people with disabilities to secure their basic human rights.

Bonus Ideas

- Consider taking a group photo and enclosing that as well as the individual family photos. On the back, consider writing, "We are all thinking of you!"

- Consider enclosing a bandage, and write a note saying, "We know this bandage won't do much, but we hope our healing thoughts will help."

- If you bring treats or small items, have families decorate the brown paper lunch bags with markers and stickers.

Operation Books & Movies

Purpose

Help troops who are deployed overseas fill their downtime by donating books, comic books, DVDs, CDs, video games, and magazines.

Possible Recipients

- Books for Soldiers at www.booksforsoldiers.com or Canadian Forces Personnel Support Agency at www.cfpsa.com/en

Time Requirement

Planning time before the project: one to two hours. Gathering materials: one hour. Setup time on the day of your project: 30 minutes to an hour. Project time: one hour.

People

This project is ideal for families with children between the ages of 3 and 18.

Materials

- The free user manual from the Books for Soldiers website at www.booksforsoldiers.com
- A list of soldiers' names and what each one has requested from the Books for Soldiers website
- A handout you create soliciting specific books, DVDs, comic books, CDs, video games, and magazines as requested on the Books for Soldiers message boards; make enough copies to publicize your project with families
- 1 large flat-rate shipping box for every soldier you're shipping to
- 1 customs form for each shipping box
- 2 to 3 rolls of packing tape
- 1 permanent marker for each family
- 2 to 3 pieces of 8½" x 11" white paper for each person
- 5 washable markers and pens for each family
- Money to ship the boxes

Families will donate the books and other entertainment items. Flat-rate shipping boxes and customs forms are available for free from the post office, or you can order them online from the United States Post Office® (www.usps.com) or the Canada Post (www.canadapost.ca).

Connecting Point

When soldiers are deployed overseas, not only do they work for their unit, but they also have downtime. Many find themselves looking for books to read, music to listen to, movies to watch, and video games to play. Help deployed soldiers find interesting things to do by donating books, DVDs, music, and video games. Using information you find at their website, talk about Books for Soldiers.

Doing the Project

1. If you wish to ship items to U.S. soldiers, become a registered volunteer through the Books for Soldiers website at www.booksforsoldiers.com before your event. This entails following steps 1 and 2 at the website home page. You will not be able to send your donations or access the message boards unless you're a registered volunteer. (It's free, and you can be removed from the mailing list at any time.) In the past, organizations could ship items "To Any Soldier," but security restrictions have eliminated that option. Organizations now need to find the names of interested soldiers, which are listed at the website.

2. If you wish to ship to Canadian soldiers, investigate current programs at www.cfpsa.com/en/corporate/newscentre/support/index.asp.

3. Note any specific requests from individual soldiers listed at the Books for Soldiers website. Create a flyer listing the books, comic books, DVDs, CDs, video games, and magazines that soldiers have requested on message boards and distribute it to families so they can locate those items and bring them to your event.

4. Purchase as many shipping boxes as you will need and gather customs forms to go with them. If you're not familiar with the customs form, review it carefully and be sure you can fill it out. Take note that it's better to use individual flat-rate boxes to ship. Larger packages (especially those weighing more than 25 pounds) often are delayed or don't get delivered at all.

5. As families arrive at your event, help them match their donations to specific soldiers.

6. Give families paper and washable markers and pens. Have them write a letter, draw a picture, and stick notes into their box along with their donated items.

7. Have families use permanent marker to write the address of the soldier on the box. Use packing tape to secure. Fill out the customs order form. Walk through the parts of the customs order form for families who may have never used one before. On the green portion of the form, have them check the box "Gift." Then have them describe the contents, note the total value, and sign at the bottom. On the white portion of the form, have them fill out their name and address, the soldier's name and address, and date and sign the form.

8. Have a volunteer bring the boxes to the post office.

9. Consider planning family service projects similar to this one a couple of times a year to keep the troops busy with books, video games, and movies.

Debriefing the Project

- Have you ever had a lot of time when you didn't know what to do? How did you figure out how to spend your time?

- What if you were a soldier overseas and you didn't have access to books, movies, or other entertainment? How would you find things to do?

- Why is it important to help our soldiers?

- How else could we help our troops deployed overseas?

Helpful Resources

- For children: *Night Catch* by Brenda Ehrmantraut (Bubble Gum Press, 2005), about how a father who is called away to serve in the military invents a game of catch with the North Star to play with his son.

- For teens: *Invasion: The Story of D-Day* by Bruce Bliven Jr. (Sterling, 2007). Written by a journalist who was there, these are the soldiers' stories of what they experienced during the storming of the beaches of Normandy in World War II.

Bonus Ideas

- The Books for Soldiers website also has a pen pal area (that you can access once you're registered). Check it out if you have families who would be interested in becoming pen pals with soldiers overseas.

- If families are interested in giving a bit more, suggest they donate a one-year magazine subscription to a service person (listed on the website) for a magazine that would interest him or her.

(61) Operation Goody Bag

Purpose

Show support for America's first responders and military men and women by making and donating goody bags.

Possible Recipients

- Operation Goody Bag at www.operationgoodybag.org, an organization that honors troops and first responders

Time Requirement

Planning time before the project: one to two hours. Gathering materials: one hour. Setup time on the day of your project: 30 minutes to an hour. Project time: one hour.

People

This project is ideal for families with children between the ages of 3 and 18. Expect each person to make one goody bag during the one-hour event.

Materials

- 1 brown paper lunch bag for each person
- 5 washable markers (make sure you have a lot of red and blue) for each person
- 1 pen for each person
- Letter templates downloaded from the Operation Goody Bag website (click on "How you can help")
- 2 pieces of 8½" x 11" paper for each person
- 1 shipping box
- 1 roll of packing tape
- 1 permanent marker

Connecting Point

Many people work hard to protect the people of the United States: soldiers, firefighters, police, rescue and ambulance personnel, and more. Operation Goody Bag shows these individuals how much we care and support their efforts. Between November 2003 and January 2010, 125,000 goody bags were shipped.

Note: Operation Goody Bag serves only U.S. servicepeople and first responders.

Doing the Project

1. Before your event, learn more about Operation Goody Bag by reading its website so you can make the case for why it's important to support it.
2. Copy the letter template from the Operation Goody Bag website and set it up (following the instructions) so you have four letters per 8½" x 11" paper. Make copies of the letters.
3. Make a goody bag so you know how it's put together and to show as an example.
4. As families arrive to your event, give each family member a brown paper lunch bag. Ask each person to color patriotic designs on one side of the lunch bag.
5. Have families write personal letters on the letter template. (You'll have four letters per page.)
6. Explain how Operation Goody Bag works. After you send the decorated bags and cards, students at East Brook Middle School in Paramus, New Jersey, will add items to each goody bag. They'll add five pieces of candy, two poems, your personal letter, and a puzzle to each bag.
7. Have families collect all the bags and put them into one pile. Then collect all the sheets with the letters on them and place them into another pile.
8. Ask for donations to help with the shipping of the materials.
9. Box up the goody bags and letters and ship them to the address listed on the Operation Goody Bag website.

Debriefing the Project

- What did you like best about this service project? Why?
- Which did you enjoy doing more: decorating the bag or writing the letter? Why?

- Why is it important to support servicepeople and first responders?
- How else can we help servicepeople and first responders?

Helpful Resources

- For children: *There Come a Soldier* by Peggy Mercer (Chronicle Books, 2007), a fictional story about a paratrooper who gets lost in the woods of Belgium during World War II.
- For teens: *Lily's Crossing* by Patricia Reilly Giff (Bantam Double Day Dell, 1999), a story about Lily, whose father enlists and leaves to fight in World War II. While he's away she befriends Albert, a European refugee.

Bonus Ideas

- Read aloud some of the letters Operation Goody Bag has received and show some of the photos of kids putting the bags together. Letters and photos are at the website.
- Consider getting patriotic stamp-making materials along with red, white, and blue stamp pads to decorate the bags.

62 Operation Phone Home

Purpose

Make it easy for deployed soldiers to phone home by donating cell phones and/or money for calling fees.

Possible Recipients

- Cell Phones for Soldiers at www.cellphones forsoldiers.com or www.cellphonesfor soldierscanada.com; or VFW Operation Uplink at www.operationuplink.org

Time Requirement

Planning time before the project: one to two hours. Gathering materials: 30 minutes. Setup time on the day of your project: 30 minutes to an hour. Project time: 30 minutes.

People

This project is ideal for families with children between the ages of 3 and 18.

Materials

- A large box for collecting donated cell phones (from a local office-supply store)
- A computer with Internet access and a printer
- Optional: Information and templates from the Cell Phones for Soldiers website

Connecting Point

More than 1.4 million Americans currently serve in the U.S. military and about 90,000 serve in the Canadian Forces. Because soldiers often work in remote places, they often do not have the ability to call home. By donating cell phones and money, we can make it easier for troops to call home and keep in touch.

Doing the Project

1. Before you do the project, visit the Cell Phones for Soldiers website and decide whether you plan to be a drop-off point. If so, go to the website and download (for free) the easy-to-use flyers, posters, collection box artwork, Internet graphics, a welcome kit, and press releases. If you plan to be an ongoing drop-off site, send press releases to the media about your event. If you wish to collect cell phones only one time (rather than be an ongoing collection site), find a local drop-off point from the website where you can donate the cell phones you collect.

2. Publicize the service project and encourage families to bring cell phones they no longer use (and wish to donate) or money to donate. Encourage families to ask their family and

friends for cell phones to donate. Explain that you need cell phones with the batteries included, even if the batteries are not in tip-top shape.

3. Collect cell phones and monetary donations from families when they arrive to your event.

4. Have families check the donated cell phones to make sure each one is turned off. Keep the battery included for each cell phone if possible.

5. Talk about the VFW Free Call Dates and Sponsors, which can be downloaded for free from the VFW Operation Uplink website. Discuss reasons why the VFW might have chosen the call dates that it did.

6. Count the number of cell phones and the amount of money donated. Have a volunteer make your group's donation to your recipient organization.

Debriefing the Project

- What do families usually do with old, unused cell phones? Why?
- Why is it a good idea to donate our old, unused cell phones?
- What would it be like not to be able to talk to someone in your family for months?
- Why is it important to keep in touch by phone? How is that different from email?

- How else can we raise funds to keep soldiers in touch with their families?

Helpful Resources

- For children: *My Big Brother* by Miriam Cohen (Star Bright Books, 2005), a story of a young boy coping with the pain and loss he feels when his older brother joins the army.
- For teens: *Flags of Our Fathers: A Young People's Edition* by James Bradley adapted by Micheal French (Laurel-Leaf, 2005). A true story about the heroic battle of Iwo Jima in 1945, as told by the son of one of the six soldiers who raised the American flag in the famous photograph.

Bonus Ideas

- Tell stories and read letters from soldiers who have benefited from this service project. Click on "Letters & Stories" on the Cell Phones for Soldiers website.
- Sign up for the free e-newsletter at the VFW Operation Uplink website. Among other news and information, you will receive free updates letting you know how phone cards lift the spirits of America's military members.
- Consider doing this project in conjunction with another short project, such as project 58: Operation GI Bracelet or 64: Operation Email.

63 Operation Give

Purpose

Collect small toys for and send a greeting to a child in a war zone.

Possible Recipients

- Operation Give at www.operationgive.org (click on "Operation Joys for Toys")

Time Requirement

Planning time before the project: one to two hours. Gathering materials: one hour. Setup time on the day of your project: 30 minutes to an hour. Project time: one hour.

People

This project is ideal for families with children between the ages of 3 and 18.

Materials

- Enough copies of the "Toys for Children in War Zones" handout (page 152) to publicize your event with families
- Lots of small toys
- 1 digital camera for every 10 families
- A way to print pictures
- 1 shipping box for every 20 to 30 toys
- 1 roll of packing tape
- 1 permanent marker

Families will donate the toys.

Connecting Point

Because of war in their countries, many children have been forced to leave their homes (and their belongings) behind. Many children no longer have much of anything, let alone anything to play with. Help make life a bit brighter for a child in a war zone by donating small toys. Using the information provided at their website, talk about Operation Give.

Doing the Project

1. Before your event, learn more about Operation Give through its website so you can make the case for why it's important to support it.
2. Distribute the "Toys for Children in War Zones" handout and encourage families to be as generous as possible.
3. At your event, have families take turns showing what they brought and explaining why.
4. Take a photograph of families holding individual toys. (If families brought more than one toy, have them take a photo with each toy brought.) Encourage families to smile. Explain how the children will each receive a toy and the photograph so they can see who gave it to them. If you have more than one camera, set up multiple photographing stations so families don't have to wait long to be photographed.

5. Place all the donated toys and photographs in a shipping box. Seal it, address it, and ship it to the address given at the Operation Give website.

Debriefing the Project

- What was it like to find a toy to donate to a child in a war zone?
- Why did we include a photograph with the toy?
- Why is it important to help children in war zones?
- What other ways could we support children living with war?

Helpful Resources

- For children: *The Soldier's Tree* by Stephanie L. Pickup (T.A.O. Army Kids Publishing, 2004), a true story about a family who sends a Christmas tree to their deployed father.
- For teens: *Saving Babylon* by Paul Holton (Perihelion Press, 2005), the true story of how Operation Give got started, written by an American soldier fighting in Iraq who befriended many Iraqi children.

Bonus Ideas

- Operation Give suggests a number of family service projects. At the website, explore other projects, such as Operation Christmas Stocking, Operation Play Baseball, Operation Play Soccer, Operation Health, Operation Clean Teeth, Operation Back to School, Operation Blossom, Operation GoodWill, Operation Troop Support, and Operation Medical Supplies.
- Incorporate some of the news items and news stories posted at the Operation Give website when you discuss the connecting point for this project. For example, families are often inspired when they hear of other groups donating toys. Click on "News" and then "News Clips."

(64) Operation Email

Purpose

Send email messages to servicepeople currently deployed.

Possible Recipients

- A Million Thanks at www.amillionthanks.org

Time Requirement

Planning time before the project: one to two hours. Setup time on the day of your project: 30 minutes to an hour. Project time: 30 minutes.

People

This project is ideal for families with children between the ages of 5 and 18.

Materials

- 1 computer with Internet access for every 2 families

Contact a local school or library that has a computer lab or a group of computers where you might be able to host this event, or perhaps you can use a room with Wi-Fi in your own building. Encourage families to bring their laptops and smart phones, too, if they have them.

Connecting Point

Many troops deployed overseas use the Internet as a way to communicate. Emails are quick and easy to send. By sending a short email message, you can let soldiers know that you're thinking of them and supporting them.

Doing the Project

1. Visit the website of A Million Thanks at www.amillionthanks.org and click on "Visit the 'America Supports You'" listed on the main page. Learn as much as you can about the organization so you can make the case about why it's important to send email to the troops.

2. Figure out the best way to set up your emailing event. Will you approach a local school or library that has a lot of computers? Does your organization have a computer room or a Wi-Fi spot where families can use laptops and smart phones?

3. When families arrive for your event, walk them through the steps of sending an email through the A Million Thanks website. Once they click on "Visit 'America Supports you'," an easy-to-use email form pops up that asks for the user's name, hometown, state, and message. Families can send as many messages as they would like.

4. If families don't know what to write (it can feel strange to send a note to someone you've never met and whose name you don't know), have them click on "Read Messages of Support" for examples. You may be able to suggest ideas, too, based on the research you've done at the A Million Thanks website.

5. Be clear that these email letters are meant to send good wishes and support. Encourage those who have different opinions or motives to channel their thoughts by writing letters to the editor or to members of Congress. This is not a forum for debating military policy.

Debriefing the Project

- How do you like to communicate best: by writing letters, sending emails, talking on the phone, or talking in person? Why?

- Why do you think email messages are so popular with troops deployed overseas?

- Why would it be harder to communicate with troops overseas via a cell phone or instant messaging?

- What else can we do to support our troops?

Helpful Resources

- For children: *Love Lizzie: Letters to a Military Mom* by Lisa Tucker McElroy (Albert Whitman, 2005), a story about nine-year-old Lizzie, who writes to her mother deployed overseas during wartime.

- For teens: *Across Five Aprils* by Irene Hunt (Berkley, 2002), a story about Jethro Creighton, who must watch his brothers go off to fight in the Civil War on opposing sides.

Bonus Ideas

- Encourage families to give each other their email addresses to build community, keep in touch, and give each other ideas on how to serve others.
- Consider being in regular contact with a specific platoon. Visit Adopt a Platoon at www.adoptaplatoon.org. This type of service project requires an ongoing commitment.
- If some in your organization have friends or family who are deployed, tell them about the free Happy Day Cards website at www .happydaycards.com. Click on "Complete listing of all the categories" then click on "Military Thank-You ecards." Encourage them to find an email card they would like to send.
- Consider doing this project in conjunction with another short project, such as project 58: Operation GI Bracelet.

(65) Operation Helmetliner

Purpose

Help deployed troops deal with subzero wind chills during the winter and extreme heat during the summer by knitting or crocheting helmet liners, scarves, and neck coolers.

Possible Recipients

- Operation Helmetliner, which is part of Citizen Support for America's Military (CitizenSAM) at www.citizensam.org. Click on "Operation Helmetliner."

Time Requirement

Planning time before the project: one to three hours. Gathering materials: one to two hours. Setup time on the day of your project: one to two hours. Project time: 90 minutes to two hours. Follow-up meeting: 30 minutes.

People

This project is ideal for families with children between the ages of 12 and 18. Expect each person to begin to knit one helmet liner during the 90-minute to two-hour event.

You will need volunteers who are good at knitting to teach family members and help people when they get stuck throughout the project. Ask one of these knitters to help gather supplies and materials.

Materials

- Soft, worsted (100 grams/3.5 ounces) wool yarn for each helmet liner in black, charcoal, brown, tan, gray, or combinations of these colors
- 1 size 8 16-inch circular needle, or size to get gauge for each person
- 1 size 8 double-point needle for each person
- 1 size 6 16-inch circular needles for each person (for ribbings)
- 1 stitch marker for each person
- 1 copy of the helmet liner knitting instructions for each person
- Shipping supplies

The helmet liner instructions are available at the Operation Helmetliner website. Have someone familiar with knitting help gather the knitting materials. Each helmet liner requires soft, worsted (100 grams/3.5 ounces) wool yarn that will knit to gauge, such as Cascade 220, with a label that states it's for size 7 needle, 5 stitches per 1 inch and for size 8 needle, 4½ stitches per inch, approximately 175 yards. The materials are available at fabric stores such as Jo-Ann Fabrics & Crafts and Hancock Fabrics.

Connecting Point

Many troops fight in extreme temperatures—bitter cold in the winter and extreme heat in the summer. They may be very uncomfortable while serving their country for us. We can help our soldiers feel more comfortable by knitting or crocheting helmet liners and scarves for the winter and neck coolers for the summer.

Doing the Project

1. Before you do this project, make sure you have carefully read the knitting instructions from the website. Learn more about the organization so you can make the case for why it's important to support it.

2. Set the date for your event and begin recruiting volunteers (both your organizing volunteers and the families you want to attend your event) about one month in advance.

3. If possible, have a volunteer knit a sample helmet liner to understand how they're made and to show families what they look like. Or print out a color photo of the helmet liner from the CitizenSAM website.

4. When families arrive at your event, distribute the materials and instructions for knitting. Have your volunteers start out by teaching people how to knit as needed. As families get started, your volunteers should answer questions as they come up, since first-time knitters often run into problems. This is a great mentoring service project that teaches others the art of knitting or crocheting.

5. Knitting and crocheting are projects that require a lot of time. This service project can only get people started. They can then take home their projects and finish them on their own. Or you can create a series of helmet liner service projects where families get together to knit and talk.

6. Set a deadline (about two weeks to one month later) for helmet liners to be finished.

(Otherwise it will be easy for families not to finish their projects.) Get together with your group to show each other your creations and ship them to the CitizenSAM (see the website for the address).

Debriefing the Project

- Have you ever been in extreme cold or extreme heat? When? What was it like?

- How did you keep comfortable when you were in extreme cold or heat?

- Why is it helpful to learn how to knit or crochet?

- Why is it good to do service projects that require more of our time and talent sometimes?

- What else could we do to support our troops?

Helpful Resources

- For children: *While You Are Away* by Eileen Spinelli (Hyperion Books for Children, 2004), a book that includes the stories of three children describing how it feels to have one of their parents away on military tour of duty.

- For teens: *Knitting for Peace: Make the World a Better Place One Stitch at a Time* by Betty Christiansen (Stewart, Tabori & Chang, 2006), a book that includes 28 contemporary knitting-for-peace endeavors along with patterns for easy-to-knit projects.

Bonus Ideas

- Tap into the interests of all kinds of different people who enjoy sewing, knitting, and crocheting and have them participate by using other patterns listed on the CitizenSAM website. The neck cooler can be made with a sewing machine or serger. The scarf can be knitted or crocheted. The helmet liner also can be made on a knitting machine.

- When you're presenting the project with the Connecting Point information, consider including news stories about Operation Helmetliner, which you can find at the website.

- The CitizenSAM website also has other projects for you to consider, such as Quilts for Our Wounded, Operation Santa, and Adopt a Soldier.

Help Create a School Kit for Children Living in War Zones

You're invited to help children living in war-torn countries by creating school kits for them. Come to our event:

Date: _____

Time: _____

Place: _____

Please bring the following NEW items:

_____ One pair of blunt-end scissors

_____ One 12-inch ruler with metric markings

_____ 12 new pencils with erasers

_____ One small pencil sharpener

_____ One large eraser

_____ One box of colored pencils (crayons melt in the summer heat of many countries)

_____ One package of notebook paper

_____ One composition book

_____ Three folders with inside pockets

_____ One zippered pencil bag

Toys for Children Living in War Zones

Because of war in their countries, many children have very little. Please help us collect small toys and donate them at our event to support children living in war zones.

Date: _____

Time: _____

Place: _____

Ideas of what to bring:

- Small dolls
- Small trucks and cars
- Balls (such as soccer balls)
- Small stuffed animals
- Small plastic animals or dinosaurs
- Small tool and cooking sets
- Small puzzles
- Basic Legos®
- Block sets
- Jump ropes
- Frisbees®
- Picture books
- Baby toys
- Stacking cups
- Shape sorters
- Chess sets
- Art supplies (such as colored pencils, pastels, markers, brushes, paint sets, paper, chalk, and so on)

Chapter 8
Projects to Celebrate Holidays and Special Occasions

Many families like to do service projects during holidays to emphasize the spirit of giving. Recipients also appreciate the gesture, because holidays can be a difficult time. Being in poor health or disconnected from family can be especially painful during times when others are celebrating.

Since many families like to do service projects particularly during the winter holidays, this section focuses more heavily on winter holidays than other holidays. Many projects can be modified, though, to be done not only during the December holidays but also on other holidays throughout the year. Some projects also are associated with a particular religious holiday or a religious organization, but these, too, can easily be modified as needed. What's important is to provide families with opportunities to enjoy "the spirit of giving."

(66) Giving Tree

Purpose

Collect new toys to give as gifts to children in need during the holidays.

Possible Recipients

- Local options: an emergency food shelf, homeless shelter, domestic-abuse shelter, community kitchen, or some other type of social agency
- Other options: The Salvation Army's Holiday Angel Tree Program (www.salvationarmyusa.org) and the Marine Toys for Tots Foundation (www.toysfortots.org)

Time Requirement

Planning time before the project: one to two hours. Gathering materials: one hour. Setup time on the day of your project: one to two hours. Project time: 30 minutes.

People

This project is ideal for families with children between the ages of 3 and 18. Expect each family to bring one gift to the 30-minute event.

You may need one or more volunteers to help cut out bulletin-board shapes.

Materials

- 1 piece of posterboard in green or brown
- Bulletin board or a blank wall
- Cutout bulletin-board shapes appropriate for winter holidays, such as snowmen, ornament balls, candles, dreidels, stars, and hearts, one for each gift
- 3 pairs of scissors
- 1 paper-hole punch
- 1 ribbon for each bulletin-board shape
- 1 thumbtack for each bulletin-board shape
- 3 fine-tip black markers
- 1 roll of masking tape

If you have access to bulletin-board paper rolls (which schools and youth organizations often have), consider using that instead of posterboard. You can buy cutout shapes or make them from colored construction paper.

Connecting Point

Many families struggle with finances over the winter holidays, and some parents have a difficult time buying gifts for their children. Make it easier for them by buying gifts that they can give. Talk about the recipient organization.

Doing the Project

1. Well before your event, call the organization you wish to serve and ask about the process for donating gifts. If they will supply a list of gift ideas, along with the age and gender of each child requesting each gift, get it.

2. Decorate a large bulletin board with a holiday theme appropriate to your organization. For example, consider making a large Christmas tree out of posterboard or construction paper.

3. If you are making your own holiday shapes, make them before your event.

4. Write a suggestion of a toy from the recipient organization's list on each cutout. If your recipient organization didn't supply a list, create a variety of ideas for both boys and girls.

5. On each decoration, list *boy* or *girl*, the age of child the gift is appropriate for, and the gift idea. Place the decorations on the paper tree by using a ribbon and thumbtack.

6. Publicize your event through your organization, giving families two to three weeks to pick a decoration off your tree and go shopping before your event. Tell them to keep their gift-idea decoration, tape it to the gift they bought, and bring the gift to your event unwrapped.

7. At your event, have families help sort the gifts first by gender and then by age. Your recipient organization will usually want the decoration with the gift information taped to the unwrapped gift.

8. Count the number of gifts given and donate them to your recipient organization.

Debriefing the Project

- What was it like to buy a holiday gift for a child you did not know?
- What do you think the holidays would be like if your family couldn't afford holiday gifts? Why?
- Why is it important to donate toys to families in need during the holidays?
- What other ways could we help families in need during the holidays?

Helpful Resources

- For children: *Happy Hanukkah, Corduroy* by Lisa McCue (Viking, 2009), a story about Corduroy celebrating Hanukkah with his friends. *Great Joy* by Kate DiCamillo (Candlewick Press, 2007), a story about Frances, who sees a sad organ grinder and his monkey performing for pennies just before Christmas.

- For teens: *Hanukkah Lights: Stories of the Season* by Susan Stamberg and Murray Horwitz (Melcher Media, 2005), a number of short stories about Hanukkah from a variety of thoughtful authors. *Love, Santa: A Different Kind of Christmas Story* by Sharon Glassman (Warner Books, 2002), a true story about the author, who wanted to make Christmas more meaningful. When she discovered the post office's "Operation Santa Claus" in New York City, she began to help kids in need.

Bonus Ideas

- Set up an actual tree (artificial or real) and place the paper gift-idea cutouts on it instead of a bulletin-board tree.
- Ask the recipient organization if you can bring the gifts wrapped (with a sticky note on top that says what the gift contains). Some organizations may appreciate your families wrapping the gifts.
- Make links from construction paper strips to create a red-and-green or blue-and-silver garland in which each link represents a gift given. Display the paper chain to show how many gifts were donated.

67 Caring Cookies

Purpose

Decorate holiday cookies to give to people who usually wouldn't receive any.

Possible Recipients

- A local nursing home, local Meals on Wheels chapter, congregation that has a number of homebound members, or some other senior agency

Time Requirement

Planning time before the project: one to three hours. Gathering materials: one to two hours.

Setup time on the day of your project: one to two hours. Project time: one to two hours.

People

This project is ideal for families with children between the ages of 3 and 18. Expect each participant to decorate about 10 to 25 cookies.

Materials

- 10 to 25 premade sugar or gingerbread cookies (plain and undecorated) for each person
- Cookie frosting in different colors, enough to decorate all the cookies you plan to make

- 3 jars of sprinkles, candies, or other sugar-cookie toppings for every 2 families
- 1 butter knife for each person
- 1 to 2 boxes of wax paper
- Shallow boxes or cookie tins to put the decorated cookies in
- 3 to 4 bottles of hand sanitizer

You can find shallow boxes or cookie tins from the baking department of a craft store.

Connecting Point

Decorated cookies are part of winter holidays, and they not only taste good but also stir up warm memories for many people. Decorate cookies to donate to those who are homebound or living in nursing homes.

Doing the Project

1. Before the family service event, purchase premade, unfrosted sugar and/or gingerbread cookies.

2. The day of your event, create family cookie-decorating stations at your meeting site by putting out lots of wax paper, cookies, frosting, cookie toppings, and knives.

3. Have families sanitize their hands before they begin to decorate cookies. If you have many preschoolers, have them add the toppings once someone older has frosted the cookies. If you have many teenagers, challenge them to create intricate designs.

4. Box up the finished cookies and have volunteers deliver them to your recipients.

Debriefing the Project

- Why are frosted, decorated cookies an important part of the holidays?
- What did you talk about as you decorated the cookies?
- Why does it matter that we think of others during the holidays?
- How else could we help those in need during the holidays?

Helpful Resources

- For children: *Baker, Baker, Cookie Maker* by Linda Hayward (Random House, 1998), a story about Sesame Street's Cookie Monster, who bakes beautiful cookies.
- For teens: *Cookie Craft: From Baking to Luster Dust, Designs and Techniques for Creative Cookie Occasions* by Valerie Peterson (Storey Publishing, 2007), which provides instructions for creating elaborately decorated cookies.

Bonus Ideas

- Some organizations assign each family to bake three dozen of their favorite holiday cookies and then bring them to an event to donate. (You'll get a large variety of cookies this way.) Other organizations have access to a large kitchen, and families spend three to four hours baking a variety of holiday cookies on-site.
- Consider having a holiday bake sale after baking and decorating cookies and donating the money you raise. Or sell half the cookies and donate the other half to the recipient organization.
- Decorated cookies are also a big hit for other holidays, such as Valentine's Day, Easter, Halloween, and Thanksgiving.
- Create personalized notes or cards to accompany the cookies.

(68) Holiday Shoe Boxes

Purpose

Pack shoe boxes with small gifts to give to children who may go without any gifts during the holidays.

Possible Recipients

- A local homeless shelter, domestic-abuse shelter, community kitchen, or some other type of shelter
- Operation Christmas Child, a program of Samaritan's Purse (www.samaritanspurse.org)

Time Requirement

Planning time before the project: one to two hours. Gathering materials: one hour. Setup time on the day of your project: 30 minutes to an hour. Project time: one hour.

People

This project is ideal for families with children between the ages of 3 and 18. Expect each family to make one shoe box during the one-hour event.

Materials

- Enough copies of the "Shoe-Box Goodies" handout (page 167) to publicize your event with families
- Empty shoe boxes with covers
- Bulk holiday wrapping paper in different styles and colors
- 1 roll of transparent tape for each family
- 1 pair of scissors for each family
- 1 to 2 pieces of 8½" x 11" white paper for each family
- 5 washable markers in various colors for each family
- 1 large rubber band for each shoe box
- 1 sticky gift label for each shoe box

Families will bring their own shoe boxes, but you may want to bring a few extra for those who forget. You can often find inexpensive, bulk wrapping paper at party-supply stores.

Connecting Point

Many children are very poor and do not receive any gifts during the winter holidays. Give them a shoe box filled with gifts to brighten their holidays. By filling up shoe boxes with gifts, we can make a difference in the holidays of the children we serve. One organization, Samaritan's Purse, has donated more than 61 million gift-filled shoe boxes around the world, thanks to caring individuals and families, since 1993. (Substitute information about whatever organization will be benefitting from your project if necessary.)

Doing the Project

1. Before your event, call the organization you wish to serve and ask about the process for donating items for this family service project.

2. Distribute photocopies of the "Shoe-Box Goodies" handout in advance, early enough so families have time to gather items.

3. Make a sample gift shoe box so you know how it's put together and to show as an example.

4. As families arrive to your event, let them circulate and see what everyone brought.

5. Have everyone wrap their shoe boxes. Make sure they wrap the cover separately from the box so it can be removed without opening the wrapping paper.

6. Give each family a sticky gift label. On it, have them note whether the box is intended for a boy or girl and the age range. Place the sticky label on top of the wrapped cover.

7. Have families fill their shoe boxes with the gift items. See if families have any extra items that don't fit into their box for another family to use in their box (or to create other boxes).

8. Have families make a handmade card using the white paper and washable markers, and place the card inside the box when they're finished.

9. Place a rubber band around each shoe box to keep it from spilling open during the drop-off.

Debriefing the Project

- What did you think about as you wrapped the box and placed the items inside?
- If you received one of these boxes, what would you think? Why?
- What else can we do during the holidays to help those with few economic resources?

Helpful Resources

- For children: *The Ziz and the Hanukkah Miracle* by Jacqueline Jules (Kar-Ben Publishers, 2006), a story about Ziz, a clumsy bird that helps the Macabees find enough oil to create a miracle. *A Charlie Brown Christmas* directed by Bill Melendez, based on the book by Charles Schulz (Paramount Pictures, 2000), a Christmas classic about Charlie Brown and the Peanuts gang discovering the real meaning of the season.

- For teens: *Thanks & Giving: All Year Long* edited by Marlo Thomas and Christopher Cerf (Simon & Schuster Children's Publishing, 2005), a collection of stories, poems, and songs by famous authors and celebrities that celebrate love, sharing, gratitude, family, and friendship.

Bonus Ideas

- If you have access to a computer, the Internet, and a projector, consider showing the video about Operation Christmas Child from the Samaritan's Purse website (www.samaritanspurse .org). View it first, however, to make sure it's appropriate for your organization.

- For one week in November every year, volunteers in 2,000 locations around the country help get the word out and provide a drop-off site for community members to create shoebox donations. Visit the Operation Christmas Child website for details if your group may be interested in doing this sometime.

69 Holiday Gifts That Matter

Purpose

Contribute to your community by giving the gift of time during the winter holidays.

Possible Recipients

- Family members, friends, extended family members, neighbors, work colleagues, or others in your community

Time Requirement

Planning time before the project: one to two hours. Gathering materials: one hour. Setup time on the day of your project: 30 minutes to an hour. Project time: one hour.

People

This project is ideal for families with children between the ages of 3 and 18. Expect each family to make one to three coupon books during the one-hour event.

Materials

- 3 copies of the "Giving Coupons" handout (page 168) for each person
- 3 pieces of 8½" x 11" white paper for each family
- 1 pair of scissors for each family
- 5 washable markers in various colors for each family
- 5 crayons in various colors for each family
- 1 stapler for every 2 families

Connecting Point

It may be easy to buy someone a gift, but often a better gift is our time. Think about people you know who would benefit from a booklet of coupons good for favors, chores, and other gifts of time from you. Maybe there's a homebound person in your neighborhood. Maybe you have a frail extended family member or you know a new mom. Think of ways you can be helpful to them and put your ideas into coupons they can redeem with you at any time.

Doing the Project

1. Before your event, make a sample coupon book to show as an example.

2. Copy the "Giving Coupons" handout so you have at least three for each person attending the event. (You can also provide blank paper and let families design their own coupons.)

3. At the event, have the group brainstorm helpful coupon ideas, such as playing a game together, mowing the lawn, running an errand, serving breakfast in bed, cleaning up your room, helping with homework, raking leaves, taking out the garbage, baking a batch of cookies, setting the table, cleaning out a closet, picking up the mail and newspapers while you're away, walking the dog, and so on. Encourage family members to write down ideas they like.

4. Have families decide if they are making one coupon book for one person or if they are making multiple coupon books for several recipients. Coupon books don't need to be thick. Sometimes three coupons is a great gift.

5. Give families time to write their names and what they're giving on each coupon. Also encourage them to draw and color pictures on each coupon to make them more festive and colorful. (Children often enjoy doing this.) Then have them cut out the individual coupons from the sheets.

6. Have families make a cover by cutting out a piece of white paper the same size as the coupons and decorating it with markers and crayons.

7. When families have finished, have them stack the coupons and the cover, and then staple their coupon books together. Allow families to take their coupon books to give as gifts.

Debriefing the Project

- How easy was it to think of someone to give your coupons to?

- How did you decide which coupons would be most worthwhile for the person you're giving them to?

- Why is a coupon book sometimes a better present than a gift you buy?

- What else can we do to help others?

Helpful Resources

- For children: *Let's Share, Grumpy Bunny* by Justine Korman Fontes (Scholastic, 2009), a story about a bunny who refuses to help others.

- For teens: *The Better World Handbook: Small Changes that Make a Big Difference* by Ellis Jones, Ross Haenfler, and Brett Johnson (New Society Publishers, 2007), a helpful book about how to be a better citizen by changing how you shop, travel, eat, spend money, and more.

Bonus Ideas

- Before the holidays, consider having a family service project where you put children and adults in different rooms and let them make gifts for each other. (This can be especially valuable if you have a community with many single-parent families, in which it can be difficult for kids to figure out on their own the logistics of getting gifts for their parents.)

- Coupon books are not only ideal for the winter holidays but also for Mother's Day, Father's Day, and Grandparents Day (the first Sunday after Labor Day). Learn more about Grandparents Day at www.grandparents-day.com.

(70) May-Day Baskets

Purpose

Brighten the day of people in your community by surprising them with May-Day baskets full of goodies.

Possible Recipients

- A local nursing home, Meals on Wheels chapter, congregation that has a number of homebound members, or some other senior agency

Time Requirement

Planning time before the project: one to two hours. Gathering materials: one hour. Setup time on the day of your project: 30 minutes to an hour. Project time: one hour.

People

This project is ideal for families with children between the ages of 3 and 18. Expect families to make 1 to 3 baskets at the event.

Materials

- 2 to 3 pieces of 8½" x 11" construction paper in a variety of colors for each person
- 5 washable markers in various colors for each family
- 1 stapler for every 2 families
- 1 roll of transparent tape for every 2 families
- Small items to place inside the baskets, such as hard candies, lollipops, mints, small bars of soap, small containers of hand lotion, small packs of nuts, small packs of granola bars, tea bags, and so on

  Ask families to donate the items to fill baskets.

Connecting Point

May Day is a holiday rooted in Celtic and German cultures, a celebration of the hard winter coming to an end for the northern climates. Traditionally, May Day has signaled the beginning of summer, and to celebrate people have anonymously left baskets of flowers and treats on people's doors. Talk about your chosen recipients and what the baskets may mean to them. Many elderly people remember the May-Day basket tradition and would enjoy the surprise of an anonymous May-Day basket left at their door.

Doing the Project

1. Before your event, publicize the event with families and ask them to bring small items to fill the May-Day baskets.

2. Make a sample May-Day basket so you know how it's put together and to show as an example. Research the history and meaning of May Day and May-Day baskets if you wish to discuss that in much depth at your event.

3. When families arrive to your event, give them a brief overview of May Day. In some cultures, it's like a Labor Day. In other cultures, it's a day to signify the beginning of summer, since warm weather tends to arrive around that day. Talk about the tradition of May-Day baskets.

4. Distribute the colored construction paper and have family members decorate it with washable markers.

5. Show families how to make a cone-shaped basket from their paper by curling it lengthwise, tightly at one end, so it forms a cone. Staple and tape the basket so the hole at the bottom is very small (and items cannot fall out).

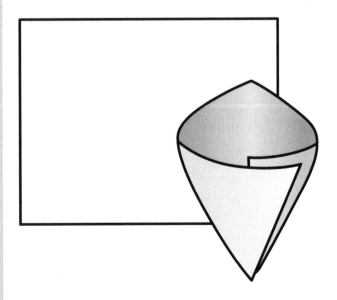

6. Make a handle out of construction paper by cutting a 1-inch wide piece that is 11 inches long. (Each sheet of construction paper should make eight handles.) Staple the handle to the May-Day basket.

7. Fill the basket with treats. Deliver them on May Day (May 1), hanging them on the recipients' doorknobs. You may want to have a volunteer deliver the baskets to one location, deliver them as a group, or let families take the baskets with them and deliver them to recipients on their own.

Debriefing the Project

- Had you ever heard of May Day before this event? When?
- Why are May-Day baskets an unusual yet meaningful service project?
- How would you react if you opened your door and found a May-Day basket hanging on it? Why?
- What else can we do to let people know that we're thinking of them?

Helpful Resources

- For children: *The Rainbow Tulip* by Pat Mora (Puffin, 2003), about first-grader Estelita who learns to love her dual Mexican-American heritage at a May-Day parade with the help of her rainbow tulip costume.
- For teens: *Beltane: Springtime Rituals, Lore, & Celebration* by Raven Grimassi (Llewellyn Publications, 2001), a book about the origins of May-Day festivals that also includes crafts and recipes to celebrate the holiday.

Bonus Ideas

- Consider buying small, inexpensive annuals and planting them in individual pots (that you can decorate) and giving them as May-Day gifts.
- Some neighborhoods are attempting to create rituals to connect neighbors and build a sense of community. Annual May-Day baskets can aid with this, although it's helpful to include a note with the May-Day basket so neighbors know why they're being given.
- Consider adding a personalized note that says "Happy May Day."

71 A Chain of Treats

Purpose

Bring Halloween to senior residents and give them a treat to enjoy for many days.

Possible Recipients

- A local nursing home, Meals on Wheels chapter, congregation that has a number of homebound members, or some other senior agency

Time Requirement

Planning time before the project: one to two hours. Gathering materials: one hour. Setup time on the day of your project: 30 minutes to an hour. Project time: 30 minutes.

People

This project is ideal for families with children between the ages of 3 and 18. Expect each family to make one chain of treats during the 30-minute event.

Materials

- 16 individually wrapped pieces of hard candy and/or lollipops for each chain (hard candy and lollipops that can be easily taped or stapled to construction paper)
- 1 roll of transparent tape for every 2 families
- 1 stapler for every 2 families
- 2 pieces of 8½" x 11" construction paper in black and orange for each chain

- 1 pair of scissors for each family
- 1 ruler, yardstick, or measuring tape for each family

Connecting Point

Many older people enjoyed Halloween when they were younger but can no longer participate in the holiday for health reasons. Bring Halloween to them (and make it last for weeks) by creating yardstick-long candy treats.

Doing the Project

1. Before your event, make a sample chain of treats so you know how it's put together and to show as an example.

2. Distribute one piece of black and one piece of orange construction paper to each family and have them cut out six 3" x 3" shapes from each piece. They may cut out circles or triangles, or even ghosts or other Halloween shapes. It's up to each family how creative they want to be.

3. Have families add one to two pieces of candy (depending on the size of the candy) with tape or a stapler to each shape.

4. Have families connect all the shapes together with tape or a stapler to create a 3-foot-long chain of treats.

5. If you have candy and construction paper left over, make more chains until you've used all your supplies. Have volunteers donate the chains to the organization you're serving.

Debriefing the Project

- What shapes did you cut out? Why?
- What would you think if you received a Halloween treat like this? Why?
- Why is Halloween a holiday for old people as well as for the young?
- How else can we connect with elderly people who may be isolated?

Helpful Resources

- For children: *Uncle Willie and the Soup Kitchen* by DyAnne DiSalvo-Ryan (HarperCollins 1997), a story about a young boy who helps his Uncle Willie at a community kitchen.
- For teens: *The Power of Giving: How Giving Back Will Enrich Us All* by Azim Jamal (Tarcher, 2009), a book that shows the benefits of giving and volunteering.

Bonus Ideas

- Consider doing this activity near Valentine's Day and make red heart shapes from the construction paper. Or cut shamrock shapes for St. Patrick's Day, Mexican flags for Cinco de Mayo, snowball shapes for the first day of winter, flower shapes for the first day of spring, yellow sun circles for the first day of summer, or leaf shapes for the first day of autumn.
- You can also get precut shapes from teacher- and educational-supply stores. (These precut shapes are often used with bulletin boards.)

(72) Valentine's Day Banners

Purpose

Remind elderly or sick people that they are cared for around Valentine's Day with a large sign.

Possible Recipients

- A local nursing home or some other senior agency, a group home for disabled adults, or a hospital pediatric ward or some other long-term clinic for kids

Time Requirement

Planning time before the project: one to two hours. Gathering materials: one hour. Setup time on the day of your project: 30 minutes to an hour. Project time: one hour.

People

This project is ideal for families with children between the ages of 3 and 18. Expect four to six people to make one banner during the one-hour event.

Materials

- 1 piece of 6-foot-long butcher paper or bulletin-board background paper (or 4 pieces of 11" x 17" paper) for every 4 to 6 people
- 5 washable markers in various colors for each family
- 1 pair of scissors for each banner
- 1 roll of transparent tape (if you're using 11" x 17" paper) for each banner

You can find rolls of white butcher paper at Office Depot or www.discountschoolsupply.com.

Connecting Point

When you're stuck in bed in a hospital, nursing home, or some other place that doesn't feel like home, you often feel alone and isolated. We can show our care for people in these situations by making a colorful banner to give them around Valentine's Day. Even though these residents are strangers, they like to be reminded that people love them. Most likely, they will remember the people they love every time they look at the banner, which is why these banners are so important.

Doing the Project

1. Before your event, make a sample banner to show as an example.

2. As families arrive to your event, have them help you unroll the butcher paper or bulletin-board paper and cut off a piece about 6 feet long for each banner you plan to make. If you're using 11" x 17" paper, tape together four pieces the long way so it's close to six-feet long. Turn it over so the tape is on the back. (It's difficult to draw with markers over tape.) Make one banner for every four to six people at your project.

3. Ask for volunteers who have good penmanship and who enjoy writing large letters. Have each of those people use washable markers to write "Happy Valentine's Day" in large letters across each banner.

4. Have families create small groups of four to six people so that each group is working on a separate banner. Have families draw pictures and add decorations to their banner with washable markers.

5. When families finish, have them sign their first names on each of the banners. Having a lot of first names shows the recipients how many people care about them.

Debriefing the Project

- What was it like to make a banner for someone you didn't know?
- How would you feel if you received a banner like this? Why?
- Why is it important to let people know they're loved and cared for?
- How else can we show people that we care?

Helpful Resources

- For children: *Somebody Loves You, Mr. Hatch* by Eileen Spinelli (Simon and Schuster, 1991), the story of how an anonymous gift changes Mr. Hatch from a crabby, lonely man into everyone's friend. *Chicken Soup for Little Souls: The Goodness Gorillas* by Lisa McCourt (Health Communications, Inc., 1997), a feel-good story about the importance of reaching out to others—even the class bully.

- For teens: *Pay It Forward* by Catherine Ryan Hyde (Simon & Schuster, 2010), a novel about 12-year-old Trevor, who does something good for three people and asks them to "pay it forward" to three more people, who in turn would help three others.

Bonus Ideas

- Share information from a thought-provoking article from the American Psychological Association, titled "What Makes Kids Care? Teaching Gentleness in a Violent World." Find the free article by searching at www.apa.org for "Teaching Gentleness in a Violent World."

- Make "Welcome Home" banners for students when they return from class trips, "Welcome to the World" banners for pediatric wards, or "Welcome to Your Family" at international adoption arrivals at the airport.

(73) Birthday Buckets

Purpose

Help a person in need have a happy birthday by supplying all the essential ingredients for a party.

Possible Recipients

- A local emergency food shelf, homeless shelter, domestic-abuse shelter, community kitchen, or other type of social agency that works with the poor

Time Requirement

Planning time before the project: one to two hours. Gathering materials: one hour. Setup time on the day of your project: 30 minutes to an hour. Project time: 30 minutes.

People

This project is ideal for families with children between the ages of 3 and 18.

Materials

- Colored bulletin-board paper, or colored construction paper to fit your bulletin board or display
- A bulletin board or a blank wall
- 1 pair of scissors for each family
- 5 washable markers in various colors for each family
- 3 to 4 pieces of colored construction paper for each birthday bucket
- 2 feet of ribbon for each birthday bucket
- 1 roll of transparent tape for every two families
- 1 empty, clean, plastic ice-cream bucket for each birthday bucket
- 1 cake mix for each birthday bucket
- 1 cake frosting in a can for each birthday bucket
- 1 box of birthday candles for each birthday bucket
- 1 package of 8 small birthday paper plates for each birthday bucket
- 1 package of 8 birthday paper napkins for each birthday bucket
- 1 bag of balloons for each birthday bucket

Ask families to donate the birthday bucket items, including the bucket itself.

Connecting Point

We often take our birthdays for granted. We have decorations. We have cake. We have presents. Every child deserves these things, but not every child gets them. Make a birthday a day of celebration for children in need by creating birthday buckets.

Doing the Project

1. Before the event, create a bulletin board or wall display (or ask for a volunteer to do this). Cut a large birthday cake out of paper. Then cut individual candles out of paper and write a different ingredient for a birthday bucket on each one. The ingredients for one bucket include cake mix, cake frosting in a can, box of birthday candles, package of eight birthday small paper plates, eight napkins, bag of balloons, and a bucket. Be sure the total number of paper candles will make enough complete birthday buckets for your group. There are six ingredients in a complete bucket, so 36 paper candles will make six birthday buckets. Place the paper candles on the paper cake on your display.

2. Publicize your event and ask families to take at least one paper candle from the display and buy the item listed on it. Allow a week or so for them to shop.

3. If you wish to get more donations, consider setting up a donation box for the birthday bucket ingredients and supplies. Sometimes families who cannot attend your event will want to contribute.

4. Consider creating a birthday-party setting for your service project. Decorate the room and serve birthday cake. (You often can purchase

sheet cake for an inexpensive price at a grocery store.)

5. Make a sample birthday bucket to show as an example.

6. When families arrive at your event, have them place their donations into separate piles— all the cake mixes together, all the birthday candles together, and so on.

7. Count up the number of buckets. Have families form groups and create stations around each bucket.

8. Have families decorate the buckets by cutting balloon shapes out of colored construction paper and adding ribbon before taping these decorations onto the sides of the buckets.

9. Once the buckets are decorated, have families line up and take one of each of the five items to place inside their birthday buckets.

Debriefing the Project

- What was it like to make a birthday bucket?

- How would you feel if your family didn't have the resources to throw a birthday party for you? Why? Why is it important to celebrate birthdays?

- How else can we help those in need?

Helpful Resources

- For children: *A Birthday for Cow!* by Jan Thomas (Harcourt Children's Books, 2008), a delightful story about Duck, who insists on adding a special ingredient to the birthday cake for Cow, while Pig and Mouse are sure it will be a disaster.

- For teens: *The Birthday Book* by Anne Druitt, Christine Tynes-Clinton, and Mary C. Rowling (Hawthorn Press, 2003), a book filled with recipes, stories, crafts, and more for birthday celebrations.

Bonus Ideas

- If the recipient agency is open to it, consider also having families make a birthday card to include with the birthday bucket.

- You also might want to consider including a birthday present for a child. Indicate whether it would be for a boy or a girl and for which age. Do not wrap the gift, but add a roll of birthday wrapping paper, scissors, and tape with it.

74 Stuffed Gift Bags

Purpose

Cheer up people in homeless or domestic-abuse shelters during the winter holidays by giving them bags stuffed with small gifts.

Possible Recipients

- A local homeless shelter, domestic-abuse shelter, or other type of shelter

Time Requirement

Planning time before the project: one to two hours. Gathering materials: one hour. Setup time on the day of your project: 30 minutes to an hour. Project time: 30 minutes.

People

This project is ideal for families with children between the ages of 3 and 18. Expect each family to make one stuffed gift bag during the 30-minute event.

Materials

- Enough copies of the "Help Create a Stuffed Gift Bag for Someone in Need" handout (page 169) to publicize your event with families
- 1 plain-colored paper gift bag with handles for each family
- 4 to 5 inexpensive items to place in each gift bag (suggestions on handout)
- 5 washable markers in various colors for each family
- Optional: Stickers to decorate each gift bag

Families will donate the gift items and bags. Inexpensive items for each gift bag can be found at discount and dollar stores. Make sure the gift bags are paper; washable markers won't work on the waxy ones.

Connecting Point

During the winter holidays, many people living in crisis don't receive gifts. We can help brighten their spirits and their holiday by filling a decorated gift bag just for them.

Doing the Project

1. About two to three weeks before your event, distribute copies of the "Help Create a Stuffed Gift Bag for Someone in Need" handout to families you hope to attract.
2. Make a sample decorated gift bag to show as an example.
3. At the event, have a gift bag show-and-tell. Ask families to connect with each other in small groups and show each other what they brought and talk about why. This often helps families see other creative ideas for future service projects.
4. Have families separate the items they brought into similar piles. For example, place all the combs in one pile, all the crossword puzzle books in one pile, and so on. Flatten all the gift bags so they're ready to decorate.
5. Give families time to decorate the gift bags with colored markers. Encourage them to draw pictures or designs that look festive.
6. Once families finish, have them collect four to five different items to put into the gift bag.
7. Place all the filled gift bags in a row and ask children to count them.

Debriefing the Project

- What was it like to buy items for the gift bag for someone you didn't know?
- Why is it important to give to those in need during the holidays?
- Why is a filled gift bag more interesting than one wrapped present?
- How else can we help those in need during the holidays?

Helpful Resources

- For children: *The Lady in the Box* by Ann McGovern (Turtle Books, 1999), a story about a young brother and sister who befriend a homeless woman in their community.
- For teens: *Service-Learning Student's Guide and Journal: Taking Action Towards Repairing the World* by Robert Schoenfeld (ServiceLearn, 2006), a journal with thought-provoking questions that help teens document and reflect on the service projects they do.

Bonus Ideas

- Instead of stuffing gift bags, consider stuffing Christmas stockings at Christmas time.
- Many military personnel are separated from their families during the holidays. Consider creating Christmas stockings for American troops through Operation Santa at www.operationsanta.info.

Shoe-Box Goodies

You're invited to give a shoe box full of holiday gifts to a child in need.
Come to our event:

Date: _____

Time: _____

Place: _____

Please bring:

An empty shoe box or small plastic container about the size of a shoe box, with cover, and new items to fill the shoe box for a child (see the suggested items below).

Please purchase items for a specific age group (such as ages 2 to 4, 5 to 8, 9 to 12, or 13 to 18) and for either a boy or a girl. If donating gifts for 2- to 4-year-olds, don't include small items that could be choking hazards.

Suggested toys:

- Stuffed animals
- Small cars
- Yo-yos
- Small balls
- Jump ropes
- Small dolls
- Kazoos, harmonicas, or other small instruments
- Toys that light up (include the batteries)

Suggested candy:

- Hard candy
- Lollipops
- Mints
- Gum
- Other candy that won't melt

Suggested school supplies:

- Writing pads or paper
- Pens and pencils
- Washable markers
- Pencil sharpeners
- Crayons
- Coloring books
- Activity books
- Picture books
- Solar calculators

Suggested hygiene items:

- Toothbrush
- Toothpaste
- Comb
- Washcloth
- Mild bar of soap (inside a plastic bag)

Giving Coupons

Coupon good for:

From:

Coupon good for:

From:

Coupon good for:

From:

Help Create a Stuffed Gift Bag for Someone in Need

You're invited to help someone in need by creating a stuffed gift bag for him or her. Come to our event:

Date: _____

Time: _____

Place: _____

Please bring:

One paper gift bag with handles (nonglossy)
Four to five small items to fill the gift bag (see the list of ideas below)

Suggested items:

- Bandages
- Bars of soap
- Batteries
- Brushes
- Candles
- Coffee
- Cologne or perfume
- Combs
- Crossword puzzle books
- Dental floss
- Dried soup mix packets
- Earmuffs
- Flashlights
- Gloves

- Hair elastics
- Hand warmers
- Hats
- Hot chocolate packs
- Lamp oil
- Lip balm
- Long-distance calling cards
- Over-the-counter medications
- Playing cards
- Reading glasses
- Scarves
- Small containers of hand lotion

- Small snack packs (such as granola bars and nuts)
- Small tools
- Socks
- Stocking caps
- Sugar-free candy
- Sugar-free drink mixes
- Sunglasses
- Tea bags
- Toothbrushes
- Toothpaste
- Underwear

Chapter 9
Projects to Help the Environment and Animals

We hear so much bad news about global warming, pollution, toxic waste, and other environmental issues that affect humans and animals. Many families want to do their part to help the environment, and family service projects can make these large, looming, complex issues easier to fathom—and to do something about. Help families feel empowered to improve our planet and help animals with these family service projects.

(75) Animal Care Boxes

Purpose

Collect much-needed items for homeless pets and pets waiting to be adopted.

Possible Recipients

- A local animal shelter, animal hospital, animal adoption center, or animal foster care home. You can search for your local animal shelter at www.animalshelter.org.

Time Requirement

Planning time before the project: one to two hours. Gathering materials: one hour. Setup time on the day of your project: 30 minutes to an hour. Project time: 30 minutes.

People

This project is ideal for families with children between the ages of 3 and 18.

Materials

- Enough copies of the handout "Help Care for Animals" (page 183) to publicize your event with families
- Animal-care items listed on handout
- 5 washable markers in various colors for each family
- 1 large box for every 4 families (sturdy enough to hold the donations)

Use the handout to ask families to donate the pet supplies.

Connecting Point

In many parts of the United States, animal shelters are filled with homeless pets. These cats, dogs, and other animals live their lives in small spaces, hoping for families to adopt them. Help make their lives a bit brighter by donating food, toys, and other items they need.

Doing the Project

1. About two to three weeks before your event, make three copies of the "Help Care for Animals" handout and check (or put a requested amount next to) two to three items on each sheet (such as the canned kitten or cat food, cat toys, and washable cat beds on one handout) so that among the three sheets every item has been accounted for. Then make multiple copies of each and distribute the copies to families.

2. When families arrive on the day of your event, have them team up with one or two other families to see what they brought and talk about why they chose those items.

3. Have families place their items into piles of similar items. For example, put all the blankets in one area, all the cat food in one area, and all the dog toys in another area.

4. Have families decorate the boxes. Encourage children to draw pictures with the washable markers. Write messages, such as "We love animals!" and "We're thinking of you." Make the boxes look festive. (The recipient organization will really appreciate it.)

5. Have families box up similar items together to be given to the animal charity you've chosen.

Debriefing the Project

- Was it easy or hard to choose what to donate to this worthy cause? Why?
- Why is it important to help homeless pets?
- Why do you think we have so many homeless pets in our country?
- What else can we do to help homeless pets?

Helpful Resources

- For children: *Jasper's Day* by Marjorie Blain Parker (Kids Can Press, 2004), a touching story about Riley's family celebrating the life of their dog, Jasper, who doesn't have much longer to live.

- For teens: Encourage teenagers to read *Careers with Animals: The Humane Society of the United States* written by Willow Ann Sirch (Fulcrum Publishing, 2000), a Humane Society publication that shows the large variety of jobs you can get to work with animals.

Bonus Ideas

- Have a newspaper-collection drive and donate the newspapers to your local animal humane society or shelter. (Most shelters need lots of newspapers because they line the cages with newspaper to make them easier to clean.)
- Collect only healthful animal food to donate. (Find out from the animal shelter which food is considered healthiest for cats and dogs.)

(76) Dog Biscuit Bake

Purpose

Bake dog biscuits to donate to an animal shelter or to sell to raise funds for an animal shelter.

Possible Recipients

- A local animal shelter, animal hospital, animal adoption center, or animal foster care home

Time Requirement

Planning time before the project: one to three hours. Gathering materials: one to two hours. Setup time on the day of your project: one to two hours. Project time: one to two hours.

People

This project is ideal for families with children between the ages of 3 and 18. Expect each family to make one batch of biscuits or team up with another family or two on each batch.

Materials

- 1 copy of the "#1 Dog Biscuit Recipe" handout (page 184) for each family
- Biscuit ingredients (see handout)
- 1 mixing bowl for each batch of biscuits
- 1 bone-shaped cookie cutter (or 1 butter knife) for each family

- 1 set of measuring cups and spoons for every 2 to 3 families
- 1 mixing spoon for each batch of biscuits
- 1 box of wax paper for cooling
- 2 cookie baking sheets for each batch of biscuits
- 1 rolling pin for every 2 to 3 families
- 2 to 4 oven mitts and spatulas
- 1 oven
- Cooling racks or a large counter
- 1 small box, plastic container with lid, or cookie tin for each batch of biscuits

Visit www.bullwrinkle.com and search for "dog treat recipes" or go to www.dogaware.com and click on "diet" and then "treat recipes" for additional recipes.

Connecting Point

Dogs love treats, but those in a shelter or foster home might not get to enjoy them very often. You can give these dogs something to be excited about by making homemade dog biscuits for them to enjoy.

Doing the Project

1. Before the family service project, decide how many batches of biscuits you plan to make. Each recipe makes about three dozen dog biscuits.

2. Make a sample batch so you know how the biscuits are made and to show them as an example.

3. When families arrive to your event, have them work in groups or as a family to make a batch of biscuits. Give each family a copy of the "#1 Dog Biscuit Recipe" handout. Have them mix all the ingredients together and roll the dough so it's about ¼" thick. Stamp bone shapes using the cookie cutters or cut them with butter knives.

4. Talk about baking safely and how to work with a hot oven so no one gets burned. Bake the biscuits for 35 to 40 minutes at 350 degrees.

5. While biscuits are baking, read aloud a picture book (see Helpful Resources) or do another activity.

6. Package the treats for delivery in the boxes or tins.

Debriefing the Project

- Have you ever made treats for dogs before? If so, when?

- What did you talk about as you made the dog biscuits?

- Why is it important to do service projects for dogs?

- How else could we help dogs or other pets?

Helpful Resources

- For children: *"Let's Get a Pup!" Said Kate* by Bob Graham (Candlewick Press, 2003), a heartwarming story about Kate and her parents visiting dogs at an animal shelter.

- For teens: *A Kids' Guide to Protecting & Caring for Animals* by Cathryn Berger Kaye (Free Spirit Publishing, 2008). This guide, developed in partnership with the ASPCA, addresses the needs of animals, including cruelty prevention, emergency readiness, wildlife rehabilitation, habitat preservation, and shelter volunteering.

Bonus Ideas

- If you have a lot of dog-loving families, consider baking other dog treats—or a variety of treats. Search for bacon bits for dogs or sweet-potato dog-chew recipes on the Internet.

- Consider creating a dog-treat cookbook and selling it to raise funds to help a local animal shelter.

 # 77 Animal Snuggle Blankets

Purpose

Help family members create cozy blankets for pets that are sick or waiting to be adopted.

Possible Recipients

- Local options: an animal shelter, animal hospital, animal adoption center, or animal foster care home

- Other options: Hugs for Homeless Animals at www.snugglesproject.org

Time Requirement

Planning time before the project: one to two hours. Gathering materials: one hour. Setup time on the day of your project: 30 minutes to an hour. Project time: 1 hour.

People

This project is ideal for families with children between the ages of 10 and 18. Expect each family to make one blanket during the one-hour event.

Materials

- 1 copy of the free Snuggles Project sheet for each family
- 2 pieces of 37" x 37" cotton or any washable fabric for each medium to large dog blanket
- 2 pieces of 25" x 25" cotton or any washable fabric for each large cat blanket or small to medium dog blanket
- 2 pieces of 15" x 15" cotton or any washable fabric for each cat blanket and small animal blanket
- 1 piece of flannel or terry cloth (not polyester or cotton batting) for filling each blanket, the same size as the blanket pieces
- 1 pair of fabric scissors for every 2 families
- 1 spool of matching thread for each fabric for each sewing machine
- 1 sewing machine for every 2 families
- Access to electrical outlets for the sewing machines
- 1 measuring tape or yardstick for every 2 families
- 1 to 2 needles for hand sewing for each family

Download the Snuggles Project sheet from www.snugglesproject.org. Click on "About" and then "Project Sheet." (The project sheet is a seven-page document.) The fabric and fabric scissors are available at fabric stores such as Jo-Ann Fabrics & Crafts and Hancock Fabrics. Also inquire if the fabric store has a bank of sewing machines (that they use for sewing classes) that you could use for your service project.

Connecting Point

Many cats, dogs, and other pets that are waiting to be adopted at animal shelters live in areas with hard floors and metal caging. A snuggle blanket helps them feel comfortable and cared for. Homeless pets can curl up in the blanket and feel a bit more at home when they're afraid.

Doing the Project

1. Read through the Snuggles Project sheet to familiarize yourself with the project.

2. Make a sample blanket so you know how it's put together and to show as an example.

3. At the event, distribute copies of the project sheet to families. Have them choose which size blanket to make and cut the fabric and filling for their blankets. Explain that it's best to add an inch to the sizes for sewing, which is why the recommended fabric sizes in the Materials list are 1 inch bigger than what's called for on the Snuggles Project sheet.

4. When the material has been cut, have families use the sewing machines to sew the filling to the unprinted side of one of the fabric pieces. Sew at a 3/8" seam.

5. Then have families lay the second fabric piece on top of the first piece *with the printed sides together.* Have them sew at a 1/2" seam most of the way around, leaving about 4 or 5 inches unsewn on one side.

6. Then have families gently turn the fabric inside-out through the four-inch hole so the printed side of the fabric emerges.

7. Have families close the 4-inch gap by folding under the unsewn edge on the two sides, placing them together while matching the fold to the already sewn seam. Then have them hand-sew the gap shut.

8. Have families make more blankets if you have materials and time.

Debriefing the Project

- How often do you use a blanket? Why?
- Why is it important for homeless pets to have blankets?
- What else can we do to help homeless animals?

Helpful Resources

- For children: *Before You Were Mine* by Maribeth Boelts (Putnam Juvenile, 2007), about a young boy who gets a dog from an animal shelter and begins to wonder what the dog's life was like before he was adopted.
- For teens: *50 Awesome Ways Kids Can Help Animals: Fun and Easy Ways to Be a Kind Kid* by Ingrid Newkirk (Grand Central Publishing, 2006), a book packed full of facts and projects for readers who love animals.

Bonus Ideas

- If you have families who enjoy knitting or crocheting, use the Snuggles Project's quick and easy patterns for those types of animal blankets. Go to the website and click on "Pattern Library."

- When working with a specific animal shelter, ask about their other needs and see if you can create related family service projects.

(78) Purr-fect Toys for Cats

Purpose

Give homeless cats in animal shelters something to do by making and donating colorful cat toys.

Possible Recipients

- A local animal shelter, animal hospital, animal adoption center, or animal foster care home

Time Requirement

Planning time before the project: one to two hours. Gathering materials: one hour. Setup time on the day of your project: 30 minutes to an hour. Project time: one hour.

People

This project is ideal for families with children between the ages of 3 and 18. Expect each family to make five or six toys for cats during the one-hour event.

Materials

- 1 new infant- or child-size crew sock for each cat toy
- 20 cotton balls or 3-inch tuft of craft stuffing for each cat toy
- 1 tablespoon of dried catnip for each cat toy
- 1 tablespoon for each family
- 5 nontoxic fabric markers for each family
- 1 bottle of nontoxic washable fabric glue for every 2 families

The fabric and fabric scissors are available at fabric stores such as Jo-Ann Fabrics & Crafts and Hancock Fabrics. Catnip is available at pet supply stores.

Connecting Point

Many cats that are housed in animal shelters do not have toys to play with. Too many of them sit, looking out of the caged bars, with nothing to do. Help make their time more comfortable and fun by making cat toys they can bat around and chase.

Doing the Project

1. Before your event, make a sample cat toy so you know how it's put together and to show as an example.
2. When families arrive on the day of your event, distribute the materials so everyone has what they need to make cat toys. Then show them how to do the project.
3. First, decorate the socks with fabric markers.
4. Then stuff the toe of each sock with one tablespoon of dried catnip.
5. Stuff the foot of the sock (over the dried catnip) with cotton balls or craft stuffing.
6. Squeeze fabric glue onto the inside of the sock's ribbing to glue the sock closed. Or knot the top of the sock to secure it.
7. Have families make several of these cat toys.

Debriefing the Project

- When have you played with a cat? What was that like?
- Why are cat toys important?
- Why is it important to care for animals in shelters?
- How else can we help cats in animal shelters?

Helpful Resources

- For children: *M Is for Meow: A Cat Alphabet* by Helen L. Wilbur (Sleeping Bear Press, 2007), a creative alphabet book about cat care, cat behavior, and cat mystery.

- For teens: *Dewey: The Small-Town Library Cat Who Touched the World* by Vicki Myron (Grand Central Publishing, 2008), a true story about a frostbitten kitten stuffed into a library book return chute who is cared for by the librarians and becomes a community builder.

Bonus Ideas

- Find other cat toys and "shelter helper projects" by downloading the free two-page brochure from the Minnesota Valley Humane Society at www.mvhspets.org. Search for "shelter helper projects."
- Make cat toys to sell and use the proceeds to support your local animal shelter.

(79) Recycling Drop-Off

Purpose

Create an easy way for people to recycle items so those items don't end up in the trash.

Possible Recipients

- A local recycling center, hazardous waste removal center, or recycling disposal center

Time Requirement

Planning time before the project: one to two hours. Gathering materials: one hour. Setup time on the day of your project: 30 minutes to an hour. Project time: 30 minutes for a kickoff event for a long-term program, or three hours for a one-time collection event, where families come and go as they drop off items.

People

This project is ideal for families with children between the ages of 3 and 18.

Materials

- A place to collect recyclables, such as at a recycling organization, a large parking lot (if you're

collecting large recyclables), or a gymnasium (for smaller recyclables)
- Containers to hold the recyclables, such as big rubber trash barrels from a home-improvement store or old milk crates
- Optional: Recycling-education materials from your local recycling provider

Connecting Point

In many parts of the country, curbside recycling programs help cut down the amount of materials that end up in a landfill. Even if your community has a curbside recycling program, most likely there are still many items that could be recycled that are not accepted by your current program. Create a way to make recycling these materials easier for people—and better for the environment.

Doing the Project

1. Call the recycling organization you wish to serve and ask about the process for donating recyclables for this family service project. To find a recycling center near you, visit

www.earth911.org/recycling and click on "Find a Recycling Center." Then search by type (such as batteries) and your zip code or postal code.

2. Ask about the details and requirements for the recycling center. These centers have to follow federal guidelines, so it's important to know what they can accept, what they can't accept, and how to provide recyclable materials to the center.

3. Choose which recyclable items you would like to collect. Common items often include batteries, paint, cell phones, computers, and other electronics. Consider picking items that your community doesn't regularly recycle and people have a hard time disposing of properly.

4. Decide if you'll host a one-time collection event or an ongoing recycling program. If you have a one-time event, consider making it a three-hour event to give families flexibility for coming and going. If you're doing a long-term recycling project (where you'll have collection containers in a permanent place), host a 30-minute event to kick it off. Publicize your recycling project to families.

5. Whether you're hosting a one-time event or kicking off a permanent drop-off spot, consider serving refreshments and providing recycling-education materials for families (perhaps from your local recycling provider). Collect recyclable items at your event.

6. If you're collecting recyclable items on an ongoing basis, make sure you have volunteers who check the bins regularly. At first, check on them daily. Estimate how long it takes for the bins to get half full. Then empty them and bring them to a local recycling center. Note: Don't let the bins gets too full because they become too heavy to move. Continue to check the bins on a regular basis, emptying them as needed, and continue to publicize your drop-off spot so people continue to donate recyclables.

7. If you have an ongoing recycling program, check in with the recycling center once or twice a year to learn about new items the center recycles or new standards to follow. This industry continues to expand and grow.

8. Either at the end of your kickoff event or periodically throughout the year for your ongoing program, publicize what your project accomplished to the families who participate.

Debriefing the Project

- What do you do with waste in your home that's recyclable? Why?

- Is it tempting to throw things out in the garbage instead of recycling them? Why or why not?

- What would our community be like if more people recycled?

- What else can we do to encourage recycling?

Helpful Resources

- For children: *I Can Save the Earth! One Little Monster Learns to Reduce, Reuse, and Recycle* by Alison Inches (Little Simon, 2008), a story about Max the monster, who always litters and never recycles. After his destructive ways cause a power outage, he discovers that he can do a lot more to make the world a better place.

- For teens: *Household Wastes* by Sally Morgan (Smart Apple Media, 2007), a book that gives detailed information about how household waste affects the environment.

Bonus Ideas

- Consider teaming up with community officials to create a recycling cleanup day, perhaps making it an annual event. In St. Louis Park, Minnesota, the community now offers such a day twice a year during which residents can donate gently used items, recycle electronics and other materials, dispose of hazardous waste in an environmentally friendly way, and get rid of large items at an economical cost through a waste disposal center. Visit www.stlouispark .org during June and October to learn more. Contact your own community (city or town council, park board, or neighborhood leaders) about doing something similar where you live.

- Inquire about your local schools composting discarded school breakfasts and lunches. Many schools are now doing this, and you can find out how to support these efforts (or get them started).

(80) Earth Day Groceries Project

Purpose

Raise awareness about Earth Day and protecting our environment by decorating recyclable paper grocery bags that will be used to sack groceries at your local grocery store.

Possible Recipients

- A local grocery store

Time Requirement

Planning time before the project: one to two hours. Gathering materials: one hour. Setup time on the day of your project: 30 minutes to an hour. Project time: one hour.

People

This project is ideal for families with children between the ages of 3 and 18.

Materials

- 3 to 5 new paper grocery bags (borrowed from a local grocery store) for each person
- 5 washable markers in various colors for each family
- Copies of 3 Earth Day Bags world templates for each participant

Grocers often are willing to let you borrow paper grocery bags to decorate (as long as you promise to bring them back). The Earth Day Bags world templates can be downloaded for free from www.earthdaybags.org; click on "Get Started" and then "World Templates."

Connecting Point

Every year, we celebrate Earth Day on April 22. This is an ideal day to raise awareness about the environment. When we decorate grocery bags that will be used by a grocery store to sack groceries, customers can see the colorful messages about taking care of our environment. Although many people now use cloth bags when they shop, a number of people still use recyclable paper bags because they can use them to hold their recyclable plastics, paper, and cans for pick up on garbage and recycling day.

Doing the Project

1. Before your event, borrow large paper grocery bags from a local grocer. Explain that your group will be decorating these bags and that you'll return the decorated bags in time to be used on Earth Day (April 22).

2. Make two or three sample decorated grocery bags to show as examples.

3. When families arrive on the day of your event, brainstorm together ideas and images that can be drawn on the grocery bags. Do not allow individuals to write their names on the bags, and make sure they make illustrations that are appropriate. For those who feel they need extra help with design, distribute the world templates. For those who struggle with what to write, show them the writing ideas on the Earth Day Bags website.

4. Give families time to decorate their bags. Encourage them to think of all the different aspects of caring for our earth: recycling, reusing materials, refilling bottles, growing gardens and flowers, picking up litter, and so on.

5. Collect all the decorated bags and count them.

6. A few days before Earth Day, have volunteers return the decorated bags to the grocer.

Debriefing the Project

- What was it like to decorate a grocery bag with Earth Day messages?
- How would you feel if you received one of these bags when you bought groceries? Why?
- Why is it important to let people know about Earth Day?
- How else can we take care of our environment?

Helpful Resources

- For children: *It's Earth Day!* by Mercer Mayer (HarperFestival, 2008), a story about Little Critter, who goes on a mission to reduce, reuse, and recycle for Earth Day.
- For teens: *The Teen Guide to Global Action: How to Connect with Others (Near and Far) to Create Social Change* by Barbara A. Lewis (Free Spirit Publishing, 2007), a groundbreaking book with inspiring stories of young people changing their world and making it a better place.

Bonus Ideas

- If you have access to a laptop computer and projector, consider showing one of the two Earth Day Bags presentations about this project. Download them for free at www.earthdaybags.org. Click on "Get Started" and then "PowerPoint."
- Get the word out about your project by taking photos and writing a news release to send to local newspapers and TV stations. The Earth Day Bags website has a ready-to-adapt news release that you can use. Click on "Get Started" and then "News Release." Your grocery store also would love the publicity if you can convince the newspaper to take photos during Earth Day at the grocery store. (Or better yet, take the photos yourself and submit them.)

81 Item Swap

Purpose

Encourage people to reuse gently used items they would typically toss, such as clothing, toys, and household items, by swapping them with others.

Possible Recipients

- The families in your community (and the earth!)

Time Requirement

Planning time before the project: one to two hours. Gathering materials: one hour. Setup time on the day of your project: 30 minutes to an hour. Project time: one hour.

People

This project is ideal for families with children between the ages of 3 and 18.

You will need several volunteers to help run the flea market. See Doing the Project steps 5 to 8.

Materials

- 5 tables for display for every 25 families
- Enough copies of the "A Free Flea Market (That's Good for the Environment)" handout (page 185) to publicize your event with families
- Copies of the "Flea Market Play Money" handout (page 186), in a different color from the other handout, about five times as many as the number of families you expect to participate
- 1 to 2 paper grocery bags per family
- 3 to 4 pairs of scissors
- 3 to 4 rolls of masking tape
- Items to swap at the flea market

Families will donate the items for the flea market.

Connecting Point

Many of us have a lot of stuff in our homes, such as clothes we no longer wear, toys we no longer play with, and household goods we no longer use. Too often, we just stuff our closets full or we end up throwing out things we no longer use (but are still in good shape). These thrown-out items sit in landfills, and many may take centuries to decompose. When we bring in our gently used (yet no longer needed) items to swap with other items we need, we reduce waste and reuse materials. *Reduce* and *reuse* are the first two of the three Rs!

Doing the Project

1. Set the date and publicize your event through your organization. Use the handout "A Free Flea Market (That's Good for the Environment)."

2. Photocopy the "Flea Market Play Money" handout and cut out the bills.

3. Before your event begins, set up lots of tables where families can place their donated items. Tape a "1" bill from the "Flea Market Play Money" handout to one table, a "2" bill to another table, and continue until you have taped the numbers 1 to 5 to each of five tables. If you anticipate a lot of people coming, consider having more tables and tape bills to them, too, but cluster the "1" tables together, the "2" tables together, and so on.

4. Tape a "1" bill to one grocery bag, a "2" bill to another grocery bag, and so on, until you have five grocery bags, each with a different bill. Have extra grocery bags and bills ready for when the first set of bags becomes full.

5. Have volunteers greet families as they arrive at the event and give them Flea Market Play Money in exchange for the items they brought to swap. These volunteers will help the family decide whether each donated item is worth "1," "2," "3," "4," or "5," with "1" being the least valuable to "5" being the most valuable. Then add up the total. For example, if a family brings in two stuffed animals that are given a "2" and a "3" and a lamp that is given a "4," that family would receive play money that equals 9.

6. Have the family move to the area with the grocery bags, where another volunteer will place each of their donated items into a designated bag (whether it was deemed a "1," a "3," and so on).

7. Another volunteer moves the items to the corresponding tables once a bag is full.

8. After all the families have traded in their donations for play money, station a volunteer at each table.

9. Give families time to shop for new items with their flea market money. They can use the bag they brought in for their new items or you can give them a paper grocery bag if they need one.

10. Enjoy exploring the flea market.

11. Have volunteers donate any extra items to a local charity such as a Goodwill or a Vietnam Veterans of America branch.

Debriefing the Project

- What was it like to go through your home and find items to donate?

- Why is it important to clean out our closets and drawers from time to time?

- What would have happened to these items if you hadn't brought them here?

- What do you think of swapping gently used items with other families?

- What other ways could we help the environment?

Helpful Resources

- For children: *Recycle Every Day!* by Nancy Elizabeth Wallace (Marshall Cavendish Children's Books, 2006), a story about Minna the rabbit who creates a calendar for her school that includes a creative recycling project for each day of the year.

- For teens: *Garbage and Recycling: Opposing Viewpoints* edited by Mitchell Young (Greenhaven Press, 2009). This book provides a number of points of view about recycling and other methods of waste reduction.

Bonus Ideas

- If you have a local charity that accepts gently used donations, inquire about what their needs are. Then have a donation drive to collect that needed item, such as winter coats.

- After you finish the swap and have extra items left over, consider pulling straws and letting families (in order of straws drawn) choose leftover items for free until they're gone. If no one wants the stuff, donate the leftovers to a Goodwill or other charity pickup.

82 Reusable Gift Bags

Purpose

Cut down on wrapping-paper use by creating cloth gift bags that families can use over and over for gift giving.

Possible Recipients

- The families and friends in your community

Time Requirement

Planning time before the project: one to two hours. Gathering materials: one hour. Setup time on the day of your project: 30 minutes to an hour. Project time: one hour if using sewing machines and two hours if hand sewing.

People

This project is ideal for families with children between the ages of 10 and 18.

Materials

- 2 pieces of 9" x 9" colorful fabric for each family
- 2 pieces of 12" x 12" colorful fabric for each family
- 2 pieces of 18" x 18" colorful fabric for each family
- 1 matching spool of thread for each fabric for every 4 families
- 1 18" fabric ribbon for each bag (match color to fabrics)
- 1 pair of fabric scissors for each family

- 1 measuring tape or yardstick for each family
- 3 sewing needles for each family
- Optional: 1 sewing machine for every 2 to 3 families

Materials are available through fabric stores such as Jo-Ann Fabrics & Crafts and Hancock Fabrics. Consider buying yards of uncut fabric and have families cut the pieces to size at your event. Gather a variety of fabric so that your families all don't receive the same fabric.

Connecting Point

People use a lot of wrapping paper for the gifts we give on birthdays, weddings, anniversaries, and holidays. Most of this paper is used once and then disposed of. To save the trees that wrapping paper is made from, make gift bags from cloth that can be used over and over again. Once families begin using fabric bags, the bags begin to cycle around as other family members—and other families—use them. Fabric bags make gift-wrapping easier and better for the environment.

Doing the Project

1. Make two sample gift bags (in two different sizes) so you know how they're put together and to show as examples.

2. When families arrive to your event, distribute the fabric among them. Have them cut two matching squares for each bag they want to make. (Consider making 9-inch, 12-inch, and

18-inch squares, since gifts can be different sizes.)

3. Have families place the two squares together with the printed sides of the fabric facing each other. Then stitch three of the sides together using a sewing machine, or stitch by hand. Leave one side open, but hem the edge using a simple zig-zag stitch.

4. Once the three sides are stitched together, have families turn the bag so the printed side is facing out.

5. Demonstrate how a gift can be inserted into a fabric bag and then tied shut with a ribbon. Have families choose a matching ribbon for their bags and tie it shut.

6. Make more gift bags in different sizes and colors.

7. Encourage families to use these gift bags for friends and family members after the event.

Debriefing the Project

- What was it like to make reusable gift bags?

- How much wrapping paper do you think ends up in landfills every year around the Christmas, Hanukah, and Kwanzaa holidays? Why?

- Why is it important to be mindful not only of the gifts we give but how we wrap them?

- What other holidays and occasions could we make gift bags for?

- How else can we help the environment?

Helpful Resources

- For children: *26 Big Things Small Hands Do* by Coleen Paratore (Free Spirit Publishing, 2008). As children learn and review their ABCs, they discover positive actions they can perform with their own small hands—like applauding, building, giving gifts made with love, helping, planting, recycling, and volunteering.

- For teens: *Don't Throw It Out: Recycle, Renew and Reuse to Make Things Last* by Lori Baird and Editors of *Yankee* Magazine (Rodale Books, 2007), a helpful book on how to recycle, renew, and reuse things in creative ways.

Bonus Ideas

- Consider selling these cloth gift bags (with matching ribbons) to raise funds for an environmental group.

- Time your event so you make gift bags before the winter holidays with festive fabric. That way, the bags can be put to use right away.

- Consider making the bags for nursing-home residents or senior citizens. These folks often have a hard time wrapping gifts, so these fabric gift bags make it much easier for them.

- Make gift bags with birthday themes for those who like to have birthday bags.

Help Care for Animals

You're invited to help homeless pets by donating needed pet food and supplies. Come to our event:

Date: _____

Time: _____

Place: _____

Please bring the following new items:

_____ Canned kitten or cat food

_____ Canned puppy or dog food

_____ Cat toys

_____ Dog toys

_____ Bath towels

_____ Blankets

_____ Washable cat or dog beds

#1 Dog Biscuit Recipe

Ingredients for each batch of biscuits

2 cups whole wheat flour
½ cup cornmeal
6 tablespoons corn oil
⅔ cup water

Instructions

Mix all the ingredients together and roll the dough so it's about ¼" thick.

Stamp bone shapes using the cookie cutters or cut them with butter knives.

Bake the biscuits for 35 to 40 minutes at 350 degrees Fahrenheit.

#1 Dog Biscuit Recipe

Ingredients for each batch of biscuits

2 cups whole wheat flour
½ cup cornmeal
6 tablespoons corn oil
⅔ cup water

Instructions

Mix all the ingredients together and roll the dough so it's about ¼" thick.

Stamp bone shapes using the cookie cutters or cut them with butter knives.

Bake the biscuits for 35 to 40 minutes at 350 degrees Fahrenheit.

A Free Flea Market
(That's Good for the Environment)

Don't throw away your gently used items! You're invited to a free flea market to find new owners for those items (and keep them out of landfills). Come to our event:

Date: _____

Time: _____

Place: _____

Please bring:

- As many gently used items as you wish to donate, such as clothing, toys, stuffed animals, games (with all their pieces), knickknacks, unused school supplies, household items, and more. You'll be able to get as much as you give!

- Shopping bags

A Free Flea Market
(That's Good for the Environment)

Don't throw away your gently used items! You're invited to a free flea market to find new owners for those items (and keep them out of landfills). Come to our event:

Date: _____

Time: _____

Place: _____

Please bring:

- As many gently used items as you wish to donate, such as clothing, toys, stuffed animals, games (with all their pieces), knickknacks, unused school supplies, household items, and more. You'll be able to get as much as you give!

- Shopping bags

From *Doing Good Together: 101 Easy, Meaningful Service Projects for Families, Schools, and Communities* by Jenny Friedman, Ph.D., and Jolene Roehlkepartain, copyright © 2010. Free Spirit Publishing Inc., Minneapolis, MN; 800-735-7323; www.freespirit.com. This page may be reproduced for individual and small group work only. For other uses, contact www.freespirit.com/company/permissions.cfm.

Flea Market Play Money

1 **one** 1 1 1	1 **one** 1 1 1
2 **two** 2 2 2	2 **two** 2 2 2
3 **three** 3 3 3	3 **three** 3 3 3
4 **four** 4 4 4	4 **four** 4 4 4
5 **five** 5 5 5	5 **five** 5 5 5

Chapter 10
Projects to
Do Off-Site

As families get used to doing service projects, they often
become interested in going off-site to do direct service projects
(and work directly with the recipients). Yet, getting started can
feel daunting and uncomfortable. The projects in this chapter are easy and
low-risk, so families can step slowly into direct service projects. Some
organizations begin to do occasional off-site projects after a year of on-site
projects and continue with a mix of on-site and off-site projects (since not all
families will be ready for off-site projects).

When coordinating off-site projects, it's important to address transportation, where
and when to introduce and debrief the project, and guidelines for conduct at the
location. It is often best to meet first at your own location so your group can carpool
and/or caravan together.

Some groups introduce the project at their location before traveling together.
Others arrive at the off-site location about five to 10 minutes early and present the
connecting point there. Most debrief at the off-site location immediately following
the project, since people often scatter quickly once the project has finished. Be sure
you and your group clearly understand guidelines for conduct. Depending on the
off-site organization, you may need to be quieter and follow more rules than
you do during projects at your location (this can be especially difficult for kids).
Find out from the recipient organization what the expectations are for
conduct before you go.

83 A Creative Nursing-Home Visit

Purpose

Brighten the day for nursing-home residents by playing board and card games with them.

Possible Recipients

- A local nursing home, senior residence, or senior agency that would know of senior care centers in your area

Time Requirement

Planning time before the project: one to three hours. Gathering materials: 30 minutes to one hour. Project time: two hours.

People

This project is ideal for families with children between the ages of 5 and 18.

Materials

- Simple board games and decks of cards

Ask families to bring games they enjoy. You may want to bring extras for those who forget. Often, preschool and early elementary games are best.

Connecting Point

Most families know that visiting people in a nursing home or senior residence can be difficult: Kids are sometimes uncomfortable. Conversations aren't always easy to have. One of the most common nursing-home visits usually entails musical talent (such as singing songs or playing a musical instrument). Connect with elderly people in a fun way for everyone by playing games with them. This eliminates the pressure of making a lot of conversation.

Doing the Project

1. Before the event, work closely with an administrator of a nursing home or senior complex to arrange a time for families to play games with residents. They'll need to get the word out to their residents just as you will need to inform your families.

2. When your group arrives at the facility, connect families with residents and start playing games. Families often feel more comfortable sticking together and playing with one or two residents rather than getting split up. Have a time limit for how long you'll play games. Consider having people play games for 30 minutes and then switch to play with other residents so they'll get to meet and interact with more people.

3. Play and have fun!

Debriefing the Project

- How did you decide which game to bring? Why?
- What tends to happen when you play games together?
- What was difficult about this visit? Why?
- What did you enjoy most about this visit? Why?
- Why is it important to play games with elderly people?
- What other activities could we do with residents of this facility that we would all enjoy doing?

Helpful Resources

- For children: *Kids and Grandparents: An Activity Book* by Ann Love and Jane Drake (Kids Can Press, 1999), a book of activities, from cat's cradle to building a family tree, that helps bridge the generational gap between kids and their grandparents.

- For teens: *The Curious Case of Benjamin Button: A Graphic Novel* by F. Scott Fitzgerald, adapted by Nunzio DeFillippis and Christina Weir (Quirk Books, 2008). A graphic novel adaptation of Fitzgerald's classic story about a boy who is born 70 years old and ages in reverse.

Bonus Ideas

- Consider having family service project activities a couple of times a year at a local nursing home. Play games one time. Sing songs another time. Decorate the lobby (with permission) for certain holidays. Deliver gifts such as in project 2: Place Mats to Go and 70: May-Day Baskets.

- Many people who work in nursing homes and elderly residences get paid little and are expected to do much. Do a service project for them, such as project 21: Caring Cards or 23: Smile Drawings.

(84) Book Buddies

Purpose

Read books aloud to increase the interest of new readers in reading and literacy.

Possible Recipients

- A local childcare center, preschool, family day care, family shelter, or elementary school

Time Requirement

Planning time before the project: one to three hours. Gathering materials: 30 minutes to one hour. Project time: 30 minutes.

People

This project is ideal for families with children between the ages of 3 and 18. Even though young children are unable to read, they enjoy being with their families for this project—and it also increases their literacy skills. Expect each family to read books with one or two children during the 30-minute event.

Materials

- Age-appropriate books to read aloud as recommended by the teacher at your recipient site, enough for each family to read 1 to 4 (depending on the length of the book)

Recommended books are available through your local library. Have one or two volunteers check out the books and bring them to your event. Families may also bring books from home.

Connecting Point

When children learn to read, they don't start reading overnight. It takes years to recognize letters, sounds, how sentences are put together, and how a story develops and unfolds. Literacy experts say that reading aloud to a child is one of the best ways to help the child learn to love reading. Research studies show that learning to read is critical to a child's success in school. *

Doing the Project

1. Before the family service event, connect with the place (such as a childcare center or school) where you'll create your book buddies. Ask a teacher there for recommendations of books for families to read aloud, or see if the organization already has books that your families can read. Some families may bring books from home, too.

---

* S. Neuman, C. Copple, & S. Bredekamp (2000). *Learning to Read and Write: Developmental Appropriate Practices for Young Children*. Washington, DC: National Association for the Education of Young Children, 3.

2. Have volunteers check out the recommended books from the library and take them to the site the day of your event. Encourage the volunteers to keep track of the due date so that all books get returned before they're due.

3. At the recipient site, try to match each adult or teen family member to read with a single child. (If you have family volunteers with young children, keep those kids with the family adults.) This ratio can be flexible depending on the size of your group compared with the number of children, but try to avoid having book buddy groups that have more than three children. Literacy research shows that reading aloud in small groups helps young children pay attention more.

4. Have families read the books aloud to the children they're paired up with.

5. After families finish reading, encourage them to ask the children to tell them a story (or read a book to them—even if they don't know how to read). Encourage families to listen and not correct the children. The point is to help the children feel comfortable telling the story and attempting to read aloud.

6. See if there's a future date when you can meet with your book buddies again (such as a month later or a few times a year).

7. Be sure to collect all the books when you leave, give them to the volunteers, and ask them to return the books to the library.

Debriefing the Project

- Have you read a book aloud to children before? What was it like?
- What was your experience with your book buddy?
- What would you do differently next time? Why? The same? Why?
- How else could we help children learn how to read?

Helpful Resources

- For children: *The Library* by Sarah Stewart (Frances Lincoln Children's Books, 2008), a story about book-lover Elizabeth Brown, who comes up with a great idea of what to do with her many books.
- For teens: *A Kids' Guide to Helping Others Read & Succeed* by Cathryn Berger Kaye (Free Spirit Publishing, 2007), a helpful workbook that includes creative ways kids and teens can help others read.

Bonus Ideas

- Consider using the book lists for preschoolers in *Playful Reading: Positive, Fun Ways to Build the Bond Between Preschoolers, Books, and You* by Carolyn Munson-Benson (Search Institute, 2005) or *The Read-Aloud Handbook: Sixth Edition* by Jim Trelease (Penguin, 2006), which includes book lists for many ages of children.
- Elderly people also enjoy having stories read aloud to them. Consider creating book buddies at a nursing home or senior care facility.

(85) Neighborhood Art Gallery

Purpose

Encourage families to create and display their art while helping neighbors connect with each other and build community.

Possible Recipients

- A local neighborhood association (or the neighborhood association where your organization is)

Time Requirement

Planning time before the project: one to three hours. Gathering materials: 30 minutes to one hour. Setup time on the day of your project: 15 to 30 minutes. Project time: one hour.

People

This project is ideal for families with children between the ages of 3 and 18. Expect each family to bring one to two pieces of art to display during the one-hour event.

Materials

- Enough copies of the "Be Part of Our Neighborhood Art Gallery" handout (page 201) to publicize your event with families
- Art created by family members
- 5 feet of rope for every 5 to 6 pieces of art
- Places to tie the rope, such as between trees
- 2 clothespins for each piece of art
- 1 8½" x 11" sheet protector for each piece of art
- 1 table for about every 10 pieces of art

Ask families to make and bring art to display. Sheet protectors are available through office-supply stores, such as Office Max and Office Depot.

Connecting Point

Many people enjoy expressing themselves through arts and crafts. Give them the opportunity to show others their creations while also building a sense of community in their neighborhood.

Doing the Project

1. Scout out a location for your art gallery. If you plan to have it outside, find places where you can hang rope, such as between trees in a neighborhood park. If you plan to have your event outside, also consider having a backup indoor plan in case of inclement weather.

2. Distribute copies of the "Be Part of Our Neighborhood Art Gallery" handout two to three weeks before the event so families have time to make something for the gallery.

3. Before the event, set up the area where you'll display the art. You can do this outside (if weather permits) or inside at your organization's building. Have tables to place work on. Secure rope so that you can display art by hanging up pieces with clothespins.

4. When families arrive to the event, help them display their art. Try to place family members' art close together so that one family member can stay with the displayed art while the others mingle.

5. Allow everyone time to view the art in your neighborhood art gallery. Encourage people to ask questions about the art and get to know the artists.

6. Sometimes someone may offer to buy a piece of art. Decide whether or not you will allow this. If you do, make sure all parties agree on the price.

Debriefing the Project

- What was it like to make something for our neighborhood art gallery? Why?
- What did you discover about the other families and their art?
- Why do you think so many people enjoy doing some type of art or craft?
- What else can we do to encourage our creativity?
- What else can we do to help build community with each other?
- What does *community* mean to you?

Helpful Resources

- For children: *Kids Art Works! Creating with Color, Design, Texture and More* by Sandi Henry (Williamson Publishing Company, 1999), project ideas organized into four sections: "Playing with Patterns," "Prints Charming," "The Sculpture Gallery," and "A Touch of Texture." *Home* by Jeannie Baker (Greenwillow Books, 2004), a wordless picture book that traces the transformation of a community.

- For teens: *145th Street: Short Stories* by Walter Dean Myers (Laurel-Leaf, 2000), 10 stories that switch between different characters' points of view to depict the powerful sense of community shared by the residents of a single city-block.

Bonus Ideas

- Some families enjoy making crafts *together*. Consider having a family service project where families bring the crafts and art they're working on. They can talk while they work, and then as a group you can brainstorm ways their creations can be sold or given to others.

- One emergency food shelf holds an Empty Bowls fundraising event every year. Children and adults create bowls and donate them. Then people who contribute money at the event are allowed to choose one empty bowl to take home. Displayed on a dining room table, the bowl is a reminder that there are people who don't have food. Some people add coins to the bowl every time they eat and donate the money to an emergency food shelf. Visit Empty Bowls at www.emptybowls.net for more information.

(86) Animal Shelter Care

Purpose

Help family members give the gift of their time to an animal shelter.

Possible Recipients

- A local animal shelter, animal hospital, animal adoption center, or animal foster care home

Time Requirement

Planning time before the project: one to three hours. Project time: one hour.

People

This project is ideal for families with children between the ages of 3 and 18, depending on the age range the shelter allows. Some shelters will allow only teenagers and adults to come and care for pets, while others may be open to families with younger children coming in.

Materials

- None needed

Connecting Point

Families with children often love pets, and they often love to help others take care of their pets. Many animal shelters need help and welcome volunteers who come in to help care for the animals.

Doing the Project

1. Before the project, work with your recipient organization to set up a time for your family service project. Work through the details of the types of projects that families can do, such as playing with animals, putting fresh water in water bowls, helping clean up, and doing other activities that the place needs help with.

2. When your group has gathered, go through guidelines of what is and is not appropriate

conduct. There may be some animals that families need to stay away from because the animals are sick.

3. When you arrive at the animal shelter, help out in ways they request.

Debriefing the Project

- Why do you think most people like pets so much?
- How did it go to help out at the animal shelter? What did you discover?
- Why is it helpful to serve together as a family?
- What else can we do to help animals?

Helpful Resources

- For children: *Buddy Unchained* by Daisy Bix (The Gryphon Press, 2006), a story about a dog's new life after being adopted from an animal shelter.

- For teens: *The Healing Power of Pets* by Marty Becker with Danelle Morton (Hyperion, 2002), an insightful book about how animals have the power to detect, treat, and cure many diseases and conditions.

Bonus Ideas

- You may discover an animal foster care home in your area that would appreciate help with walking dogs and playing with cats.
- If the animal shelter is having trouble getting pets placed with families or needs funds, consider doing a fundraiser or a promotion to get the word out about animal adoptions.
- Do one of the other animal service projects such as project 75: Animal Care Boxes, 76: Dog Biscuit Bake, 77: Animal Snuggle Blankets, or 78: Purr-fect Toys for Cats and donate the items you create to the shelter.

87 Birthday Pals

Purpose

Celebrate a homebound person's birthday with him or her to help that person feel remembered and appreciated.

Possible Recipients

- A local nursing home, Meals on Wheels chapter, congregation that has a number of homebound members, or some other senior agency

Time Requirement

Planning time before the project: one to three hours. Gathering materials: 30 minutes to one hour. Project time: one hour.

People

This project is ideal for families with children between the ages of 3 and 18.

Materials

- 1 birthday cake
- 20 birthday candles
- 1 set of matches
- 1 knife to cut the cake
- 1 paper plate for each person eating the cake
- 1 napkin for each person eating the cake
- 1 plastic fork or spoon for each person eating the cake
- Children's birthday picture books to read aloud, such as *A Birthday for Bear* by Bonny Becker (Candlewick Press, 2009), a story about Mouse, who makes sure Bear doesn't ignore Bear's birthday; *Otis & Sydney and the Best Birthday Ever* by Laura Joffe Numeroff (Harry N. Abrams, 2010), a story about Otis planning a surprise birthday party for Sydney

and making a huge mistake; and *A Birthday for Cow!* by Jan Thomas (Harcourt, 2008), a story about Duck adding a special ingredient to Cow's birthday cake

See if a local bakery will donate a sheet cake, or collect donations to purchase the cake and supplies. Make sure you get a cake that will feed your whole group, including the recipients. You may need more than one cake if your group is large. Check out the recommended picture books from your local library.

Connecting Point

A birthday is an important day in people's lives. But when you're alone, the day can become a painful reminder of how isolated you are. Make someone's birthday much more memorable and bright by celebrating it with him or her.

Doing the Project

1. Before you do the project, work with an agency, a senior residence, or a nursing home to set up the birthday celebration. Find out the names of the people whose birthdays you're celebrating. For example, you could celebrate all the March birthdays of senior residents by throwing a March Birthday Party at a nursing home or senior care center. Or you could celebrate the birthday of an individual who is homebound, if you have a small group of families (too few could be uncomfortable and awkward for the individual, but too many could be overwhelming).

2. When you arrive at the location, greet the people you're visiting. Read aloud the birthday picture books to the seniors. Even though they're books for children, elderly people enjoy the illustrations and short stories.

3. Sing happy birthday to the seniors. (If you are singing to a lot of people, have a printout of all their names. Sing the song, and say the names one by one in unison when you get to that part of the song. Encourage families to say the names slowly so that each birthday person hears his or her name.)

4. Light the candles on the cake and have the birthday person (or people) blow them out. (If the person is unable to do so, ask the person to choose a child to blow out the candles with him or her.)

5. Serve the cake and eat.

6. Have volunteers from your organization interact with the seniors and introduce family members to them. For families who are new to this, it helps to have someone they know introducing and starting the conversation for them.

7. Clean up before you leave. Say good-bye to the birthday people, and thank families for coming and contributing.

Debriefing the Project

- Why is a birthday an important day?
- What would it feel like if nobody celebrated your birthday with you?
- What did you think of this birthday celebration? Why?
- What else can we do to let homebound people know that we're thinking of them?

Helpful Resources

- For children: *Helping Out and Staying Safe* by Pamela Espeland and Elizabeth Verdick (Free Spirit Publishing, 2004), a book full of stories and ideas of how to help others.

- For teens: *Life as a Daymaker: How to Change the World by Making Someone's Day* by David Wagner (Jodere Group, 2003), a true story about a hairdresser who makes people's days by listening to them, talking with them, and being kind.

Bonus Ideas

- Consider making personalized birthday cards beforehand and taking them to the recipient for the birthday celebration.

- Consider taking balloons and crepe-paper streamers to decorate the party area. (Get permission first.) At a nursing home or senior care center, they often leave up these decorations for a long time.

88 Plant a Bulb

Purpose

Plant bulbs in the fall so flowers can bloom in the spring and brighten someone's spirits.

Possible Recipients

- A local nursing home, senior care center, residential home, school, community park or roadside area, church, temple, mosque, or the flower bed of a homebound person. Even though some of these organizations may have a gardener or groundskeeper, most are on tight budgets and open to letting groups plant bulbs.

Time Requirement

Planning time before the project: one to three hours. Gathering materials: 30 minutes to one hour. Project time: 30 minutes.

People

This project is ideal for families with children between the ages of 3 and 18. Expect each family to plant about 20 bulbs during the 30-minute event.

Materials

- Flower bulbs that can be planted in the fall, 20 for each family
- 1 trowel or bulb-digging tool for each family
- 1 12" ruler for each family

Connecting Point

Flowers that emerge from bulbs in the spring give people hope after a long winter. In New York City, a citywide initiative was started (called the Daffodil Project) after the attacks of September 11, 2001. More than 4 million daffodil bulbs have been planted by more than 20,000 volunteers between 2001 and 2010, making spring in New York City an incredible sight. (Visit www.ny4p.org to learn more. Click on "Beautify," then "The Daffodil Project.") Even planting 10 to 100 bulbs can make a big difference for people who rarely get out, don't have much to look at out their window, or regularly drive past an eyesore. Planting bulbs can transform an area, brightening people's spirits. Talk about the place where you'll be planting bulbs and who will benefit from it.

Doing the Project

1. Before you do the project, get permission from the official at the place where you wish to plant the bulbs. Find out exactly where and what you are allowed to plant.

2. Choose bulbs that will be maintenance free. If there are rabbits, deer, or squirrels in the area, they may dig up all your tulip bulbs. Check with a gardening expert to see what he or she suggests.

3. When your group arrives at the location, give clear directions of where you can plant bulbs. Also inform families about how deep the bulbs need to be planted and how far apart. Bulbs that are planted too shallow or too deep will not grow well and flower. (Ask for planting tips at the garden store where you buy the bulbs, if there are no instructions with them.) Use 12" rulers for guidance.

4. Plant bulbs, lots of bulbs!

5. Write a reminder note to yourself to check the area in the spring when the bulbs are blooming. Get permission to take photos to show families.

Debriefing the Project

- Which flowers do you enjoy seeing in the spring? Why?
- Why are flower gardens important?
- Why do fresh flowers boost people's spirits?
- What was your experience in planting bulbs?
- What else can we do to beautify an area?

Helpful Resources

- For children: *Circles of Hope* by Karen Lynn Williams (Eerdmans Books for Young Readers, 2005), a story about a young Haitian boy who struggles against the elements to plant a tree for his new baby sister.

- For teens: *The Power of Kindness: The Unexpected Benefits of Leading a Compassionate Life* by Piero Ferrucci (Tarcher, 2007), a book that examines how being kind is linked with your own well-being.

Bonus Ideas

- You can also plant trees on Arbor Day. Visit www.arbor-day.net for a list of Arbor Day celebrations for each of the 50 states.
- If you're looking for a larger project, consider planting a community garden or creating a garden for a nursing home. This requires ongoing care for watering, weeding, and maintenance.

(89) Celebrate New Parents

Purpose

Help parents of newborns feel cared for and celebrated by visiting them in the hospital.

Possible Recipients

- The maternity ward at a local hospital

Time Requirement

Planning time before the project: one to three hours. Gathering materials: 30 minutes to one hour. Project time: one hour.

People

This project is ideal for families with children between the ages of 12 and 18.

Materials

- A fresh rose in a vase for each new mom
- A candle in a candlestick with matches for each new mom
- A congratulations card signed by the families for each new mom

Connecting Point

Giving birth to a child is a life-changing event. It also is an exhausting event. In our society, a lot of the excitement of a new birth centers on the baby, not the mother. Congratulate the mother (or the parents) of a newborn by taking a small gift (rose, candle, and card) to her and by spending time with her to hear her birthing story.

Doing the Project

1. Connect with a hospital administrator and get permission to visit newborn parents for your family service project. (There may be a few steps required with getting permission first from the hospital and then from individual mothers in the hospital.)

2. Once you have permission, ask the hospital to determine which new moms your group should visit. Some new mothers like privacy (and prefer not to have a visit from strangers), whereas others are open to and touched by visits from caring strangers, especially families with kids. Also inquire about hospital regulations for bringing a candle and lighting it, since candles may not be allowed in some rooms.

3. Buy congratulations cards (or make them) before your event. Have family members sign their first names.

4. Have two families team up to celebrate (visit) each new mother you have permission to visit. Have them present the rose in a vase and introduce themselves. They should explain that they're there to celebrate the heroic efforts

of giving birth and becoming a new mom. Light the candle to honor the mom (if you have clearance from the hospital to do so). Then ask the mom to tell them the story of the birth and her hopes for her newborn child. Encourage families to pay close attention to signals from the mother about their presence. If she seems to be enjoying having visitors, they can engage in a longer conversation about the baby. If not, their stay should be brief.

5. End the visit by giving the mom the congratulations card.

Debriefing the Project

- What was it like to sign a congratulations card for someone you did not know?

- How might you feel if you were a new mom in the hospital and you received a visit like this? Why?

- Why is it important to let new moms know they're cared for?

- How else can we show moms of newborns that we care?

Helpful Resources

- For children: *Generosity* by Cynthia Klingel (Child's World, 2008), a book about the value of being generous with others.

- For teens: *Random Acts of Kindness* by the Editors of Conari Press (Conari Press, 2002), stories and ideas of small ways to make a difference in people's lives.

Bonus Ideas

- Find gifts you can give to the dads, such as a knickknack or plaque that says "#1 Dad." Figure out ways to celebrate the dads as well.

- You can also make "Welcome Home" banners for new parents you know and place them outside their home.

- Consider cooking a meal for the parents of a newborn once they arrive home.

- Celebrate with adoptive parents on or near the arrival day of their adopted child.

90 Wagging Tails

Purpose

Bring your pet to visit and brighten elderly or lonely people's days.

Possible Recipients

- A local hospital ward (that allows visiting pets), congregation that has a number of homebound members, group home for disabled adults, nursing home, senior care center, or some other senior agency

Time Requirement

Planning time before the project: one to three hours. Project time: one hour.

People

This project is ideal for families with children between the ages of 3 and 18.

Materials

- Each family's pet on a leash or leader or in a pet carrier

- A copy of each pet's vaccination record (that includes vaccinations for rabies)

Connecting Point

Few people don't brighten up when a friendly dog or cat greets them. Most people who are homebound, hospitalized, or isolated from others rarely get the chance to see and interact with pets. Brighten their day by bringing in your friendly pet for a visit.

Doing the Project

1. Before the event, work with the administrator of the care center to ensure you can bring pets in (and, in particular, the *kinds* of pets you intend to bring). Also find out what necessary documents they need (such as a current vaccination record). Never bring a pet into a facility without prior permission and authorization.

2. When your group arrives at the location, ensure that all pets are in carriers or on leashes. Create ways to keep dogs separate from cats so that you don't have any animal skirmishes.

3. Split up the pets so they're visiting different parts of the site (or different locations). The purpose is to try to provide as much one-on-one time between a pet and the person the pet is visiting.

4. If families do not have a pet (or have an unfriendly pet), encourage them to pair up with a family that does have a pet. (The residents in these places enjoy human visitors as well as animal ones!)

5. Encourage families to teach the resident how to best pet or hold the animal so that it's a positive experience for everyone. (For example, many cats are more open to being petted from behind by a stranger.)

6. Visit and have fun interacting with the residents. Pets have a way of getting people to open up and talk.

Debriefing the Project

- What was it like to bring your pet to this facility?
- What surprised you about the visit? Why?
- Did having the pet there make it easier or harder to talk to this person? Why?
- How else can we brighten people's days?

Helpful Resources

- For children: *W Is for Woof: A Dog Alphabet* by Ruth Strother (Sleeping Bear Press, 2008), a creative alphabet book that helps readers learn about dog behavior, grooming, and more.
- For teens: *Real Kids, Real Stories, Real Change* by Garth Sundem (Free Spirit Publishing, 2010), a book full of true stories about kids around the world who used their heads, their hearts, their courage, and sometimes their stubbornness to help others and do extraordinary things.

Bonus Ideas

- If the agency or facility is open to it, consider scheduling a once-a-month visit by families and their pets. (Not all families need to participate every month. You can create a rotation so that families volunteer two to six times a year, depending on their interest.) This type of long-term service project will help build relationships and create a sense of hope among the recipients, who will look forward to the monthly visits.
- If someone has an unusual pet (such as a talking bird or a pet that does tricks), consider creating a pet show for the residents where they can watch the pets do their interesting feats.

(91) Park Spruce-Up

Purpose

Spruce up a park, community area, or your organization's outdoor area by cleaning it and making it more beautiful than before.

Possible Recipients

- A local community parks-and-recreation department, nature center, neighborhood association, church, temple, mosque, or a nonprofit organization

Time Requirement

Planning time before the project: one to three hours. Gathering materials: 30 minutes to one hour. Project time: one hour.

People

This project is ideal for families with children between the ages of 3 and 18. If you'd like to clean up a park or community area, you'll need about 10 to 20 families.

Materials

- 1 rake for each family
- 1 pair of gloves for each person for yard work
- 2 to 3 trash bags for each family
- Optional: bulbs, trees, bushes, or other plants appropriate for the planting season

Connecting Point

With resources being tight for so many communities and organizations, most organizations would welcome a group of volunteers to come in and clean up a park area and make it more beautiful. A place feels more welcoming and inviting when it's filled with beauty—rather than filled with litter and debris.

Doing the Project

1. Before you do the project, connect with a parks-and-recreation department or organization that would be willing to allow your group to clean up a park. Find out exactly what you are allowed to do. (For example, some communities employ master gardeners, and they require any new plants and trees to fit with the master gardener's plan.) If the organization or community you choose does have a grounds-keeper or master gardener, see if you can also talk to that person to find out what more your group can do, beyond cleaning up an area.

2. When you arrive at the location, begin by having families spread out and pick up litter and debris. Note: Be aware that some debris can be very dangerous. You may discover discarded syringes, broken bottles, or other hazardous items. Only adults should clean up these types of litter. Be sure to wear gloves.

3. If possible (and with permission from the recipient organization), plant bulbs, trees, shrubs, or other plants.

4. If you notice that there are no places for people using the park to toss their garbage, see if the community or organization can add garbage cans and create a maintenance plan to empty the trash on a regular basis.

5. Notice the progress you made after you finish.

Debriefing the Project

- What did you think of this area before we started to clean it up? Why?
- What did you think after we finished? Why?
- Why is it important to keep our park areas clean?
- Why is it important to beautify the areas around us?
- How else can we make our area look better?

Helpful Resources

- For children: *The Tree* by Karen Gray Ruelle (Holiday House, 2008), which provides a look at history through the lens of an elm tree and the land where it grows; readers see 250 years pass by in Madison Square Park in New York City.
- For teens: *A Kids' Guide to Climate Change & Global Warming* by Cathryn Berger Kaye (Free Spirit Publishing, 2009), a workbook full of practical, creative ways to help the environment.

Bonus Ideas

- If you live near a beach, consider sprucing up a beach. (It's alarming how much debris gets left in the sand or washes ashore.)
- The Wilderness Project (www .wildernessproject.org) has an Apprentice Ecologist Initiative. Families can take photos of an area that they've cleaned up, write an essay, and get published at the site. (Click on "Volunteers," then "Apprentice Ecologist" at the website.) Reading other people's essays and looking at their photos could also provide more information for you to share with families prior to this project.
- Consider reading *Ancient Ones: The World of Old-Growth Douglas Fir* by Barbara Bash (The Sierra Club, 1994), a book that captures the majesty of the forest through text and water-color paintings, while relating information about the wildlife that lives there.

Be Part of Our Neighborhood Art Gallery

You're invited to display a piece of art or a craft that you've created at our neighborhood art gallery. If you don't have any art you've created, it's not too late to make something. Come to our event:

Date: _____

Time: _____

Place: _____

Please bring something you created, such as:

- A painting
- A drawing
- A clay pot or piece of pottery
- Embroidery or needlework
- Scrapbook
- Hand-made greeting cards
- Hand-made jewelry
- Collages
- Something you've knitted, crocheted, quilted, or sewn
- Woodwork
- Metal work
- A photograph you took
- Any type of creation you can think of and enjoy doing!

Chapter 11
Projects Families Can Do on Their Own

As you host family volunteer projects at your organization, you might become aware of families who are interested in doing additional service projects on their own. You can act as a resource to those families, providing ideas for one-time or ongoing opportunities, in addition to the group projects you offer.

The projects in this chapter are especially appealing to families because many of them can be completed without ever having to leave home. Families can do these projects when it's convenient for them and still get the satisfaction of helping out in ways that make a difference. Simply explain the project to interested families and provide them with the accompanying handout that introduces the project and offers step-by-step instructions. It also provides tools for encouraging education and reflection among family members, making the projects deeper and richer for both adults and children.

The point of these projects is to encourage families to begin weaving service into their lives. But it's not always easy for families. While some families will jump in, complete the projects, and begin making connections with recipient organizations, others will be hesitant. For that reason, you or someone from your organization might want to take on the responsibility of researching and contacting possible recipient organizations, removing one more obstacle for families who are reluctant to reach out in that way.

Consider suggesting projects from this chapter following a group family service project that ties into the same theme. For example, project 100: Floral Friends and 101: Giggle Book are great take-home projects for families to do following many of the projects in chapter 1 or chapter 3.

To inspire families, point them to true stories of family volunteers making a difference in *Family Fun* magazine. Go to www.familyfun.go.com and search for "volunteers." Click on the volunteers contest for the current year. In the article, you'll find links to winners of previous years. Each year in its April issue, *Family Fun* magazine recognizes families who are serving others together. Perhaps, as a result of your efforts, families from your organization will be featured in next year's issue.

92 Help the Hungry

Become more aware of hunger and donate funds to organizations that help those who are hungry.

Possible Recipients

- Local options: a community kitchen, homeless shelter, domestic-abuse shelter, food shelf, or some other type of social agency that would collect donations for hunger relief
- Other options: Share Our Strength (www.strength.org), Feeding America (www.feedingamerica.org), or World Food Programme (www.wfp.org)

Time Requirement

About 5 to 10 minutes a day for a month

People

This project is ideal for families with children between the ages of 3 and 18.

Materials

- Rolls of pennies (or other coins)
- A container (box or jar) for the coins

Get rolls of pennies from your bank, or set aside the loose coins in your home.

Doing the Project

Use the "Hunger Calendar" on the back of this page. Starting on the first day of the month, do the activity that corresponds with that date (so, do activity 1 on the first day of the month, and so on). For each day's activity, you will come up with a numerical answer. Add that number of pennies (or other coins) to the box or jar you're using for your hunger collection.

Use this project as an opportunity to talk about the issue of hunger with family members. Discuss what other ways you can make a difference for those who don't have enough to eat.

Talking Points

- What did you think of these daily hunger activities? Why?
- Why is it hard to picture what it's like to be hungry if your needs are always met?
- Why do you think some people don't get enough food to eat?
- Why is it important to help hungry people?
- What else could we do to help those who are hungry?

Helpful Resources

- For children: *Armando and the Blue Tarp School* by Edith Hope Fine and Judith Pinkerton Josephson (Lee & Low Books, 2007), a moving story about Armando and his father, who are trash-pickers in Tijuana, Mexico. Based on a true story.
- For teens: *Hunger: An Unnatural History* by Sharman Apt Russell (Basic Books, 2006), a thought-provoking book about hunger and famine.

Bonus Ideas

- Consider not eating out for one month (or one week). Set aside the money you typically would spend to eat out in that period of time. Give the money to a hunger organization or food shelf.
- Set an empty bowl on your table during meals. Talk about the people you don't see who are hungry. Use the empty bowl as a reminder that there are people who don't have food to eat.
- Create a "giving box" by decorating a coffee can, shoe box, or other container. Place the coins you collect in this special container each day.
- Learn more about hunger issues by visiting www.feedingamerica.org and taking the hunger quiz.

Hunger Calendar

1 Count how many pairs of shoes you have in your closet.	**2** Count how many times you eat today (meals and snacks).	**3** Count how many items are on your top refrigerator shelf.	**4** Count how many boxes of cereal (or breakfast bars) you have.	**5** Count how many bottles or cans of soda you have.
6 Count how many pieces of fruit are in your home.	**7** Count how many pairs of pants you have.	**8** Count how many rooms you have in your home.	**9** Count how many shelves of food you have in your home.	**10** What do you collect? Count how many items you have in your collection.
11 Count how many stuffed animals you own.	**12** Count how many pairs of socks you have.	**13** How full is your freezer? If it's completely full, use the number 20. If it's half full, use the number 10.	**14** Count how many cans of food you have in your home.	**15** Count how many closets are in your home.
16 Count how many food items you store in your refrigerator door.	**17** Count how many shirts you have.	**18** Count how many times you throw food away each month (e.g., off plates or when cleaning out refrigerator).	**19** Count how many minutes you bathe or shower each week.	**20** Count how many loads of laundry your family does each week.
21 Count how many books you have in your home.	**22** Count how many drawers are in your home.	**23** Count how many pieces of candy (or snacks) you have in your home.	**24** Count how many coats you have.	**25** What kind of food do you have the most of? Count how much you have.
26 Count how many containers of food you have (such as ones that hold flour, rice, and so on).	**27** Count how many movies (such as DVDs or VHS tapes) you have in your home.	**28** Count how many hats (or caps) you have.	**29** Count the number of times you go grocery shopping each month.	**30** Count how many faucets are in (or outside) your home.
31 Count how many music CDs (or digital music files) are in your home.				

(93) Creative Shopping for Those Who Are Homeless

When you eat out at fast-food restaurants, think of those who can't afford to eat, and buy something for them.

Possible Recipients

- A local community kitchen, homeless shelter, domestic-abuse shelter, food shelf, or some other type of social agency that would collect this type of donation. (Or family adults can simply hand the gift certificates to folks they see on the streets.)

Time Requirement

About 5 to 10 minutes

People

This project is ideal for families with children between the ages of 3 and 18.

Doing the Project

People who are homeless often don't know where their next meal is coming from. Instead of giving cash to people on the streets, consider purchasing gift certificates from fast-food restaurants to donate to them. You can keep the certificates in your car, backpack, or purse to give to people who are homeless whenever you meet them, or you can donate them to a shelter to be passed out to residents.

Talking Points

- Why do you suppose it is easy to take what we eat for granted?
- What was your experience in giving away these fast-food gift certificates?

- How do you feel when you see someone on the street asking for money? How do you think you should respond?
- Which would you prefer to give to a homeless person: cash or fast-food gift certificates? Why?
- How else could we help people who are homeless and hungry?

Helpful Resources

- For children: *A Shelter in Our Car* by Monica Gunning (Children's Book Press, 2004), a story about Zettie, who lives in a car with her mother while they both go to school and try to find a more permanent home.
- For teens: *Kids with Courage: True Stories About Young People Making a Difference* by Barbara A. Lewis (Free Spirit Publishing, 1992), a book about 18 remarkable kids who speak out, fight back, come to the rescue, and defend their beliefs.

Bonus Ideas

- On the Internet, search for the name "Trevor Ferrell." You will find newspaper stories and video clips about this 11-year-old who became concerned about homeless people and started doing something to help.
- Volunteer at a community kitchen or a food shelf to get a more hands-on experience of helping the homeless and hungry. To find an opportunity, visit www.volunteermatch.org.

94 Fabulous Fringe Scarves

Many homeless people don't have proper winter wear to keep them warm. Make a simple, no-sew scarf (or two) to help people who are homeless.

Possible Recipients

- A local homeless shelter, domestic-abuse shelter, community kitchen, food shelf, or some other type of social agency that would collect these types of donations

Time Requirement

About one hour

People

This project is ideal for families with children between the ages of 3 and 18.

Materials

- 2 yards of colorful fleece fabric
- 1 pair of fabric scissors
- 1 tape measure or yardstick

Doing the Project

1. For a diagram of how these scarves are made, visit Home Made Simple at www .homemadesimple.com. Click on the language you speak. In the search engine at the top of the page, type in "no-sew scarf."

2. Purchase two yards of colorful fleece fabric from a fabric store for each scarf.

3. Cut the piece of fleece 27 inches wide by 72 inches long. (The 72 inches equals 2 yards.)

4. Decide how long you want the scarf fringe to be. Choose between 5 to 9 inches. Cut a square from each corner of your 27" x 72" piece. (For example, if you want the fringe to be 5 inches long, cut a 5" x 5" square piece from each corner.)

5. Fold the fabric in half lengthwise with the wrong sides together so the outside of the fabric faces out. The fabric is now 13½" x 72".

6. Begin by cutting fringe (at the length you had determined before, such as 5 inches) at intervals of about one-half inch. Do this around the entire border of your scarf but be careful so that the top side doesn't get cockeyed from the bottom side. (It's often helpful to cut the long side first and then tie it before cutting the other sides.)

7. Knot the top and bottom fringe pieces (that line up) together. Continue until the entire scarf is fringed.

8. Deliver the scarves to the recipient agency.

Talking Points

- What was it like to make a scarf for someone you didn't know?
- What did you discover as you made the scarf?
- Why do you think people become homeless?
- What do you think it would be like to live in a shelter, in your car, or on the street?
- What else can we do to help homeless people keep warm?

Helpful Resources

- For children: *I Call My Hand Gentle* by Amanda Haan (Viking, 2003), a book about a girl who describes her gentle hands and how they can do helpful things.
- For teens: *A Kid's Guide to Giving: By Kids for Kids* by Freddi Zeiler (Innovative Kids, 2006), a book written by a 14-year-old who researched many charitable organizations to find which ones had the most meaning to her.

Bonus Ideas

- Make the scarves more festive by slipping beads onto the fringe and tying them in place. Add seam sealant to secure them. (Find seam sealant at craft stores such as Michael's.)
- Consider making scarves with holiday designs or colors for certain holidays, such as Thanksgiving, Valentine's Day, and Halloween.

95 Take a Volunteer Family Vacation

If you're interested in taking a vacation that offers a deeper level of satisfaction, and that allows you to connect with a different culture, immerse yourself in that way of life, and work together with the people to make a real difference in their community, then consider family volunteer travel.

Possible Recipients

Global Volunteers (www.globalvolunteers.org), Global Citizens Network (www.globalcitizens .org), or Cross-Cultural Solutions (www.crossculturalsolutions.org)

Time Requirement

Approximately one to two weeks, depending on the trip chosen. Volunteer travel also requires weeks of planning.

People

This project is ideal for families with children between the ages of 8 and 18, depending on the program requirements.

Doing the Project

1. Find an organization that offers volunteer travel for families. Be aware that while the organizations listed on this page, and a number of other volunteer travel organizations, include families with children on their trips, Global Citizens Network focuses special attention on that effort, trains its staff to work with families, and offers child-friendly resources to enhance the experience.

2. Ask these questions of any organization you're considering:

   • What projects will we be working on?

   • How much time will we be committing?

   • What is the cost? What is included in the fee?

   • What are the accommodations like? Will our family be housed together? Where and what will we be eating?

   • Is there leisure time?

   • What is the minimum age for volunteers?

   • Are there medical facilities at the site?

   • What is the application process?

   • Will there be other family volunteers on the trip?

3. Once you've decided on traveling with a particular organization, spend time preparing your family for the trip. Let your children know what to expect and explain any rules of behavior. If you're traveling abroad, learn as much as you can about the country or culture you'll be experiencing.

4. Take the trip and have fun!

Talking Points

• What was different about doing a family volunteer vacation from our usual family service projects?

• What was the most difficult part of the trip? What was the most valuable?

• What surprised you the most?

• What did you learn?

• What are the stories you want to tell others about the trip?

• Do you have a different view of your own culture now? In what way?

• Would you do another family volunteer vacation? Why or why not?

• What else can we do to make a difference through family service?

Helpful Resources

- For children: *Be Polite and Kind* by Cheri J. Meiners (Free Spirit Publishing, 2004), a helpful book about how to be polite, kind, courteous, and respectful toward others.
- For teens: *Volunteer Vacations: Short-Term Adventures That Will Benefit You and Others* by Bill McMillon, Doug Cutchins, and Anne Geissinger (Chicago Review Press, Inc., 2009), a helpful guide with more than 2,000 volunteer vacations worldwide.

Bonus Ideas

- A number of books are available on volunteer vacations, but you have to sift through the information to discern which ones are open to families with children. Two helpful books include *The 100 Best Volunteer Vacations to Enrich Your Life* by Pam Grout (National Geographic, 2009) and *How to Live Your Dream of Volunteering Overseas* by Joseph Collins, Stefano DeZerega and Zahara Heckscher (Penguin, 2001).
- If you belong to a religious community, ask about family volunteer camps. A number of religious denominations offer these to families.

(96) Chemo Angel

Going through chemotherapy is an arduous journey. Many people get sick and extremely fatigued. Even though you'll never meet the person you're helping through this activity, you can make a difference by sending cards and small gifts to let the person know you're thinking of him or her.

Possible Recipients

- Chemo Angels (www.chemoangels.net)

Time Requirement

Approximately 15 to 30 minutes a week

People

This project is ideal for families with children between the ages of 3 and 18.

Materials

- Cards, envelopes, and stamps
- Small gifts

Doing the Project

1. Visit the Chemo Angels website and learn the requirements and responsibilities for becoming a Chemo Angel. Take on this project only if you have the time and energy to follow through. It's a long-term commitment—you could be corresponding with someone for one to three years or more.

2. Once you become an "angel," support the person you've been matched with in the ways that best fit your family. If you have young children, have them draw pictures. If you have teenagers, have them write letters, record a song they're composing, or create something else that fits with your child's passions and hobbies.

3. Keep messages upbeat and avoid writing "get well soon" since the person may never get well.

4. Send something to this person at least once a week throughout the duration of the chemotherapy treatment.

5. Don't expect replies. Many of these people get sick and weak from chemotherapy.

Talking Points

- What is it like to support someone you don't know?
- How is giving weekly support different from doing something for someone only one time?
- Why does it matter so much that we keep our commitment to this person?
- What do you think it might feel like to have a serious illness?
- What else can we do to help those going through chemotherapy?

Helpful Resources

- For children: *Kathy's Hats: A Story of Hope* by Trudy Krisher (Albert Whitman & Company, 1992), a touching story about a child who lost her hair to chemo.
- For teens: *Teens with Courage to Give: Young People Who Triumphed Over Tragedy and Volunteered to Make a Difference* by Jackie Waldman (Conari Press, 2000), a book that includes 30 true stories about teenagers who use their own difficulties to help others.

Bonus Ideas

- Become a Senior Angel through the same website (www.chemoangels.net). Support elderly people by sending them notes and small gifts on an ongoing basis.
- Read some of the thank-you notes from recipients at the website. People appreciate being cared for—even by people they've never met.
- Read *H Is for Hair Fairy: An Alphabet of Encouragement and Insight for Kids with Cancer* by Kim Martin (Trafford Publishing, 2005) or *Chemo Girl: Saving the World One Treatment at a Time* by Christina Richmond (Jones & Bartlett Publishers, 1996).

97 Sponsor a Family in Need

For families living in poverty, trying to make ends meet is difficult. The Box Project connects families in poverty with families that have more resources who can help them meet their needs. Each month, send a box and notes to the recipient family. Over time, this support can help families in poverty become more self-sufficient.

Possible Recipients
• The Box Project (www.boxproject.org)

Time Requirement
Approximately 90 minutes once a month

People
This project is ideal for families with children between the ages of 3 and 18.

Materials
• About $50 each month to spend on box items (or part of that amount if you pair up with another family or two)
• Shipping boxes and postage
• Information and directions from the Box Project website

Doing the Project
1. Before you begin this project, examine your family budget to ensure that you have about $50 a month that you can responsibly spend to help another family. If you don't, figure out how much you *can* spend each month, and team up with other families so that together you can give $50 a month.
2. Contact the Box Project through its website to sign up as a sponsor. The Box Project will match you with a recipient family.
3. About once a month, purchase items to ship in a box to the family you're helping. You will receive suggestions from the project regarding what types of items would be most useful. Or

ask your recipient family what they need. You can also send letters and cards.
4. Learn as much as you can about the family.
5. Include children in the project. Go shopping together. Have children draw pictures to include with the letters. Encourage kids to help choose items to ship, and (if you wish), include photos of your family.
6. Research the region and services that could be available to the recipient family. Think of your family as an advocate for the other family. Look for other sources of help and assistance for them.
7. Continue to be supportive and caring; work to build a relationship with the family over time.

A Team Effort
If you're working with other families to send a box each month, it's often helpful to designate a team leader who makes sure the project gets done each month.

Talking Points
• What is it like to sponsor a family over time?
• How is that different than just sponsoring a child?
• Would you be interested in talking to our "match" family by phone? Would you like to visit them sometime?
• What is most difficult about this project? What is most fun?
• Why is it important for families with resources to support struggling families?
• What else can we do to help families in poverty?

Helpful Resources

- For children: *Reach Out and Give* by Cheri J. Meiners (Free Spirit Publishing, 2006), a picture book that explores the power of gratitude and gives ideas on how to help others.

- For teens: *Giving: How Each of Us Can Change the World* by Bill Clinton (Alfred A. Knopf, 2007), a book written by a former U.S. president about the power of giving money, time, things, and skills.

Bonus Ideas

- You might also want to sponsor a family through Family-to-Family (www.family-to-family.org).

- When you ship your box each month, consider decorating the box on the outside so that it looks festive.

- Although most of the items you'll ship will be items of necessity, consider adding some comfort items that show you care, such as a stuffed animal or a personalized blanket.

98 Support a Candidate

Running for office requires a lot of volunteers. How can your family support a candidate running for office?

Possible Recipients

- A local school board candidate, a city council member candidate, a candidate for mayor, or a state or federal political candidate for any office

Time Requirement

From 30 minutes a month to several hours a month, depending on your interest and involvement

People

This project is ideal for families with children between the ages of 10 and 18. Younger children can be included in some campaign events.

Doing the Project

1. Research candidates who are running for office. Learn about their policies on issues that are important to you and choose a person who fits best with your family's hopes.

2. Contact the candidate's office and ask how your family can help.

3. Consider which volunteer activities work best with your family's interests and timeframes. Some common volunteer activities include stuffing envelopes, making telephone calls, writing a letter to the editor, going door to door talking about the candidate, putting up lawn signs, distributing campaign literature, attending a campaign rally, and more.

4. Pace yourselves. There is always lots to do in a political campaign, and candidates can keep asking for more and more. Don't burn yourselves out.

5. Talk about the political process with your family. Model how important it is to vote and be politically active. If possible, attend a caucus or a primary as a family so your children (even when they're too young to vote) can see the political process in action.

Talking Points

- What do you like best about the candidate? Why?

- What do you find most interesting about the volunteer work that we're doing? Why?

- Which of the issues our candidate supports matters most to you? How else can we advocate for that issue?

- Why is it important to support political candidates?

- How else can our family support the political process?

Helpful Resources

- For children: *America: A Patriotic Primer* by Lynne Cheney (Simon & Schuster Children's Publishing, 2002), an alphabet book that celebrates American history, principles, and famous political leaders.

- For teens: *Politics for Dummies* by Ann DeLaney (For Dummies, 2002), an introductory book about the American political process.

Bonus Ideas

- A fun, interactive, informative website is the PBS Kids Democracy Project at www.pbs.org. Search for "the Democracy Project." On this site, kids can learn about the role of government, voting, and voting rights.

- Help family members become informed voters by learning about candidates' views on issues. Visit Project Vote Smart at www.vote-smart.org.

(99) Effective Lice Kits

Head lice is a common problem, one that can be expensive to treat. Help create lice kits for families who may not have the resources to purchase their own medications.

Possible Recipients

- A local school health office, childcare center, shelter, or agency that works with families

Time Requirement

About one hour

People

This project is ideal for families with children between the ages of 3 and 18.

Materials

These materials will create one lice kit.

- 2 bottles of lice-treatment medication (with pediculicide) that you can purchase over the counter in pharmacies or in the healthcare sections of discount stores
- 1 quality nit comb
- 1 copy of the "Get Rid of Lice For Good" handout (page 214)
- 1 gallon-size zip-top plastic bag

Doing the Project

Place the two bottles of lice treatment, the nit comb, and the photocopy of instructions in the gallon-size, top-zip bag. Deliver your completed lice kit(s) to your recipient organization.

Talking Points

- Have you ever had head lice? If so, what was it like? If not, have you heard of others getting head lice?
- Why is it important to treat head lice right away?
- Why is treating head lice so difficult if you don't have much time or money?
- What did you think of making head lice kits?
- How else can we help families in need?

Helpful Resources

- For children: *Yikes—Lice!* by Donna Caffey (Albert Whitman & Company, 2002), a book that diminishes the stigma of getting lice through a delicate combination of fact and fiction.
- For teens: *Head Lice to Dead Lice* by Joan Sawyer and Roberta MacPhee (St. Martin's Paperbacks, 1999), a practical book on how to get rid of head lice.

Bonus Ideas

- If no one in your family has ever had head lice, read more about the condition. Look at pictures. A helpful article titled "Head Lice Treatment for Kids" by Vincent Iannelli, M.D., is available at pediatrics.about.com. Search for "Head Lice Treatment for Kids" and click on the July 11, 2009, article.
- Consider making a card of support to place inside the gallon zip-top bag. Sign your first names and let the person know you're thinking of him or her.

Get Rid of Lice for Good

Follow these simple instructions to use this get-rid-of-lice kit, and you should be able to get rid of lice—for good.

1. Make sure a responsible adult is helping apply the treatment to ensure safety.

2. Apply one lice treatment (from one of the bottles) to the hair. Follow the directions on the bottle.

3. Change and wash your clothes after treatment. (This helps keep the lice from spreading.)

4. Wash all bedding, clothes, and towels in hot water. Vacuum the mattress thoroughly.

5. After about 12 hours (from when you used the lice treatment), use the nit comb to remove dead lice.

6. Do not wash or condition the infected person's hair until one to two days following the lice treatment.

7. Use the nit comb every two to three days to continue removing dead lice.

8. After 10 days, repeat the process using the second bottle of lice treatment. (Lice eggs may have hatched in the meantime, and the second treatment will make sure that the lice stay away for good.)

(100) Floral Friends

Whom do you know who needs a boost? Is it an elderly person who lives alone? Someone who has gotten sick—or is going through rigorous medical treatments? Or someone grieving the loss of a family member? Consider visiting the person as a family and bringing some flowers.

Possible Recipients

- An elderly or sick neighbor, an extended family member, someone from your office, someone from your congregation, a bedridden student, someone at a nursing home, a homebound person, or a family member of a friend

Time Requirement

Approximately one hour

People

This project is ideal for families with children between the ages of 3 and 18.

Materials

- Bouquet of flowers
- Vase

Doing the Project

1. Identify someone you'd like to bring flowers to. Think of neighbors, extended family members, someone at your office—anyone you might know who could use some cheering up. Maybe someone is going through chemotherapy. Maybe someone just had a death in the family. Maybe someone has been sick or sad lately.

2. Purchase a bouquet of flowers. You often can find inexpensive bouquets at a grocery store. Also purchase a vase for the flowers.

3. Call the person you'd like to visit. Arrange for a time to visit.

4. Deliver the flowers as a family. Tell the person how much you've been thinking of him or her.

Talking Points

- What did you think of our visit? Why?
- How hard was it to think of someone to visit?
- Why is it thoughtful to bring flowers?
- How else can we boost someone's spirits?

Helpful Resources

- For children: *How Kind!* by Mary Murphy (Walker Books Ltd., 2004), a story that begins with Hen giving Pig an egg, which sets off a domino effect of kind deeds.

- For teens: *How to Be an Everyday Philanthropist: 330 Ways to Make a Difference in Your Home, Community, and World—At No Cost!* by Nicole Bouchard Boles (Workman Publishing, Co., 2009), a collection of easy, creative ways to take action and bring positive change to your community.

Bonus Ideas

- Consider growing flowers in your garden to give away. Gladiolas are easy to cut and give.

- Consider decorating a terra cotta pot with terra cotta paints (which you can find at a craft-supply store). Then buy a small flowering plant from the nursery and plant it in your homemade pot to give away.

- Consider creating a greeting card or note to accompany the flowers.

(101) Giggle Book

Everyone enjoys a good laugh. That's why the daily comics are such a big hit in newspapers. Consider making a giggle book of comics to cheer up someone who is sick or lonely.

Possible Recipients

- An elderly or sick neighbor, an extended family member, someone from your office, someone from your congregation, a bedridden student, someone at a nursing home, a home-bound person, or a family member of a friend

Time Requirement

Approximately one to two hours

People

This project is ideal for families with children between the ages of 3 and 18.

Materials

- About 25 pieces of 8½" x 11" white paper
- 1 half-inch binder or report cover that will hold the 8½" x 11" paper
- 1 or more daily or Sunday newspapers (or magazines that feature comics, such as *The New Yorker* or *Mad* magazine)
- Markers in various colors or other art supplies
- 1 pair of scissors for each family member
- 1 roll of double-sided tape

Doing the Project

1. Before you do the project, decide whom you wish to give your giggle book to. Find out which comic strips that person likes or what type of humor tickles his or her funny bone.

2. Cut out comic strips from newspapers or magazines. Feel free to print out comics from websites if they give permission to do so. (Be sure not to make or distribute multiple copies of copyrighted work, which is illegal.)

3. Tape one comic strip or cartoon onto each separate sheet of 8½" x 11" paper. (Use both the front and back of the paper.) If you're going to use a binder, make sure you leave space for the binding. Place the pages in order if you're using a series of comic strips in which a story builds from strip to strip.

4. Make a creative cover page.

5. Bind the pages together.

6. Deliver the giggle book to your recipient.

Talking Points

- What did you think of this service project? Why?
- Why do you think people read comic strips?
- Why is it important to laugh—even when life is hard?
- How else can we lift someone's spirits?

Helpful Resources

- For children: *Giggle, Giggle, Quack* by Doreen Cronin (Atheneum, 2002), a hilarious book about a duck who creates trouble when Farmer Brown goes on vacation.
- For teens: *The Learning Power of Laughter: Over 300 Playful Games and Activities that Promote Learning with Young Children* by Jackie Silberg (Gryphon House, 2004), a book packed with more than 3,000 games and activities that help young children laugh and learn.

Bonus Ideas

- If you enjoy jokes and riddles, check out these types of books from your local library. Copy your favorite jokes and riddles to make a joke and riddle book. (Cite the source of the jokes and riddles and don't make copies to distribute.)
- Take photos of funny facial expressions of people (or pets) and create a funny photo album to give away.

Chapter 12
Community-Building Games

For a family service project to be successful, family members need to know each other—and be comfortable with each other. Open each family service project with a game to help build community and camaraderie in your group.

The games in this chapter are simple icebreakers that are easy to play, so you can keep the focus on building community rather than complex rules. These games help families get acquainted and all games are appropriate for families with children ages three and older.

As families get to know other families in your group, they're more likely to come to your family service projects—not only to serve and make a difference, but also to see other people who are becoming friends.

Name Game

Playing the Game

1. Have families sit in a circle. If more than 15 people are present, form groups of about 12 to 15 people each. (It's easier to get to know people when the groups are smaller.) If family members are age six or younger, make sure they sit next to an older family member who can help them if needed.

2. To begin, one person says her first name only, such as Brianna, and then names an object that starts with the same letter as her first name, such as bananas. Encourage that person to remember the object he or she named because it will be used later.

3. After the first person does this, have everyone in the group say, "Hi, Brianna!" (or whatever the first name of the person is).

4. Then go to the person on the right and repeat the process, with the person stating his or her name and an object that starts with the same letter the name does. If it's a young child or someone who is shy, have a family member help out.

5. Continue until you've made it around the circle.

6. Then start around the circle again. This time, have the person name only the object. For example, Brianna would say, "Bananas." Then give people in the circle time to guess her first name. If no one can remember it, she tells them.

7. Then go to the next person on the right, continuing around the circle.

8. Once you finish, go faster with each person naming the object and people shouting out the person's name. (This is fun and can get quite wild as it goes faster and faster.)

9. End the game and begin your family service project.

M&M® Moments

Materials

- 1 1-pound bag of M&M candies for every 25 individuals or so
- 1 plastic or paper cup for each group of 15
- 1 plastic spoon for each group of 15
- 1 paper napkin for each person

Playing the Game

1. Pour M&M candies into a plastic or paper cup. Distribute a paper napkin to each person.

2. Have families sit in a circle. If you have more than 15 people present, form groups of about 12 to 15 people each. If family members are age six or younger, make sure they sit next to an older family member who can help them if needed.

3. Ask each person to take two to 10 M&M candies by scooping them out of the cup with the plastic spoon and placing the candies onto their paper napkin. Explain that they cannot eat the candy now, but they will be able to do so later.

4. Go around the circle until everyone has taken some candy.

5. Choose someone to go first and explain that the person must name one attribute, interest, or interesting fact about him- or herself for each piece of candy taken. (You'll most likely hear the people who took 10 pieces of candy groan.) For example, if Sten took four pieces of candy, he could say he likes to play soccer, his favorite color is green, he broke his leg falling out of a tree in first grade, and his favorite class is math. Once the person has spoken, he or she can eat the candy taken.

6. Go on to the next person and continue until you've made it around the circle.

7. End the game and begin your family service project.

Birthday Buddies
Playing the Game

1. Have families stand up.

2. Explain that you're going to name the 12 months of year and point to a different area of the room for each month. When people hear the month they were born in, they should go to that area of the room. (If you have young children who are scared to get separated from their parents, they can remain with their parents. Or their parents can decide to go to the month of the child's birth.)

3. Start with January. Point to one area of the room and have all the people with January birthdays gather in that part.

4. Call out each of the months, one by one, designating separate areas in the room for each.

5. Once everyone is in their groups, have them introduce themselves to the people in the group and determine the ascending numerical order of their birth dates in the month (not years). See if anyone has the same birthday. Note: Some people get worried that you'll ask for their age or year of birth. Explain that this game is only about the date of birth within the month. It's meant to help people get to know people who have birthdays near theirs.

6. Ask for all the people who share birthdays. (You may have a few.) See if there are any days that have more than two people sharing it.

7. End the game and begin your family service project.

You're Fooling
Playing the Game

1. Have families sit in a circle. If more than 15 people are present, form groups of about 12 to 15 people each. If family members are age six or younger, make sure they sit next to an older family member who can help them if needed.

2. Ask everyone to think of two true things about themselves and one false thing. Explain that they will say this list of three things (and they can decide if the false thing will come

first, second, or third) to the group when it's their turn. People in the group will then have to guess which thing is false.

3. Give the group a minute or two to think of their lists.

4. Choose someone to go first, and ask that person to tell the group his or her list.

5. Have people in the circle take turns guessing which item is false. (Consider starting with the person who got up earliest this morning and then going around the circle clockwise.) Continue until a person guesses the false thing.

6. Continue with the next person on his or her right. Play the game until you've made it around the circle.

7. End the game and begin your family service project.

Zip, Zip, Zoom
Playing the Game

1. Have families sit in a circle. If more than 15 people are present, form groups of about 12 to 15 people each. (It's easier to get to know people when the groups are smaller.) If family members are age six or younger, make sure they sit next to an older family member. The younger child can decide whether he or she wants to play or just watch.

2. Explain how the game is played. One person in the circle will start. That person will say his first name only, such as Sam. Then the person sitting on Sam's right will say his or her first name.

3. Continue around the circle until everyone has said his or her first name.

4. Then go around the circle again, but this time have people say their names faster.

5. Repeat but even faster.

6. Continue repeating until the game is impossible to play.

7. End the game and begin your family service project.

Group Juggle
Materials

- 1 soft ball (for about every 15 people present) that group members can toss to each other without getting hurt

Playing the Game

1. Have families sit in a circle. If more than 15 people are present, form groups of about 12 to 15 people each. If family members are age six or younger, make sure they sit next to an older family member. The child can decide whether to play or just watch.

2. Give one person in the group a soft ball. Have that person say one thing about him- or herself. For example, Kay may say, "My favorite color is red."

3. Everyone who shares the opinion or personal fact that the speaker mentions should raise a hand. In this case, everyone whose favorite color is red would raise a hand. Kay then will gently throw the ball to one of those people.

4. That person catches it (or retrieves the ball) and says something different that is true about him- or herself. For example, Jamal may say, "I like to play volleyball."

5. The people who share that opinion or personal fact raise a hand. In this case, anyone who likes to play volleyball would raise a hand. Jamal then gently throws the ball to one of those people. Encourage members of the circle to throw to different people so that everyone is included.

6. Continue until every person has touched the ball at least once or twice.

7. End the game and begin your family service project.

Camera, Set, Action
Playing the Game

1. Have families stand up and form a circle. If more than 15 people are present, create circles of about 12 to 15 people. If you have young children present, have them stand near a family adult.

2. Explain how the game is played. Each person will take a turn saying his or her first name, naming an action, and doing that action. Then everyone repeats the action. (It can be fun to have the action start with the same letter as the person's name—for example, Julie could say "jumping jack" and lead the group in doing one jumping jack, or Karl could say "kick" and lead the group in doing one kick.)

3. Choose a person to start and say, "Camera! Set! Action!"

4. After the first person says his or her name, says an action, and does it, everyone repeats the action. Then the next person in the circle repeats the process with his or her own name and action.

5. Go around the circle once.

6. When you get back to the first person, have people shout out that person's first name (if they know it) and try to remember the action by doing it. (This can be funny since people will remember different actions.) After the group tries an action, have the person named do the correct action.

7. Go around the circle again, repeating this pattern.

8. End the game and begin your family service project.

Beach-Ball Shout
Materials

- 1 inflatable beach ball (that you can write on) for each group of about 15 people
- 1 black permanent marker

Playing the Game

1. Before families arrive, inflate the beach ball(s) and write a category on each panel of the ball(s) with a permanent black marker. Players will name their favorite in these categories. Consider categories such as these: color, food, activity, school subject, sport, TV show, music group or singer, movie, animal, time of day, vacation or getaway, holiday, place, and hobby.

2. Have families sit in a circle. If more than 15 people are present, form groups of about 12 to 15 people each. If family members are age six

or younger, make sure they sit next to an older family member who can help them if needed.

3. Explain that you'll throw the beach ball to one person in the circle, who will catch it. That person reads what's written in the panel where his or her left thumb is when it's caught.

4. The person then names his or her favorite in that category. For example if a person's left thumb is touching "place," he or she might say "library" or "my bedroom"—whatever his or her favorite place is.

5. The person then tosses the beach ball to another person in the circle who does the same thing.

6. After a while, switch to having people name their least favorite in the category.

7. Go back to "favorite" after a while. Then end the game and begin your family service project.

Clap, Clap
Playing the Game

1. Have families sit in a circle. If more than 15 are people present, form groups of about 12 to 15 people each. (It's easier to get to know people when the groups are smaller.) If family members are age six or younger, make sure they sit next to an older family member who can help them if needed.

2. Create a rhythm by clapping twice, then stomping first with your right foot and then with your left. Continue this four-part pattern: *clap, clap, stomp, stomp*. Invite others to do it with you two or three times.

3. Once everyone is clapping and stomping in rhythm, begin the game by saying your first name on the first clap of the rhythm only. The clapping and stomping rhythm continues. After the second clap and two stomps in the rhythm, the person on your right says his or her first name on the first clap of the rhythm.

4. Continue around the circle, each person in turn saying his or her name on the first clap, until everyone has had one turn: *Sandy, clap, stomp, stomp, Darlene, clap, stomp, stomp, Jackson, clap, stomp, stomp*, and so on.

5. Once you reach the beginning of the circle, repeat—but this time, have everyone say the person's name *together* while that person raises his or her hand on the first clap.

6. Continue until you've made it around the circle again.

7. End the game and begin your family service project.

Electricity
Playing the Game

1. Have families sit in a circle. If more than 15 are people present, form groups of about 12 to 15 people each. If family members are age six or younger, make sure they sit next to an older family member who can help them if needed.

2. Have everyone hold hands. Start by having one person give a nonverbal "electrical pulse" by doing two quick hand squeezes to the person on his or her right. That person then gives two quick hand squeezes to the person on his or her right. Continue until you make it around the circle.

3. Explain that you're going to name a topic. The first person will quickly respond to the topic and then give two quick hand squeezes to the person on his or her right. That person then answers the question and gives two quick hand squeezes to the person on his or her right. Continue until you make it around the circle.

4. Consider topics such as favorite candy, favorite item to shop for, favorite charity, favorite website, favorite musical instrument, and favorite sound effect.

5. Pick another topic and repeat.

6. End the game and begin your family service project.

Alphabet Hop-Up
Playing the Game

1. Have families sit in a circle. If more than 15 people are present, form groups of about 12 to 15 people each. If family members are age six or younger, make sure they sit next to an older family member who can help them if needed.

2. Explain that you're going to say letters of the alphabet (in order). When people hear the first letter in their first name, they should hop up and shout out their name before sitting down. If you have a lot of people with the same first letter, stop the game at this point and repeat the letter—but have each person whose name starts with that letter hop up and stand without making a noise. Then point to each person, one at a time. The person you point to shouts out his or her name before sitting down. Continue until everyone is sitting down again.

3. Play once going in order of the alphabet from A to Z.

4. Then repeat the game, but this time mix up the letters. Or consider playing the game using the first letters of people's last names.

5. End the game and begin your family service project.

On a Rainy Day
Materials
- Stuffed animal

Playing the Game

1. Have families sit in a circle. If more than 15 people are present, form groups of about 12 to 15 people each. If family members are age six or younger, make sure they sit next to an older family member who can help them if needed.

2. Explain that you're going to give one person a stuffed animal. Then you'll ask that person a question related to the weather, such as "What do you do on a rainy day?" That person should say his or her first name followed by a favorite thing to do in that kind of weather. Then that person will hand the stuffed animal to the next person, and that person will say his or her name followed by a favorite thing to do in that kind of weather.

3. Continue until you've made it around the circle.

4. When you've made it back to the first person who started, choose a different weather condition, such as a snowy day, a stormy day, the hottest day of the year, the coldest day of the year, a windy day, or a perfect day. Pass the stuffed animal around the circle and play the game again.

5. End the game and begin your family service project.

Hello, Star
Materials
- 1 self-adhesive name tag for each person
- 1 pen for each person
- 5 to 10 self-adhesive stars for each person

Playing the Game

1. Have everyone get a self-adhesive name tag, write his or her first name on it, and place the name tag on his or her shirt. Then give each person a bunch of self-adhesive stars (about five to 10 per person).

2. Explain how the game is played. When you say "start," people mill around the room and introduce themselves by saying, "Hi, I'm _____ (say first name). Nice to meet you, _____ (say first name of person they're talking to by reading that person's name tag)." When that's happened, the person who introduced him- or herself can place a star on the other person's name tag.

3. People continue milling around the room introducing themselves to other people until all their stars are gone.

4. At the end of the game, most people will have stars on their name tags. If anyone is missing stars or has only one or two stars, introduce yourself and place a star on that person's name tag, and ask others to do the same. (Sometimes you'll get a bunch of people who want to give one person stars, which can brighten the day of someone who is typically quiet.)

5. End the game and begin your family service project.

Here or There
Playing the Game

1. Have families gather in the middle of a large open area. Explain that you're going to make a statement, and they should decide if they agree with it or not. If they agree, they should move to one area of the room (point to that area). If they don't agree, they should move to another area of the room (point to the opposite area of the room).

2. Make statements such as these:
   - More families should do family service projects.
   - Even helping someone a little is actually a big help.
   - I got up way too early this morning.
   - I wish I had more time to read books.
   - I'm hungry right now.
   - I wish I could travel to Asia.
   - I wish students had a longer school day.
   - I think daydreaming is a waste of time.
   - I wish the day was longer.
   - I think the TV is on too much in our home.
   - I wish I lived in the woods.
   - I find all this new technology confusing.
   - I think everyone needs a helping hand from time to time.
   - I like to sing.
   - If I could, I would wear pajamas all day.

3. Give family members time to move to a different part of the room (or stay) after each statement. Notice when certain groups are larger than others—or if there are any questions that almost everyone answers the same way.

4. End the game and begin your family service project.

Multiply
Playing the Game

1. Have families stand up. Ask each person to find one partner. If you have an odd number of people, join in with the game so that everyone has a partner.

2. Have partners introduce themselves to each other by saying their first names and what kind of pet they have (or wish they had).

3. When they finish, have pairs find another pair, and have the four of them take turns saying their first names and what kind of pets they have (or wish they had).

4. Have these foursomes connect with another foursome, so they're a group of eight, and repeat.

5. Continue until you have a group (or groups) of 16.

6. End the game and begin your family service project.

Age Index

Age 3

Project numbers: 2, 3, 4, 6, 8, 10, 12, 15, 16, 18, 19, 20, 22, 23, 25, 26, 28, 29, 33, 34, 35, 36, 38, 39, 40, 41, 43, 44, 45, 46, 47, 49, 52, 54, 55, 57, 58, 60, 61, 62, 63, 66, 67, 68, 69, 70, 71, 72, 73, 74, 75, 76, 78, 79, 80, 81, 84, 85, 86, 87, 88, 90, 91, 92, 93, 94, 96, 97, 99, 100, 101

Age 4

Project numbers: 2, 3, 4, 6, 8, 10, 12, 15, 16, 18, 19, 20, 22, 23, 25, 26, 28, 29, 33, 34, 35, 36, 38, 39, 40, 41, 43, 44, 45, 46, 47, 49, 52, 54, 55, 57, 58, 60, 61, 62, 63, 66, 67, 68, 69, 70, 71, 72, 73, 74, 75, 76, 78, 79, 80, 81, 84, 85, 86, 87, 88, 90, 91, 92, 93, 94, 96, 97, 99, 100, 101

Age 5

Project numbers: 1, 2, 3, 4, 5, 6, 8, 9, 11, 12, 13, 15, 16, 17, 18, 19, 20, 21, 22, 23, 24, 25, 26, 27, 28, 29, 30, 31, 32, 33, 34, 35, 36, 37, 38, 39, 40, 41, 42, 43, 44, 45, 46, 47, 49, 51, 52, 54, 55, 56, 57, 58, 59, 60, 61, 62, 63, 64, 66, 67, 68, 69, 70, 71, 72, 73, 74, 75, 76, 78, 79, 80, 81, 83, 84, 85, 86, 87, 88, 90, 91, 92, 93, 94, 96, 97, 99, 100, 101

Age 6

Project numbers: 1, 2, 3, 4, 5, 6, 8, 9, 11, 12, 13, 15, 16, 17, 18, 19, 20, 21, 22, 23, 24, 25, 26, 27, 28, 29, 30, 31, 32, 33, 34, 35, 36, 37, 38, 39, 40, 41, 42, 43, 44, 45, 46, 47, 49, 51, 52, 54, 55, 56, 57, 58, 59, 60, 61, 62, 63, 64, 66, 67, 68, 69, 70, 71, 72, 73, 74, 75, 76, 78, 79, 80, 81, 83, 84, 85, 86, 87, 88, 90, 91, 92, 93, 94, 96, 97, 99, 100, 101

Age 7

Project numbers: 1, 2, 3, 4, 5, 6, 8, 9, 11, 12, 13, 15, 16, 17, 18, 19, 20, 21, 22, 23, 24, 25, 26, 27, 28, 29, 30, 31, 32, 33, 34, 35, 36, 37, 38, 39, 40, 41, 42, 43, 44, 45, 46, 47, 49, 51, 52, 54, 55, 56, 57, 58, 59, 60, 61, 62, 63, 64, 66, 67, 68, 69, 70, 71, 72, 73, 74, 75, 76, 78, 79, 80, 81, 83, 84, 85, 86, 87, 88, 90, 91, 92, 93, 94, 96, 97, 99, 100, 101

Age 8

Project numbers: 1, 2, 3, 4, 5, 6, 7, 8, 9, 10, 11, 12, 13, 14, 15, 16, 17, 18, 19, 20, 21, 22, 23, 24, 25, 26, 27, 28, 29, 30, 31, 32, 33, 34, 35, 36, 37, 38, 39, 40, 41, 42, 43, 44, 45, 46, 47, 49, 51, 52, 54, 55, 56, 57, 58, 59, 60, 61, 62, 63, 64, 66, 67, 68, 69, 70, 71, 72, 73, 74, 75, 76, 78, 79, 80, 81, 83, 84, 85, 86, 87, 88, 90, 91, 92, 93, 94, 95, 96, 97, 99, 100, 101

Age 9

Project numbers: 1, 2, 3, 4, 5, 6, 7, 8, 9, 10, 11, 12, 13, 14, 15, 16, 17, 18, 19, 20, 21, 22, 23, 24, 25, 26, 27, 28, 29, 30, 31, 32, 33, 34, 35, 36, 37, 38, 39, 40, 41, 42, 43, 44, 45, 46, 47, 49, 51, 52, 54, 55, 56, 57, 58, 59, 60, 61, 62, 63, 64, 66, 67, 68, 69, 70, 71, 72, 73, 74, 75, 76, 78, 79, 80, 81, 83, 84, 85, 86, 87, 88, 90, 91, 92, 93, 94, 95, 96, 97, 99, 100, 101

Age 10

Project numbers: 1, 2, 3, 4, 5, 6, 7, 8, 9, 10, 11, 12, 13, 14, 15, 16, 17, 18, 19, 20, 21, 22, 23, 24, 25, 26, 27, 28, 29, 30, 31, 32, 33, 34, 35, 36, 37, 38, 39, 40, 41, 42, 43, 44, 45, 46, 47, 49, 50, 51, 52, 53, 54, 55, 56, 57, 58, 59, 60, 61, 62, 63, 64, 66, 67, 68, 69, 70, 71, 72, 73, 74, 75, 76, 77, 78, 79, 80, 81, 82, 83, 84, 85, 86, 87, 88, 90, 91, 92, 93, 94, 95, 96, 97, 98, 99, 100, 101

Age 11

Project numbers: 1, 2, 3, 4, 5, 6, 7, 8, 10, 11, 12, 13, 14, 15, 16, 17, 18, 19, 20, 21, 22, 23, 24, 25, 26, 27, 28, 29, 30, 31, 32, 33, 34, 35, 36, 37, 38, 39, 40, 41, 42, 43, 44, 45, 46, 47, 49, 50, 51, 52, 53, 54, 55, 56, 57, 58, 59, 60, 61, 62, 63, 64, 66, 67, 68, 69, 70, 71, 72, 73, 74, 75, 76, 77, 78, 79, 80, 81, 82, 83, 84, 85, 86, 87, 88, 90, 91, 92, 93, 94, 95, 96, 97, 98, 99, 100, 101

Age 12

Project numbers: 1, 2, 3, 4, 5, 6, 7, 8, 10, 11, 12, 13, 14, 15, 16, 17, 18, 19, 20, 21, 22, 23, 24, 25, 26, 27, 28, 29, 30, 31, 32, 33, 34, 35, 36, 37, 38, 39, 40, 41, 42, 43, 44, 45, 46, 47, 48, 49, 50, 51, 52, 53, 54, 55, 56, 57, 58, 59, 60, 61, 62, 63, 64, 65, 66, 67, 68, 69, 70, 71, 72, 73, 74, 75, 76, 77, 78, 79, 80, 81, 82, 83, 84, 85, 86, 87, 88, 89, 90, 91, 92, 93, 94, 95, 96, 97, 98, 99, 100, 101

Ages 13–18

Project numbers: 1, 3, 5, 6, 7, 8, 10, 11, 12, 13, 14, 15, 16, 17, 18, 19, 20, 21, 22, 24, 25, 26, 27, 28, 29, 30, 31, 32, 33, 34, 35, 36, 37, 38, 40, 41, 42, 43, 44, 45, 46, 47, 48, 49, 50, 51, 52, 53, 54, 55, 56, 57, 58, 59, 60, 61, 62, 63, 64, 65, 66, 67, 68, 69, 70, 71, 72, 73, 74, 75, 76, 77, 78, 79, 80, 81, 82, 83, 84, 85, 86, 87, 88, 89, 90, 91, 92, 93, 94, 95, 96, 97, 98, 99, 100, 101

Topical Index

Bibliography

Benson, Peter L., *All Kids Are Our Kids: What Communities Must Do to Raise Caring and Responsible Children and Adolescents,* Second Edition (San Francisco: Jossey-Bass, 2006).

Benson, Peter L., *Sparks: How Parents Can Help Ignite the Hidden Strengths of Teenagers* (San Francisco: Jossey-Bass, 2008).

Boraas White, Stephanie, "Volunteering in the United States, 2005," *Monthly Labor Review,* February 2006, pp. 65–70.

Buckley, Jack; Schneider, Mark; and Shang, Yi, "The Effects of School Facility Quality on Teacher Retention in Urban School Districts," February 2004, posted by the National Clearinghouse for Educational Facilities.

Center on Philanthropy at Indiana University, "America Gives: Survey of Americans' Generosity after September 11," (Indianapolis: Center on Philanthropy at Indiana University, 2002).

Conference Board, *Philanthropy and Business: The Changing Agenda* (The Conference Board, 2006).

Corporation for National and Community Service, *Volunteering in America: State Trends and Rankings* (Washington, DC: Corporation for National and Community Service, Office of Research and Policy Development, June 2006).

Family Strengthening Policy Center, *Family Volunteering: Nurturing Families, Building Communities,* Policy Brief No. 17. (Washington, DC: National Human Services Assembly, November 2006).

Friedman, Jenny, *The Busy Family's Guide to Volunteering* (Beltsville, MD: Robins Lane, 2003).

Gill, Zoe, *Family Volunteering* (Adelaide, Australia: Government of South Australia, Office for Volunteers, 2006).

Grimm, Robert; Dietz, Nathan; Spring, Kimberly; Arey, Kelly; and Foster-Bey, John, *Youth Helping America* (Washington, DC: Corporation for National and Community Service, November 2005).

Hegel, Annette, *Volunteer Connections: Family Volunteering—Making It Official* (Ottawa, Ontario: Volunteer Canada, 2004).

Hegel, Annette, and McKechnie, A.J., *Family Volunteering: The Final Report* (Ottawa, Ontario: Volunteer Canada, 2003).

Henderson, Anne. T.; and Mapp, Karen L., *A New Wave of Evidence: The Impact of School, Family, and Community Connections on Student Achievement* (Austin, TX: Southwest Educational Development Library, 2002), p. 24.

Hodgkinson, Virginia A., editor, *Volunteering and Giving* (Washington, DC: Independent Sector, 1997), p. 23, 25.

Independent Sector, *Engaging Youth in Lifelong Service: Findings and Recommendations for Encouraging a Tradition of Voluntary Action Among America's Youth* (Washington, DC: Independent Sector, 2002).

Jalandoni, Nadine; and Hume, Keith, *America's Family Volunteers* (Washington, DC: Independent Sector, 2001).

Kaye, C. B., "What Is Service-Learning? A Guide for Parents" (Scotts Valley, CA: National Service-Learning Clearinghouse, 2007).

Littlepage, Laura, *Family Volunteering: An Exploratory Study of the Impact on Families* (Indianapolis: Center for Urban Policy and the Environment, 2003).

Markitects, Inc., *Power Skills: How Volunteerism Shapes Professional Success* (Wayne, PA: Markitects, Inc., 2006).

McKaughan, Molly, *Corporate Volunteerism: How Families Make a Difference* (New York: The Conference Board, 1997).

National Service-Learning Clearinghouse, *Reflections in Service-Learning: Selected Resources* (Scotts Valley, CA: National Service-Learning Clearinghouse, 2007).

RMC Research Corporation, *Standards and Indicators for Effective Service-Learning Practice* (Scotts Valley, CA: National Service-Learning Clearinghouse, 2008).

RMC Research Corporation, *Parent and Family Involvement* (Web page) (Scotts Valley, CA: National Service-Learning Clearinghouse, 2004).

Roehlkepartain, Eugene C., and Friedman, Jenny, *Engaging Families in Service: Broadening Service-Learning's Reach, Impact, and Support* (Web page) (Scotts Valley, CA: National Service-Learning Clearinghouse, 2009).

Roehlkepartain, Eugene C., "Engaging Families in Service: Rationale and Resources for Congregations," *Family Ministry,* Volume 17, Issue 3, 2003, pp. 22–41.

VolunteerMatch, *Measuring Corporate Volunteerism* (San Francisco: VolunteerMatch, 2005).

Woods, Mike; and Freeman, Andrea, "Volunteers and Community Development," Oklahoma Cooperative Extension Fact Sheet, AGEC-907 (Stillwater, OK: Oklahoma State University, Division of Agricultural Sciences and Natural Resources 2000).

About the Authors

Jenny Friedman, Ph.D., is founder and executive director of Doing Good Together and a leading national expert on family volunteerism. She is the author of *The Busy Family's Guide to Volunteering* (Robins Lane Press, 2003) and magazine articles published in *Parents, Parenting, American Baby, Nick Jr.,* and *Childcare Exchange.* She works with schools, businesses, youth-serving organizations, and religious groups in addition to families and groups of families. Jenny also speaks nationally on family volunteering and has been a guest speaker or workshop leader at the National Service-Learning Conference, the National Conference on Volunteering and Service, Search Institute's International Healthy Communities/Healthy Youth Conference, the National Conference for the General Federation of Women's Clubs, and MOPS (Mothers of Preschoolers). She is frequently called on by national magazines as an expert in the area of family volunteering, and she has been interviewed by *Family Circle, Good Housekeeping, Money* magazine*, Better Homes and Gardens, Newsday,* the Associated Press, Knight Ridder, and *Child* magazine.

The Doing Good Together website (www.doinggoodtogether.org) highlights a number of family service projects and partnerships Jenny has developed. She has volunteered with her own family of three children for more than 20 years. Jenny lives in Minneapolis, Minnesota.

Jolene Roehlkepartain is the author of more than 30 books, including *Teaching Kids to Care and Share, 101 Great Games That Keep Kids Coming, Parenting Preschoolers with a Purpose,* and *Raising Healthy Children Day by Day.* She writes in the areas of family advocacy, education, parenting, personal finance, recreation, youth development, and community building. Jolene has been interviewed by National Public Radio, *The Washington Post, U.S. News & World Report, Time* magazine, *Glamour* magazine, *Ms.* magazine, and *Woman's Day.* She is president and chief creative officer of Ideas to Ink, LLC, a company that develops creative, practical ideas. Jolene lives in St. Louis Park, Minnesota. Learn more about her work at www.booksbyjolene.com.

Teachers, Administrators, Librarians, Counselors, Youth Workers, and Social Workers
Help us create the resources you need to support the kids you serve.

Join the Free Spirit Advisory Board

In order to make our books and other products even more beneficial for children and teens, the Free Spirit Advisory Board provides valuable feedback on content, art, title concepts, and more. You can help us identify what educators need to help kids think for themselves, succeed in school and life, and make a difference in the world. Apply today! For more information, go to **www.freespirit.com/educators.**

More Great Books from Free Spirit

The Complete Guide to Service Learning
Proven, Practical Ways to Engage Students in Civic Responsibility, Academic Curriculum, & Social Action (Revised & Updated Second Edition)
by Cathryn Berger Kaye, M.A.

288 pp., softcover, 8½" x 11".
Teachers grades K–12.

Reach Out and Give
by Cheri J. Meiners, M.Ed.

48 pp., softcover, color illust., 9" x 9".
Ages 4–8.

Going Blue
A Teen Guide to Saving Our Oceans, Lakes, Rivers, & Wetlands
by Cathryn Berger Kaye, M.A., and Philippe Cousteau with EarthEcho International

160 pp., softcover, color photos & illust., 6" x 9". Ages 11 & up.

The Kid's Guide to Service Projects
Over 500 Service Ideas for Young People Who Want to Make a Difference (Updated 2nd Edition)
by Barbara A. Lewis

160 pp., softcover, 2-color, photos, 6" x 9". Ages 10 & up.

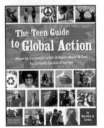

The Teen Guide to Global Action
How to Connect with Others (Near & Far) to Create Social Change
by Barbara A. Lewis

144 pp., softcover, 2-color, illust., 7" x 9". Ages 12 & up.

The Kid's Guide to Social Action
How to Solve the Social Problems You Choose—and Turn Creative Thinking Into Positive Action
by Barbara A. Lewis

244 pp., softcover, BW photos & illust., 8½" x 11". Ages 10 & up.

Interested in purchasing multiple quantities? Contact edsales@freespirit.com or call 1.800.735.7323 and ask for Education Sales.

Many Free Spirit authors are available for speaking engagements, workshops, and keynotes. Contact speakers@freespirit.com or call 1.800.735.7323.

For pricing information, to place an order, or to request a free catalog, contact:

Free Spirit Publishing Inc. • 217 Fifth Avenue North • Suite 200 • Minneapolis, MN 55401-1299
toll-free 800.735.7323 • local 612.338.2068 • fax 612.337.5050
help4kids@freespirit.com • www.freespirit.com